THERON F. SCHLABACH is a close student of twentieth-century welfare developments. He has published a number of articles and a monographic study of one of Andrew Carnegie's philanthropies, *Pensions for Professors* (1963). More recently, under a Social Security Administration grant, he has undertaken a study of the social insurance movement in America before 1935. He is associate professor of history in Goshen College, from which he received his B.A. degree in 1960. Like Edwin Witte, Professor Schlabach is a product of the University of Wisconsin, where, as a Danforth Fellow, he earned his M.S. and Ph.D. degrees.

WILBUR J. COHEN, Dean of the School of Education in the University of Michigan and former Secretary of Health, Education, and Welfare, was one of Edwin Witte's students at the University of Wisconsin.

Edwin E. Witte

CAUTIOUS REFORMER

Edwin E. Witte
CAUTIOUS
REFORMER

By THERON F. SCHLABACH

With a Foreword by
WILBUR J. COHEN

STATE HISTORICAL SOCIETY OF WISCONSIN

MADISON : MCMLXIX

FOREWORD

PROFESSOR SCHLABACH's biography of Edwin E. Witte is an excellent description of the life-time adventure of a remarkable man. Reading this book brought back fond and rewarding memories of my thirty-year association with this truly fine man. He was my teacher, my colleague, and my friend.

I first met Ed Witte in 1933. He was one of the professors at the University of Wisconsin who guided me into my own life work. In those days, ideas and innovations were flourishing at the university. Witte was one of the leading advocates of the "Wisconsin Idea" of public service in a period when the university was pioneering in this field. With John R. Commons, Selig Perlman, the La Follettes, E. A. Ross, Arthur Altmeyer, and other distinguished people, he investigated controversial social problems. And he believed that the university should make major contributions to the clarification and resolution of public policy issues. The current debate about the university's role in the community would have been no problem for Witte; he firmly believed in the university's obligation to the community and was prepared to help meet that obligation.

Witte combined the values and experiences of a political scientist, social reformer, and historian. In his lectures he emphasized the importance of the diffusion of economic power. He was influenced by the La Follette progressive movement and worked closely with many of the progressive leaders and their legislators. His identification with the "little man," with the individual farmer and worker, and with the needs of individuals who were unemployed, sick, or aged, made him conscious of the need for far-reaching social reforms.

He was often critical of the power and influence of large impersonal corporations, of private insurance companies, of Wall Street, and of professors from eastern universities in government, business, and labor. Yet he was never hostile or bitter towards those he disagreed with. He instilled in his students a sense of optimism, and a belief in human progress.

Professor Witte's greatest reward in life may have been his influence on and through his students. Although he was also a social reformer and a public servant, he was primarily a teacher, in and outside of the classroom. He gave unselfishly of his time and energy to his students.

After Ed left the university to become Executive Director of President Franklin D. Roosevelt's Committee of Economic Security, he asked me if I would like to come to Washington as his research assistant. Although I had planned to go to graduate school, I accepted and arrived in Washington on August 14, 1934, one year before the enactment of the Social Security Act. Never have I regretted it. Working with and learning from Ed Witte during the next few months was one of the most rewarding periods of my life.

He was a human dynamo. In six months' time he compiled voluminous reports and drafted one of the most important pieces of legislation enacted in the nation's history. I doubt that anything like that could be accomplished today. Professor Schlabach has aptly described the task that confronted Witte: he started from scratch in setting up an organization; he had to balance the interplay of ideas and interests among many groups; there were violent differences of opinion, and petty jealousies. There were no statistics on which to base accurate reports. There were no demonstration projects from which to benefit. "It was," as Frances Perkins described it "like driving a team of highstrung unbroken horses"—and, I add, to do an impossible task.

Yet what resulted from his patience, his intelligence, level-

headedness, and ability was a monumental report and a set
of recommendations for a plan that has proved viable and effective, yet amenable to amendments when needed over the
past third of a century. His success as a mediator and his over-
riding drive and ability enabled him to accomplish in six months
what would have taken any other human being much longer.

We worked long hours in those days. Ed had a zest for encyclopedic knowledge. He wanted to know everything there was
to know about foreign social insurance systems. He gave close
attention to detail, yet he was a master at sorting out the details,
delineating the issues, evaluating alternatives, and analyzing and
synthesizing ideas for practical application.

His task was not over, however, with completion of the report and the drafting of the bill. He found himself explaining
and defending the proposed legislation before both the House
Committee on Ways and Means and the Senate Committee on
Finance. He sat in the executive sessions of both committees,
on the floor of the Senate and in conference committees, helping to mold the technical and legal modifications and policy
compromises. Here Witte practiced the art of combining economics, politics, and conciliation in the crucible of hard reality.
This book gives a lively description of this period of Witte's
life.

After he returned to Madison, I continued my association
with Ed up until the time of his death in 1960. We met many
times and carried on a voluminous correspondence. He continued his interest in social security, serving frequently as advisor and consultant to federal and state agencies, speaking to
many groups, and writing often on the subject of social security.
The high point of this period of his career was when he was
elected president of the American Economic Association in 1956.
His selection came as a surprise to him because he staunchly
defended institutional economics at a time when the Keynesian
and other new schools of economics were becoming more popular. He was an economist who taught political economy, a subject which became sharply split among the social sciences. He was

not comfortable with the socio-scientific vocabulary. Nor did he express his theories in mathematical formulas. He had little time for micro-economics, for his concern was with the whole institution and how it related to society.

A complex but humble man, he always disclaimed fame for his many accomplishments. Although many people called him the Father of Social Security, he unhesitatingly gave the credit to others. He was an ordinary man in many ways, unimpressed by superficialities. He loved his family and his home. He was a man on whom you could depend. Regardless of the problem, his students, his friends and associates knew that Ed Witte would find the time and energy to help find a solution. He was a source of great strength, a compassionate and kind man of absolute integrity.

In the pages that follow Professor Schlabach conveys to the reader the many Edwin E. Wittes: the reformer, the teacher, the mediator, and the administrator.

WILBUR J. COHEN

PREFACE

FOR VALID HISTORICAL REASONS, Edwin E. Witte is most remembered for his roles as the so-called "Father of Social
Security": directing the forces that created the Social Security Act of 1935, convincing skeptical congressmen and senators that
the program was practical, and thereafter giving advice and comment on social security's development. But Witte's interests were
broader. At the University of Wisconsin, he helped to keep alive
the John R. Commons tradition of institutional economics and
distinguished himself as a teacher in his own right. As an expert on labor law he wrote the official dissent to the labor provisions of the 1914 Clayton antitrust bill, helped draft the Norris-La Guardia Act of 1932, and gave advice to labor-minded
legislators such as Robert M. La Follette, Jr., and Robert F.
Wagner. In the role of labor mediator he served on the World
War II National Labor Relations Board, the postwar Atomic
Energy Labor Relations Panel, and other agencies.

Edwin E. Witte: Cautious Reformer aims to tell the story
of Witte's many interests. It reveals the techniques, ideas, and
outlook of a pragmatic practitioner of reform. Often the story
is one of struggle between Witte and other reformers whose ideas
were more highly theorized, and more bold, but probably less
realistic and practical. Edwin Witte was a man who advocated
change, but always with caution. And as such, he was effective
in transforming reform ideas from amorphous proposals into
concrete, working institutions.

To write a book is to incur debts. All of the persons who

ix

helped me in interviews, through correspondence, and in other ways deserve my explicit thanks, but I can mention only a few. Messrs. Murray Latimer, Wilbur J. Cohen, and David Saposs, all of Washington, D. C., were exceptionally clear and candid as they recalled events and offered insights. In the Manuscripts Division of the State Historical Society of Wisconsin, Mrs. Margaret Hafstad and Miss Josephine Harper put the Witte Papers in highly usable form and made my access to them most convenient. Officials in various government offices in Madison and in the National Archives belied all the usual clichés about government bureaucrats. Miss Elizabeth Brandeis of the University of Wisconsin in Madison, Professor Walter Trattner of the University of Wisconsin–Milwaukee, and Professor Ralph Pumphrey each read the manuscript at one or another stage, and offered lucid suggestions. Most of all I wish to thank Mrs. Florence Witte of Madison, Wisconsin, and my graduate school professor, Dr. Irvin G. Wyllie, now Chancellor of the University of Wisconsin Parkside Campus. Mrs. Witte helped me immeasurably by discussing her late husband's life and manners, by opening the Witte Papers, and by giving me access to additional family documents. Dr. Wyllie very carefully read and criticized my manuscript in its early stages, tried unflaggingly to impress upon me high standards of scholarly excellence, and gave personal encouragement. Without such people an author is helpless.

THERON F. SCHLABACH

Goshen College
November 30, 1968

CONTENTS

1

From Ebenezer to Madison

IN THE RURAL AREA OF EBENEZER, four miles south of Watertown, Wisconsin, Emil and Anna Witte lived and reared their second son, the third of five children. Edwin Emil Witte was born on January 4, 1887, into a community secure on its religious, ethnic, and economic foundations. The farms were on fertile hardwood soil. The Witte farmhouse was unpretentious, but it was new, two-storied, and built solidly of brick. A mile from the Witte home the Ebenezer Moravian Church watched over the countryside from a site on a hill. Edwin Witte was a member of the community's third generation, both his grandfathers having immigrated from Prussia in the 1850's. One, Julius Witte, had been among the dozen Moravian families who founded the Ebenezer church. The other, Carl Yaeck, repelled by his fellow Lutherans' "worldliness," had soon joined the Ebenezer group.[1]

The Moravian faith resembled a very low-church form of Lutheranism, having taken its character from the pietistic movement that spread across Germany in the eighteenth century, instilling in the faithful the quest for a consciousness of a vital faith inwardly, and for right conduct outwardly. For Edwin Witte, in his childhood, those were personal quests; but they were also a part of home and community traditions. His parents made Bible reading and prayers, quite as much as farm chores, a part of their daily routine. Anna Witte lived her pietism with a quiet efficiency, and her son caught from her a gentle sensitivity that he kept for life. Dancing and smoking were forbidden, and even the alcoholic beverages of the German fathers were becoming taboo. The religious traditions shaded off into the ethnic. *Plattdeutsch* being the dialect of home and community, the Ebenezer church instructed young Witte in the reading and writing of German along with his catechism.[2] He was part of a community knit together by faith, tradition, language, and occupation.

The community offered security and a base, not necessarily a limitation. The Ebenezer Moravians wore their pietism comfortably, and Edwin Witte scarcely missed the superfluous sins. For fun he had the gay parties that the church's *Jugenbund* sponsored along with its religious exercises, and the pleasures of constant holiday celebrations, family gatherings, church picnics, and neighborly visits. He might play whist or mill, or (though normally he was not mischievous) help hoist a bed to the roof at his favorite sister's wedding. His father, never one to confuse pietism with quietism, found horse breeding and spirited discussions of local issues much more interesting than the daily routine of his 113 acres, and, until he died of diabetes and an infected ax wound when his son was sixteen, the community rewarded him with positions of leadership: church committeeman, president of the mutual fire association, town clerk, tax assessor, and justice of the peace. Like his father, the young Witte soon looked beyond the farm. He dutifully helped with the chores, and would continue to do so when he returned home as a university student. But as a lad he preferred to calculate the number of cornstalks in an acre to hoeing its weeds, and preferred the tiny Ebenezer school to the barn. So quickly did he advance at the one-room school that he often recited with students much older than he, and, according to a fellow student, even "teached the teachers."[3]

In Jefferson County at the turn of the century only one pupil in ten went beyond the eighth grade. The Wittes made sure that their bright son was among the few. In 1901 they enrolled him in high school, even though it meant boarding him with relatives in the city of Watertown five days each week. Watertown, lying midway between the state's capital and its largest industrial city, was a well-established municipality of 8,000 people. Among the institutions that its New Englanders, free-thinking German Forty-eighters, and other settlers had established were numerous churches, a Catholic college, an opera house, a Turner hall, a dramatic society, and several factories with products as diverse as shoes and cash registers. Already Edwin's older brother Max had studied several terms at its German-speaking Lutheran *gymnasium*. Witte, however, attended the English-speaking four-year public school.[4]

In high school Witte was an unpolished country boy with an awkwardness that he never quite outgrew, even later in adulthood. Combs, inkwells, and his own feet were his natural enemies, and already he had the habit, which he kept conspicuously for life, of chewing pencil ends to prime his mental apparatus. Yet his classmates accepted him. Though not athletic, he took a vicarious interest in sports, and he amused his fellows with a dry but contagious sense of humor. Moreover, his mind was agile, and the students soon learned that an easy solution to academic problems was to "ask Witte." As freshmen they made him president of their class—then they kept him in office for each of their four years. He was self-assertive in intellectual matters, especially on social and political issues, with history and civics his favorite academic subjects. Ever quick with proposals and arguments on public policy, he took up debating and by his senior year was the school's champion debater. If judged by debating rather than mere oratorical skill, reported *The Watertown Gazette* in the spring of 1905, he was a very able debater—but admittedly "not the most graceful." In the same spring the awkward country boy was also valedictorian of his graduating class.[5]

Witte's next step took him farther from Ebenezer, to the University of Wisconsin. He and his family had long assumed that he would get a higher education. The state university was only forty miles from home, and offered a broad course of instruction.[6]

Attempting explicitly to be democratic, it welcomed students of modest means and unsophisticated manner. So in September Witte boarded the train for Madison, taking with him his interest in public questions, his debating skills, and his unpolished ways.

*   *   *   *   *

Edwin Witte's peculiar intellectual talent was his ability to grasp quickly ideas in the air around him, synthesize them, and put them to use. In his maturity it was this aptitude, rather than an outstanding ability to generate startlingly new, original, untested ideas, that underlay his reformism; hence its cautious bent. At the University of Wisconsin he demonstrated his peculiar talent by quickly absorbing the atmosphere of the campus.

Witte had scarcely found his way about the university when sophomores, observing a yearly ritual, planted a flag atop a telegraph pole near the lake at campus edge, challenged freshmen to remove it, and touched off what became reputedly the hardest fought "freshman rush" in the university's history. Witte was slight of build, and the weapons of the battle—fire hoses, clubs, bare fists, and heavy boots—were hardly for the delicate. Nevertheless he found the struggle "inspiring," and joined with gusto. One especially brutal sophomore had his ribs broken, another student suffered a broken leg, another a skull fracture. Witte was fortunate—he only got bruised, took a mud bath and a ducking in Lake Mendota, and lost his shirt and one suspender. He did not even lose his trousers, as he had feared. What inspired him was the way the rush initiated him to the campus atmosphere. "Before the rush the Freshman feels that the university is something beyond him," he later recalled. But "in the rush he catches the Wisconsin spirit, and becomes a true stude."[7]

The campus atmosphere competed with Moravian piety. Apparently Witte's faith had already begun to wane at Ebenezer and Watertown, for when on the day of his departure from home his mother tearfully advised him to seek God's assistance in all his "many troubles," Witte felt like a "vagrant son." Within the next few weeks he resolved to "lead a better life" and to regain the religious faith of his childhood. But his resolutions did not wear well at the university. He determined to read his Bible each day, and on Sunday to attend church in the forenoon, the Young Men's Christian Association in the afternoon, and Christian Endeavor in the evening. When his determination faltered, he devised a system of reading an extra chapter of the Gospels for every omission. But his system was not yet a day old when he neglected his YMCA and Christian Endeavor meetings. Three Sundays later he attended no service at all. "This is terrible," he confessed, "but I cannot really get concerned about my future faith." As penance he read thirty-two chapters of the Gospels in three hours. But it was to no avail, and during the remainder of his freshman year his religious resolves dwindled to insignificance. Upon his return as a sophomore, after a summer of Moravian piety, he took up a course at the YMCA and once again tried to discipline himself to read his Bible. But again to no avail. By the time he graduated in 1909, he had lost all interest in pious religious exercises.[8]

But in his personal code of behavior, Witte retained a kind of pietism in secularized form. While some of his close friends drank alcohol quite freely, he rarely indulged beyond a glass of beer. The only occasion of his entire life when he was known to get drunk was during his junior year, when, having won election to Phi Beta Kappa, he mixed wine and hard drinks too freely. He did not smoke. Although he once toured Chicago's red-light district with a classmate, he apparently did so quite innocently, and he took a dim view of burlesque and similar divertissements. His widowed mother he held in exceptionally tender regard, and he was concerned especially that his education not burden her financially, even to the point of using his concern as an excuse to eat irregularly and dress poorly. Actually Mrs. Witte, while not affluent, was by no means in want,[9] and his concern and parsimony were evidence more of his sensitive, quasi-pietistic nature than of circumstances. Throughout his life the same traits made him almost fastidiously conscientious on matters such as truthfulness, helpfulness, fair treatment of associates, and complete honesty in financial dealings down to the smallest expense account.

Whatever piety Witte retained, he did not remain an Ebenezer Moravian. When as a graduate student he once heard an Ethical Culturist declare that Christianity was not the only true religion, and that men should concentrate upon a code of ethics drawn from the teaching of all religions, he confessed that this was an "ideal program," "my belief." Later, in 1922, a half-dozen years after he married, he affiliated with his wife's church, the First Methodist Church of Madison. But though he retained his membership throughout life, it was little more than nominal. In 1938 he confessed to a friend that he had not taken his Bible from its shelf for many years. When he was once asked to discuss how religion might help bring harmony between capital and labor his wife thought it a great joke that he should be delivering a "sermon," and he admitted that he was not "much of a church man."[10] In his later years he grew more and more inclined to hark back to fundamental traditions, and he often emphasized that both industrial harmony and social security were true to Christian precepts. But in clear contrast to his usual style, which was to be highly specific, he kept such references most vague. For him to say that social security fit the basic concepts of a "civilized and Christian society" meant about the same as his alternate phrase, that it was "a recognized part of the American way of life."[11] The pietistic church of Witte's boyhood had not phrased its teachings in terms readily applicable to the social issues with which Witte dealt in the university and in later life. Nor did the university challenge him to pursue theology and ethics at a level commensurate with his intellectual growth in other fields. At the university he absorbed a set of operative beliefs, but without the dimension that a religious tradition, with its ethical insights and its sense of historical rootage, might have offered.

Witte himself later thought that he had retained something from his rural community heritage, if not specifically from its piety. In 1948 he publicly deplored "the engrossment of so many college graduates in individual success without a sense of social responsibility," but declared that he still had faith in "the many college graduates, who like . . . myself, come from the farms and small towns to the cities." They offered much that was creative, "although their lives are fragmented and their interests do not center in an old-style community."[12] Whatever the truth of Witte's assumptions, the ideal of social responsibility was at least as strong at the University of Wisconsin as at Ebenezer, and Witte drew most heavily on the university atmosphere and ideas when he gave the ideal specific content. For the operative beliefs he absorbed were those of the Wisconsin progressivism that happened at the moment to permeate the campus and the state.

Dominating Wisconsin in Witte's student years was Robert M. La Follette, the state's reforming Republican governor and after 1905 its most famous United States Senator. La Follette and his progressive political faction were filling Wisconsin with a renewed concept of government for the benefit of the independent farmer, the worker, and the small businessman, expressed in such reforms as the direct primary, the revision of railroad taxation, and the regulation of industry. The university was a center of the progressive spirit. President Charles R. Van Hise was leading it through a golden age, expanding its facilities, extending its influence to every hamlet in the state through a growing extension service, inviting qualified youth to seek higher education regardless of social standing, encouraging professors to lend expert advice to state government, and in every way putting the facilities of the university at the service of the people and the state.[13] For Witte, Wisconsin's progressivism came to mean, as a practical matter, government for the protection and welfare of the common man, especially the industrial laborer; and personal devotion to public affairs, according to the "Wisconsin Idea" of the intellectual committed to the service of the state.

Helping Witte to internalize the campus atmosphere was a

small group of friends in the Athenaean Society, a literary and forensic group that Witte joined early in his freshman year because of his debating interests. John Dorney was a red-haired Irish Protestant who eventually became an attorney in Milwaukee. Myron (Mike) Utgard was an agricultural student, later the manager of a corporation farm in Virginia. David Saposs, a Milwaukee Jew, advocated the mild Milwaukee brand of socialism. Like Witte he became a student of Wisconsin's labor economist John R. Commons, and in later life a researcher, government official, and writer on labor matters. Douglas Anderson, from the upstate community of Rhinelander, was a poker-playing extrovert, sometimes frustrating to Witte but too likeable to shake off, who eventually became head of the field service of the United States Internal Revenue Service and a roving organizer of Democratic political campaigns. On the periphery of the group but a close friend of Witte was Chester Griswold, son of a Waukesha judge, who was intensely religious and went on to a theological seminary. To these friends, Witte was plain "Ed," "Wit," or "Dutch."

There were no co-eds in the group. In high school Witte had felt attracted to his class secretary-treasurer, Eugenie Abele, and in his first days at the university he fancied himself very much in love with her. But she, a town girl from a wealthy but broken home, was of a different temperament than he and the friendship never matured. While a university student he kept up very infrequent contacts with her, but finally as a graduate student he decided that she had "no time for any of my notion of 'service to mankind.' Success is her one ideal." Apart from remembering "Genie," as a student Witte showed no taste for a social life that included the opposite sex. Once, after he attended a country party back at Ebenezer, he confessed that while he had amused the crowd he had only disgusted himself. He never learned to dance, more out of social backwardness than out of fidelity to pietism. Above all, the style of life that he and his inner circle of friends led provided neither the inclination nor the contacts for dating.[14]

"Intellectual monks," Saposs later characterized the group. They lived with very little money, and if one ran too low to pay room rent, the others found a corner for him. Meals they took at cheap boardinghouses, or at a favorite saloon, where with a glass of beer one bought generous sandwiches for a pittance. Clothes and appearances mattered little. For recreation Witte enjoyed playing handball or running. He and his friends were avid sports fans, and Witte amazed those around him with his copious mastery of baseball statistics. None in the group was an athlete. Yet they loved combat: their outlets were student politics and debating.[15] Both battles conditioned them for absorbing Wisconsin's progressivism.

In campus politics Witte and his friends became leaders of the "barbarians," a faction which attacked the fraternities on the grounds that they were socially undemocratic and enabled a minority to control campus politics. The dispute was much larger than Witte and his fellow monks. In 1901 the Wisconsin legislature had entertained a bill to abolish fraternities, but had not passed it. The dispute smoldered on, and in 1909 the legislature resolved that the university's Board of Regents should investigate the controversial organizations. The next year a faculty committee to whom the regents had delegated the investigation admitted that fraternities interfered with academic effort, but declared that they were not as undemocratic as their accusers charged, and that they provided needed housing, boarding, and social facilities. So the fraternities survived.[16] Meantime Witte and his fellow barbarians fought the battle at the student level. First they threatened to break the fraternities' monopoly hold on the Student Conference—a body Van Hise had introduced to give students a semi-governing voice—by organizing every student rooming house in the city as a fraternity and flooding the Conference with their representatives. When the faculty report of 1910 moved fraternities to support a reform that opened representation in the Conference to classes and colleges as well as themselves, the barbs responded with what Saposs later described as "Tammany Hall tactics of the clean type"—a political machine without bribery. They surveyed Madison businesses to learn where students might find part-time employment, then dispensed job information as patronage. Mike Utgard acted as political organizer in the agricultural school, and just when the frats were confident of an election victory, marched his platoon of aggies to the polls. With such tactics the barbs won control of the student court and reformed the annual student prom, a fraternity-sorority affair which they considered too expensive to be democratic.[17]

Typical of his role with reformers in later life, Witte supplied a voice of pragmatism and moderation among the barbs. He operated behind the scenes, taking a prominent part in barb caucuses, writing publicity pieces, and negotiating with the enemy when necessary. He was afraid to destroy the fraternities entirely lest the university lose public support in its period of growth, so he worked closely with history professor Alfred Dennis to protect Dennis' position as a moderating voice in the frats' camp. Although sometimes his own statements needed softening, he co-operated with the editor of the student newspaper, John Childs, to get both sides to tone down their public accusations.[18]

To Witte, both the barbs' crusading against undemocratic elements and his own circumspection were consistent with his growing progressivism. In 1910 he was an officer in a campus La Follette Club, and when the group formed a new Progressive Club to work in the 1910 state elections, Witte became chairman of their platform committee. That summer he performed a bit of organizational and publicity work in his native Jefferson County for the La Follette Congressman John M. Nelson, and in the fall he helped in Madison to deliver the student vote for the progressive faction. At home he took pains to convince his brother Max to vote the progressive Republican ticket, in an area where most German farmers, probably including Witte's own father before he died, were by tradition conservative Democrats.[19] He participated in the campus Commonwealth Club, which was quite preoccupied with progressive issues. Witte was active also in the university's Socialist Club, but in his cautious way supported socialism only in its mildest form. Early in 1910, as a graduate student, he cheered the city election victory of socialists in Milwaukee, who were nonradical and hardly distinguishable from other progressives. But at other times he criticized socialists for being "very dogmatic" as "true idealists." "I am in less probability of entirely endorsing the socialist program than I was about a year ago," he declared late in the year. He expected to vote Socialist many times in the future, "but I haven't yet made up my mind that theoretical socialism is the 'cure-all' for all present day ills."[20] Already Witte had passed his peak of sympathy for socialism. It was too theoretical, too doctrinaire, and too radical for Witte's cautious, pragmatic turn of mind. He was a progressive, not a socialist.

More important even than political activities for developing Witte's progressive ideas was his debating. Not that he was always a winner; teams on which he served, often in the key position of closer, lost some very important debates. After failure—and even after winning—Witte frequently berated himself for poor delivery, although seldom for poor preparation. His friends later insisted that he was excessively self-critical, and never made a really poor showing, but his self-criticism had substance. Witte never was a polished orator. His senior yearbook commented of him that "speeches cannot be made long enough for the speakers, nor short enough for the hearers."[21] As in later life, Witte was more effective behind the scenes, preparing the argument that he or a fellow-debater might make, than in the limelight. It was in study for debates, not in the debates themselves, that he profited most. He sought to acquaint himself with every relevant source and fact. As a debater and student he developed a practice characteristic of his later research: that of carrying small cards, jotting down assorted bits of information as he came across them, and filing them in a vast index for future use.[22] His card-file was particularly Wittean, a symptom of thoroughness and extreme, even excessive, attention to small detail in research.

Through Witte's debating his progressive outlook deepened.

The Athenaean Society was the stronghold of progressivism on campus, having been the debating society of both President Van Hise and Senator La Follette in their undergraduate days. The questions for debate usually incorporated such timely progressive issues as governmental regulation of industry, the income tax and other tax reforms, and legislation protecting workers' safety, their right to organize, and their economic security. In the course of preparing, Witte made the close acquaintance of progressive leaders such as Charles McCarthy of Wisconsin's Legislative Reference Library and "discovered" his future teacher, John R. Commons. One of the first major debates Witte attended on the campus concerned compulsory workmen's compensation for industrial accidents, soon to become America's first form of social insurance and harbinger of other social security programs. Debating sharpened and developed his thinking. In an early debate he was to defend the proposition that cities should relieve unemployment through public works projects. At first he thought that he had drawn "the rotten side of this socialistic measure"; but after study he decided that he had the better side of the argument.[23]

Most importantly, debating gave Witte's progressivism specific substance by grounding him in the reform around which he would build his early career. For an important 1908 debate in which Witte acted as closer, his team submitted the question of whether in cases of labor disputes courts should have power to interfere with boycotts, blacklisting, strikes, lockouts, and peaceful picketing. Nineteen hundred and eight was the year in which the United States Supreme Court had set a precedent against labor organization by upholding a suit for triple damages against a hatters' union at Danbury, Connecticut, for the union's boycott of an employer. Witte's team drew the side favoring restriction of the courts, and in the course of their research they travelled to Chicago and Milwaukee to interview numerous labor leaders. Witte became convinced of the correctness of labor's position, and began to express his convictions in other forums. When he was selected as one of five seniors to deliver an oration upon his graduation in 1909 he called boldly for courts to adopt a more liberal attitude towards labor. Later he used the topic of the courts' role in labor disputes for his Ph.D. dissertation and for his major published book. Always he advocated restricting the courts' role.[24]

Witte's extracurricular activities at the university suggested his future style. His fellow "intellectual monks" and "barbarians" replaced the fellowship of rural community and church. In later life he found his companionship not in social affairs, neighborly, or religious groups, but in a faculty discussion group and even more among those with whom he worked in some common cause, often of reform. He spent some of his best intellectual energies in debating activities. Throughout his life his style of treating problems and issues was the flexible debate manner, finding the idea or the argument best suited to the immediate occasion. His senior oration drew protests to university officials from William D. Hoard, a prominent Wisconsin agricultural leader and university regent, who thought trade unionism "a species of Socialism." Perhaps partly because of Hoard's displeasure, Witte later declared that he was trying not to be openly controversial in his discussions of the courts and labor,[25] and throughout his life he tried to avoid sharp polemic, covering his reform ideas with layers of passivity and apparent objectivity. Most of all, the extracurricular activities gave direction to Witte's shift of loyalties from Ebenezer to Madison, from Moravian piety to progressivism.

* * * * *

Putting the finishing touches on Witte's new outlook was his academic work. At Wisconsin, Witte had as teachers a roster of outstanding professors, some of them famous for progressive ideas as well as scholarship. Dana Munro, a prominent medievalist, was to Witte an especially friendly teacher. The versatile American historian, Carl Russell Fish, attracted him temporarily to the idea of taking a graduate degree in American history. Frederick Jackson Turner impressed him not only with his "frontier thesis" but also with his incisive comments in seminars, and Witte was disappointed when Turner left Wisconsin for Harvard in 1909. Supplementing Turner's democratic outlook, Witte attended the courses of two reform-minded sociologists, Edward A. Ross and Frank Lester Ward. In economics he studied not only under John R. Commons but under Commons' German-educated, anti-laissez-faire teacher, Richard T. Ely, and under another of Ely's students, William Scott.[26] His was an education of exceptional quality, and one liberally infused with progressive ideas.

Witte's academic career did not always proceed smoothly. In it he exhibited a lifelong tendency to let large, remote tasks go undone in favor of numerous smaller and immediate ones. It was a tendency that reinforced the immediate, practical bent in his reformism, as opposed to pursuit of more distant and theoretical goals. He was not lazy or disorganized; he was simply most stimulated by immediate problems, which he attacked with prodigious energy and great attention to detail. In his undergraduate and early graduate years he majored in history, and, chiefly because Munro wanted him to mine a German-language source, he planned to write his bachelor's thesis on the question of how much actual fighting had occurred during the medieval crusades. He graduated without having completed the thesis, decided to use it for a master's thesis, failed to complete that, and finally by-passed the Master's degree for the Ph.D.[27] Even then he became so preoccupied with immediate tasks, often educational and rewarding to be sure, that he did not receive his degree until 1927.

Despite his frequent procrastination, for which he constantly chided himself, Witte succeeded academically. His mind absorbed facts in encyclopedic quantities, and he had a phenomenal ability to study and recall information under pressure. In all but a few of his courses he received grades in the middle nineties, and was elected to Phi Beta Kappa in his junior year. In 1916, when he took his preliminary doctoral examination, he won exceptional praise from the famed economist Richard T. Ely, as he often had from other professors for specific papers and reports. His professors encouraged him, seeming sometimes to compete with each other to keep him in their respective academic fields.[28]

Despite Witte's favored status, during his first year of graduate study he toyed with the idea of transferring to Columbia. John B. Andrews, a former student of Commons' and secretary of the American Association for Labor Legislation, tentatively offered him a part-time position as researcher on the Association's staff. Although Witte for a time felt "sick and tired of staying in Madison" and wanted "a change of scenery," he did not push the plan to fruition.[29] Though made by default, the decision could hardly have been more definitive for his career. Thereafter, although he left Madison from time to time for extended periods, he retained intellectual and emotional loyalties to Wisconsin, and always returned. Had he transferred he might have grown more cosmopolitan, and his reformism might have been less distinctly colored by Wisconsin progressivism.

Other important decisions followed. In 1910, at the beginning of his second graduate year, through Commons' influence, he had opportunity to become Municipal Reference Librarian of Milwaukee, investigating industrial conditions and drafting corrective ordinances for the city's Socialist administration. But he chose for the time to remain academician rather than activist, reasoning that "I can make a name for myself more surely by doing up my 'Development of the Law of Labor Combination.'" At that time he was an American history major, Professor Fish having assured him that his study of labor law would be an acceptable dissertation in history, and the history department having given him an assistantship which the economics department had failed to match. But before his third graduate year, he made another decision. For 1911–1912, Commons sought his help to teach the "Labor Problems" course. The economist-reformer was much interested in Witte's labor law research, and Witte in turn had appreciated Commons' courses, seminar, and advice on debate topics. Before leaving Wisconsin, Frederick Jackson Turner had advised Witte that Commons, though an economist, was the best historian on the Wisconsin campus.[30] In the spring of 1911 Witte therefore switched to economics, to study under John R. Commons.

2

John R. Commons' Student

DURING THE YEARS IMMEDIATELY PRECEDING World War I it was thus Witte's good fortune to be a student and a friend of a man intensively and effectively seeking answers to pressing social questions. John R. Commons led young scholars not only intellectually, for, through the force of his personality and ideas, he also imprinted his answers upon them and changed their social values and their lives. Personally he was moody and hounded by tragedy. But he was also sensitive, generous, and completely earnest. Intellectually he was complex and rambling, and often unclear to the point of mystery. He was, however, also tenacious and original. To Witte he was "the most lovable man I have ever known."[1]

"I owe to Commons my entire outlook on life and a great many of my ideas," declared Witte pensively in 1945.[2] It was exaggerated but true. From his teacher Witte had absorbed most of the attitudes and assumptions for his reformism, including his caution. Commons was a reformer to the marrow of his bones, but he fully accepted private capitalism and democratic procedures, and insisted that reforms should build on well-established practices and traditions.

After an erratic undergraduate career oscillating between study at Oberlin, work as a union-shop printer in Cleveland, and recovery from a nervous breakdown, Witte's teacher had gone to graduate school in the late 1880's at Johns Hopkins, where he

19

studied economics under Richard T. Ely. Ely espoused reforms ranging from factory legislation, through trade unionism, to municipal and national ownership of public utilities, basing his doctrines on notions of Social Gospel benevolence, an ordered and organic society, and German-style state paternalism. For a time in the 1890's Commons' thought resembled that of Ely. But in the early years of the twentieth century he began to shift away from Christian ethics and state paternalism and to base his anti-laissez-faire reformism on the ideas of an "institutional" economics.[3] It was Commons' institutionalist assumptions that Witte, as a student, absorbed.

Commons was not satisfied with the classical economics of Adam Smith, David Ricardo, and others, who had taught a concept of automatic equilibria in response to purely economic stimuli. And hedonistic economics based on consumer satisfaction seemed to him little better. From his vast reading Witte's teacher was attracted to the nineteenth-century German school of historical economists, who explained economic decisions by evolution, custom, property concepts, and conflicts of interests. He called the writings of his fellow-institutionalist Thorstein Veblen brilliant, especially Veblen's doctrine that a proper theory of value rested on the evolution of habits and customs of men acting together in society.[4] For, even more than from books, Commons derived his institutional economics from a highly pragmatic contemplation of actual experience. Economics to him was not a matter of abstract "economic man" responding to "natural economic law," but a process by which breathing men and groups of men came together in fluid social encounters, amid a flow of time and myriad rational and irrational influences, to make valuations, apportionments, and exchanges.[5] His basic economic unit was not the classic product of labor, or the hedonic commodity of consumption, but rather one of social activity: the transaction. Commons of course recognized that economic forces such as cost of production on the supply side and desire to consume on the demand side set outer limits on the transaction, but he thought they impinged imperfectly and left a wide range for discretion. Within that range there was room for human volition based on non-economic considerations, which created a "negotiational psychology."[6] It was to the question of how negotiators made economic decisions largely on non-economic grounds that Commons addressed his attention.

John Commons was foremost a labor economist, and his thought at many points was an elaboration and a generalizing of the philosophy of collective bargaining. His view of society resembled a vastly enlarged picture, in motion, of management and union representatives around the negotiating table. One way in which the negotiators made decisions, Commons believed, was by "working rules," a concept that he admitted grew out of the "shop rules" by which organized capital and organized labor agreed to restrictions of output. "Working rules" was a broad term, for Commons wanted to include all of reality in his scheme, not merely to isolate one or two factors for hypothetical study. The term covered all impingements—from informal custom and norms of conduct, through private organizations' dicta such as union rules and the business ethics of trade associations, to formal laws and judicial decisions. Working rules gave continuity to the economic order, yielding the precedents of the past as a guide for present conduct and the patterns to expect in future conduct. They were the stuff from which institutions were made. They set a *collective* standard for individual and group action.[7]

Accepting collective standards, Witte's teacher fully endorsed the early twentieth-century trend towards greater organization and associationalism in American economic life. A champion of trade unionism, he declared in 1925 that he had been a follower of Samuel Gompers since before 1900, and praised the president of the American Federation of Labor as "one of the ten or twelve great Americans." Gompers' "slow-minded" learning from patient experimentation, he declared, was more "scientific" than the theories of the labor intellectuals who criticized Gompers.[8] Unlike some progressive reformers, Commons championed incorporation of business and development of employers' associations as well as organization of labor. Organized businessmen, by evolving corporation policies, business ethics, and trade association practices, helped to create the "working rules" that would bring order into economic life. Rather than denouncing monopoly, or pursuing the chimerical goals of keeping economic units small and restoring perfect competition, Witte's mentor emphasized that business incorporation laws of the mid-nineteenth century had begun the stabilization of capitalism. Moreover, organized interest groups, both of business and of labor, could become building blocks for democracy. "Individuals seldom act as individuals," Commons declared. Instead they acted in association, and to deny them an organized voice was to deny them representation. By allowing association government could bring conflicting interests into countervailing equilibrium. Thus associations served a "public utility" function, and democracy became "the partnership of classes." It was not easy to achieve the equilibrium, he conceded, "but what else is there to do?"[9]

Of all forms of organized activity, that which most impressed Witte's teacher was the work of the courts, despite their seeming hostility in his day to collective bargaining. Commons considered law and its interpretation as overarchingly important in economic transactions, and the prime example of working rules. Hence his keen interest in Witte's study of the role of judicial decisions in labor disputes. The manner in which court decisions had transformed customs into collectively sanctioned and enforced doctrines of common law epitomized the evolution of all working rules. Commons gave special attention to two doctrines that were current and that impinged most directly on his interests: that restraint of trade by a business corporation was permissible if it was "reasonable"; and that business "goodwill" was a form of property.

To Commons the doctrine of reasonableness was a vital, evolving concept, as necessary to his view of economics as transaction and bargaining. When the United States Supreme Court sanctioned "reasonable" restraint of trade in its 1911 decision dividing up the Standard Oil Company, it had merely recognized the right to exercise bargaining power. "For," wrote Witte's teacher, "restraint of trade is bargaining power, and reasonable restraint of trade is reasonable bargaining power." Somewhere within the limits for negotiation that economic forces set there were narrower limits of reasonableness at which the courts considered the bargains made to infringe upon the public interest. Within those limits negotiations involved persuasion. Outside them it became unfair coercion. Commons recognized that the courts' definitions of unfairness and coercion, and therefore of reasonableness, were highly subjective, and that sometimes they allowed the strong wider limits than the weak. Yet they had the virtue of being practical rules made in real situations. Commons' quarrel with the courts was not that the doctrine of reasonableness was wrong, but that the judges failed to see the public utility in labor organization, and so refused to allow labor unions much range in which to exercise restraint of trade.[10]

Upon the doctrine of reasonableness Commons reconstructed his social ethics. Where earlier he had based his ethics on Christianity, by the time Witte was his student he had adopted a secular criterion which he named Pragmatic Idealism. By his new standard the goal in industrial reform was to legislate those practices whose prior adoption by the most progressive firms attested their workability. "The problem of social idealism through collective action," he declared, "consists in bringing the 'average' and those below the 'average' up to the level" of the best.[11] His was an ethics for reform, but hardly for radicalism. Commons rejected the doctrines of Karl Marx. Marx had been a very great thinker, Witte's teacher conceded in 1925, but unfortunately he had formed his ideas at the very nadir of the capitalistic system. So he had not foreseen the regenerative potentialities of capitalism.

Capitalism had partly regenerated itself since the time of Marx by using the corporate form of organization and by developing trade associations with their business ethics. Regeneration had partly been forced on it from the outside, through the application of common law, antitrust legislation, regulative commissions, and the Federal Reserve system. Where Marx prescribed dogmas, moreover, Commons ascribed to the instrumentalist version of pragmatism, which tried to establish social ideas through science and experimentation. The virtue of making the practices of advanced firms the reform goal, he argued, was what they could "be investigated and tested as to facts." In that goal lay the "upper practical limit of idealism," and hence reasonableness. His reasonable limit allowed reformers "plenty of room for enthusiasm and propaganda."[12] For Commons and for Witte, purposeful but evolutionary and cautious reform was the true expression of reasonableness.

Closely related not only to Commons' reformism but specifically to the place of labor within a system of private property was the second judicial doctrine which impressed Commons, the concept of business "goodwill." In cases such as that of the Danbury hatters' boycott in 1908, the Supreme Court ruled that intangibles such as accessibility to labor and to markets were goodwill, which in turn constituted a form of property deserving full legal protection. Commons agreed that value lay in intangibles, and argued that indeed the value of property depended on a whole cluster of them, e.g., the various rights and powers property conferred upon its owner, the corresponding duties and liabilities it lay on others, and owners' accessibility to its use. Intangibles also gave property a dimension of "futurity," so that its value was bound up with the expectations and potential it represented to the owner for his future use.[13] All the working rules of the entire social, economic, and legal system converged to secure and give value to those expectations, and to make a business—to use his favorite phrase—"a going concern." To Witte's teacher, property was a matter of vital social relationships and collective controls, not of individual or static natural rights.

Commons appropriated the goodwill concept just as he had that of reasonableness. This time he used his acquisition for a theory of labor relations. He rejected the popular notion that because the price of labor fluctuated with supply and demand, economists must treat labor like any other commodity. In the labor transaction, he pointed out, there was no permanent exchange, only an offering and an acceptance of services, subject to termination at any moment. He encouraged employers instead to build their labor relations on an alternate idea of "industrial goodwill." Industrial goodwill was not a matter of virtue or altruism, but of management and labor mutually making concessions to each other's personal and class interests, even passions and prejudices, in order to create the expectation of continuity in the tenuous labor transaction. To supplement goodwill and to help make it operative, he suggested also a "public-utility theory of labor": a recognition that labor's welfare extended beyond class to the public interest and that legislation beneficial to labor would benefit the public.[14] But the task of management he would leave to the managers. He admired successful capitalists, and supported the idea that labor could gain more by bargaining with them than by displacing them and their entrepreneurial skills.[15]

Thus Commons accepted capitalism, and even the essence of reactionary court decisions. His strategy was to transform judicial doctrines that were seemingly adverse to labor into arguments for class harmony within capitalism, and for labor reform. He gave early expression to a conservative philosophy of trade unionism. It was within this framework of cautious reformism that Edwin Witte would build his career.

*   *   *   *   *

Commons experienced difficulty in articulating his doctrines, and had not yet set them forth systematically when Witte began to study under him. He did, however, convey very convincingly their practical applications, by taking his students with him into many field investigations and into his work as government adviser. More than absorbing Commons' opaque verbiage, Witte's education under the prominent reformer consisted of undertaking a series of practical tasks which formed a virtual microcosm of his later career. In August, 1912, Witte went to work for the Wisconsin Industrial Commission.

No institution demonstrated better than the Industrial Commission Commons' ideas of interest groups coming together and negotiating the rules whereby industry would function. Commons was chief architect of the commission when the legislature created it in 1911,[16] and served as one of its three original commissioners until 1913. His particular contribution to the industrial commission device was to adapt a pattern already used in railroad and public utility regulation which combined the function of investigation with those of order-making and administration, all in one permanent agency. Largely at his suggestion, the 1911 legislature repealed much of Wisconsin's specific legislation affecting working conditions, and replaced it with only the very general requirement that places of industrial employment be "reasonably" safe, healthful, comfortable, and conducive to good morals. It gave to the commission, along with other duties such as industrial mediation and regulating child labor, the task of deciding what was reasonable and then issuing and enforcing the specific rules. Witte's teacher thought that the commission was better equipped than the legislature to make technical judgments, and that its enforcement was better than the courts' because it could bypass formal, rigid procedures and respond to social and economic facts that courts seldom considered. In practice the commission appointed advisory commissions with representatives from interest groups such as the Wisconsin Manufacturers' Association and the Wisconsin Federation of Labor as well as from the public. Commons' theory was that courts would accept as "reasonable" rules made by such representatives more readily than they would the autocratic pronouncement of experts, and that to consult all interest groups would fulfill the courts' rule that regulation should involve "due process of law." In practice he and his colleagues found also that persons affected, especially employers, complied far more readily when their recognized spokesmen had agreed in advance to a particular order. Commons termed the Industrial Commission a "fourth branch of government."[17] It was a concept of government built on the rationale of collective bargaining.

A major task for which the legislature created the commission in 1911 was to administer Wisconsin's new workmen's compensation law, providing employer-financed insurance to workers against industrial accidents. Witte's position in 1912 was that of statistician, and for six months he worked chiefly at compiling a bulletin on rates for workmen's compensation insurance. He and his colleagues indicted insurance companies for discriminating against the new law, which was still optional, and suggested that corrective legislation might be in order. In 1913 the legislature gave the Industrial Commission power to supervise the rates.[18] The commission assignment gave Witte intimate involvement in the practical functioning of Commons' economic ideas, his first direct contact with social insurance and labor law, and his first opportunity to influence legislation.

Meantime Commons helped Witte get a new position, beginning in December, 1912, as secretary to John M. Nelson, the Congressman from the Madison area for whom Witte had once done a bit of party footwork. By the arrangement Nelson got an aide upon whom he depended for economic advice. Witte in turn got to move beyond Wisconsin for a time, and also to associate with the Insurgent Republican faction of congressional progressives.[19] In 1914 Witte had the opportunity of working on the historic Clayton antitrust bill, since it was assigned to the House Judiciary Committee of which Nelson was a member. Nelson opposed the measure, and Witte wrote a minority report that Nelson and a fellow dissenter submitted.[20] It was not that Nelson disliked the bill's central idea of curbing monopoly. He supported a companion measure, based on the ideas of reform attorney Louis Brandeis, who wanted a federal trade commission. Witte's report objected that the Clayton bill's language was too weak to prevent the practices it purported to outlaw. His indictment extended to the clause exempting labor unions from antitrust action.[21] He further doubted, with considerable prescience, the effectiveness of a section declaring labor not to be a commodity, the section Gompers hailed as labor's "Magna Carta."[22] The bill passed, but Witte's involvement in it demonstrated Witte's growing facility to bring to the drafting of law, especially labor law, highly specific and technical considerations. Far from satisfying him, it whetted his interest in a truly adequate labor disputes law.

For a time, from 1913 to 1915, it appeared that Witte might have the chance to generate such a law. Commons was serving as a member of a United States Commission on Industrial Relations, and arranged for Witte to become one of its investigators, beginning late in 1913.[23] In the following year and a half Witte and an assistant compiled more than twenty-five research reports on such subjects as antitrust law and unions, damage suits in labor cases, boycotting, and picketing. His main report was on the subject of his own academic study, the courts' role in labor disputes, and foreshadowed his most substantial later writings. Witte recommended to the commissioners a labor relations law on the lines of the British Trades Disputes Act of 1906, whose central idea was that the government should leave its hands off labor disputes, regardless of how much one side coerced another, so long as the parties did not use criminal methods.[24] In the end the commission had no effect on legislation, largely because it suffered an inglorious demise when a quarrel broke out between Commons and the commission's chairman, Frank P. Walsh, with Commons criticizing Walsh for turning investigations into a muckraking exposé rather than pursuing solid research.[25] Both factions, however, accepted Witte's ideas in their final reports.[26] Witte, in turn, had taken a long stride in developing his ideas for a labor relations law.

Being a protégé of Commons took Witte into still other tasks. In 1915 he contributed anonymously a section on the law of labor combinations to Commons' and John B. Andrews' book, *Principles of Labor Legislation*. (Although usually self-effacing, a decade later he described the section as "still the best popular account" of the subject.) During the next few years Commons and his associates also drew heavily on Witte's researches for sections of their landmark *History of Labour in the United States*.[27] In 1916, under a special assignment for the Wisconsin

Industrial Commission he stepped for the first time into the role of labor mediator, by attempting to forestall a strike of Milwaukee machinists. At that he did not succeed.[28] But each task under Commons, whether advising the Industrial Commission on workmen's compensation, advising Nelson on legislation, researching and recommending labor law, contributing to books, or acting as industrial mediator, gave Witte opportunity to put some idea of Commons' into practice, and foreshadowed some part of his future career.

In 1916 Witte returned temporarily to his formal academic studies, and prepared for his preliminary doctoral examination. When he took it in August, Ely praised his performance and that of his fellow student of Commons, Selig Perlman, as the best in Ely's quarter century at Wisconsin.[29] That done, the twenty-nine-year-old Witte turned once again to other matters, and not until 1927 did he receive his Ph.D. degree.

For one matter, Witte had met a young lady while working in Chicago for the United States Industrial Relations Commission in 1915. Florence Rimsnider was a trained librarian of the Commission staff, in her mid-twenties. She had been reared in Madison, and, like Witte, was a participant in the pursuit of progressive legislation, having worked for five years in the Wisconsin Legislative Reference Library. Their first date was in the summer, and Witte took her to a baseball game. She did not care for baseball, but she did care for Witte. Within three weeks they were engaged. Because she decided to carry through a previous commitment to work for nearly a year in New York cataloguing material in the Columbia Law Library, Witte courted her largely by correspondence—plus several visits to her city. Back at Madison on September 2, 1916, they were married in a small ceremony on the porch of her family's Lake Waubesa cottage.[30]

Witte's life thereafter centered in his work, his home, and a few commonplace diversions. Apart from his professional accomplishments he was quite an ordinary man. In his moments of relaxation he was an avid sports fan, annually cultivated an exceptionally beautiful flower garden, and traveled. For his deepest friendships outside the family he looked to a small faculty men's dining club and to people with whom he worked.[31] He had little taste for the stylish but superficial type of social life. In 1931 he once promised Mrs. Witte to take her out more, noting ruefully that if he did he would have to "learn the game of light chatter which bores me so much." And then he let his professional aspirations get in the way, for with unconscious contradiction he determined at the same time also to work harder at writing and publishing. In the Depression, he thought, "real economic leadership is needed. . . . I feel that in this time I really have something to contribute and I am going to work hard to make good."[32] Work was always Witte's overwhelming preoccupation.

Yet he found time to enjoy his family, with profound loyalty and deep affection. The Wittes' first son died a few hours after birth, but another son, John, born in 1918, and two daughters, Margaret and Elizabeth, born in 1922 and 1926, grew to complete their family circle. Witte was fond of small children, both his own and eventually his ten grandchildren, and he often read or played games with them. While far too busy to be a "little league" type of father, he especially enjoyed taking his family on outings and picnics. As his children grew he granted them a large measure of independence. John, ironically, chose to join a fraternity at the University of Wisconsin and later to become an independent retail merchant in nearby Fort Atkinson. Yet the relationship between father and son remained warm, and on most political and social questions the son adopted his father's views.[33]

Mrs. Witte, her husband once declared, was "the real center of our family." She was an energetic woman, more active than he in local civic and church affairs. It was her role to see to life's details, partly because Witte was busy, and partly because he had a penchant for overlooking small matters, constantly losing his hat or his shaving kit, or forgetting his coat or briefcase. She brought to the marriage a strong pride and encouragement in Witte's professional attainments, and on large decisions as well as small he considered her wishes. Her deep attachment to Madison was important in keeping his career centered there. There they owned and lived in the same modest bungalow home from 1919 until his death in 1960.[34] Between them the bond was strong and genuine.

* * * * *

In the fall of 1916, after his marriage, Witte returned to the university as an assistant in political economy. His assignment was to teach "Labor Legislation and Administration" in Commons' absence, to help supervise Commons' students, and to help Ely revise several books. In taking the post he understood that he might later receive the offer of a position on the Wisconsin faculty. Shortly after the academic year began, however, the Wisconsin Industrial Commission invited him to become its executive secretary. Commons encouraged the move, declaring that "the future of the Commission depends on having this kind of man." At first Witte hesitated. He was uncertain that the Commission was the best route to his professional future.[35] He also feared that his name might become a political issue in the imminent state elections. Conservative Republicans wanted the legislature to weaken the Commission's authority over workmen's compensation insurance companies, just opposite to what Witte had recommended in 1912. But after the election, in which progressives won enough seats to stay the hand of conservative Governor Emanuel Philipp, Witte accepted.[36] His decision harbingered a characteristic of his reform career: his contribution would not be to add much to Commons' theories and ideas, but to work them out in practice.

In Witte's graduate student days Commons was preoccupied with practical questions. His and Andrews' 1916 book, *Principles of Labor Legislation*—which outlined laws to facilitate collective bargaining, minimum wage laws, regulation of workmen's hours and safety, social insurance, and measures such as public works and public employment offices to reduce unemployment—reflected this practical emphasis. Witte kept in touch with his teacher as Commons moved into a more theoretical period in the 1920's. But he confessed that he got "lost" in Commons' theories.[37] What Witte inherited from Commons, consequently, was not a system of thought so much as a set of assumptions useful for practical reformism: that a wide variety of practical and noneconomic considerations impinged upon the making of any economic decision, law, or institution; that laws worked out by the persons whom they would effect were usually superior to those of theoreticians; that associationalism was an irreversible fact and the best means of harmonizing groups in conflict lay in collective bargaining and negotiation; that where voluntary action failed to protect the economically weak the state should rectify the imbalance; and most of all, that social change could come through a pragmatic and democratic approach, without veering from America's capitalistic and constitutional traditions. These assumptions made up the essence of his progressive approach to reform.

3

Servant of Wisconsin

WHEN WITTE MOVED HIS OFFICE from the University of Wisconsin to the state capitol in January of 1917 he did not intend to renounce an academic career, but not until 1933 did he finally retrace the steps back to the campus. For the first five years he worked as secretary of the Wisconsin Industrial Commission, and then, for eleven years more, he was chief of another agency closely associated with Wisconsin progressivism, the Legislative Reference Library. Both positions helped to mold Witte's matured reformism. They offered opportunity for investigation and research, always Witte's forte. They immersed him in the legal aspects of labor policy and economics. They kept him confined largely within the boundaries of state legislation rather than the broader field of national action on labor and welfare problems. And they kept him in very close touch with legislators, employers, and trade-union leaders who made their judgments on the basis of the detailed, everyday ramifications of economics and public policy, more than with academic scholars whose views were larger but less immediately practical. The effect was that Witte became preoccupied even more than his great teacher Commons with the immediate and the actual, and much less with abstract styles of thought. He developed an operational pragmatism and a genuine respect for practical politicians, both of which pleased men in government and prepared him for his numerous governmental advisory roles.

In the Wisconsin Industrial Commission Witte worked in a context of practical, flexible problem-solving. The state legislature had, of course, built into the agency Commons' twin ideas of combining the functions of investigation, order-making, and enforcement, and of having the commission spell out rules giving specific content to regulative laws stated only in general terms. By the time Witte became secretary in 1917, the agency and its advisory committees had already written most of the safety and sanitation codes governing working conditions in Wisconsin. Yet each year Witte oversaw the development of further such orders,[1] and as supervisor of a staff of engineers, inspectors, deputies, examiners, and clerical workers he learned the art of making orders effective.

Witte's involvement in one of the leading labor reforms of the day—the regulation of children's and women's labor—demonstrated his and the commission's methods. At about the time he took up his post, the Wisconsin Federation of Labor, the Milwaukee Council of Social Agencies, and the Wisconsin Consumers' League presented the commission a major petition reminding it that the law gave it the power to set limits on working hours for women. Earlier the commission had created a special Women's Department to see that women and children worked in safe and healthy environments, but had done little to limit women's hours. Witte arranged hearings throughout the state, where commissioners could gather the opinions of employers, workers, and members of the public who felt directly interested in the proposed regulations. He personally compiled a report on practices in Great Britain. Witte found that the British had concluded that excessive work caused physical harm, but he candidly admitted that they had not proven that the reformers' ideal eight hours was necessarily the proper working day. In June, 1917, the commission issued orders forbidding employment of women at night in factories and laundries, and despite Witte's admission, applied the eight-hour standard to their night work in other establishments.[2]

Witte and his staff applied the new orders flexibly, however.

As was typical for the commission, they proceeded to modify their own promulgations with extensions and exemptions to cover special cases.[3] And they enforced them with a degree of opportunism. In one case the streetcar workers' union in Kenosha staunchly opposed the employment of women as conductors, while operators insisted just as adamantly that they had to employ women because of World War I labor shortages. The commission issued orders forbidding use of women conductors during night and rush hours—a blatant compromise.[4] In another instance the agency struck an informal bargain with an employer in La Crosse, allowing the employer to employ women temporarily at night, contrary to the spirit of the law, if he would raise their wages to a decent minimum.[5] Such was the context of negotiation and flexibility in which Witte worked.

The commission's efforts on behalf of working women and children gave Witte a first-hand lesson in the fine art of framing labor reform legislation so as to circumvent objections from the courts. In 1919 the agency issued orders gradually introducing minimum wage standards for women. Five years later a Wisconsin company challenged the minimum wage orders in the courts. Witte helped the state's attorney general, Herman Ekern, prepare the brief to fight the challenge. But the state lost the decision in the case of adult women. Thereupon the legislature passed a new law stating only that firms could not employ women under "oppressive" conditions, including wages of less than "reasonable and adequate compensation." But the commission, accepting the realities of the situation, did not re-establish specific minimum wage standards. Instead it used the new law as a tool to bring pressure on the lowest-paying firms to raise wages.[6] Such a technique did not offend the courts; it applied Commons' principle of trying to bring backward firms up to the standards of the best; and it demonstrated a method less offensive than blind coercion based on rigid legal standards.

Working as the Industrial Commission's secretary reinforced in Witte a willingness pragmatically to abandon any theory that did not pass the test of experience, and also a distrust of federal as opposed to state administration in reform programs. The commission had legal responsibility to try to stabilize employment in Wisconsin. One of the most popular approaches at the time was to establish systems of free public employment offices which supposedly would centralize the labor market, match workmen to suitable jobs and to localities where jobs were open, and reduce labor turnover and unemployment. During Witte's secretaryship the Wisconsin commission co-operated closely with the wartime United States Employment Service, set up twenty-five new employment offices throughout the state, and thus vastly expanded upon the few employment offices already existing in Wisconsin cities.[7] Witte, however, soon concluded that in practice the new offices did not perform as theory had predicted. They were useful, but they did not significantly centralize the labor market.[8] Moreover, he criticized the federal government's role, not merely because Washington cut off funds at the end of the war just when the employment offices were most needed for postwar readjustment, but also for overstaffing with unqualified personnel, for prolabor bias, and for general inefficiency.[9] Willingness to abandon theory in the face of experience, suspicion of federal action, and concern that reforms not be too partisan all became permanent features of Witte's reformism.

The Industrial Commission extended Witte's experience with America's initial form of social insurance, workmen's compensation. His appointment in 1917 occurred just after thirty-four American states, in the years 1911 to 1916, had brought the American social insurance movement its first significant results by passing laws creating the new form of insurance for industrial accidents. Wisconsin's law, passed in 1911, was the first such state law to go into effect, prove successful in operation, and stand the test of the courts. Designed by Commons, it fit well with the Wisconsin approach to reform that was so much a part of Witte's outlook. The Industrial Commission was to supervise its administration. Yet the legislation neither created a state insurance fund, as did a Washington State law of the same year, nor even make the compensation system compulsory. A

Wisconsin employer could elect either to operate under the new law, which had the advantage of making compensation in fixed amounts automatic and predictable, or he could continue to operate under the risk of lawsuits based on traditional liability laws. To induce employers to adopt the new system, the law relieved from traditional common-law liabilities those who did so, and denied important legal defenses to the employer who was inclined to take his chances under the old common law. Moreover, it allowed employers to form mutual insurance companies, rather than leave them at the mercy of commercial insurance carriers.[10] The law's semivoluntarism was in part a technique to make the system less vulnerable to attack in the courts, but it also fit Commons' preference for inducing all affected parties to co-operate with reforms voluntarily or semivoluntarily, rather than submit to naked coercion.

Witte directed his main efforts in workmen's compensation toward making the institution more effective, through careful attention to procedure and technical detail. By the time he became secretary the reform was well established in Wisconsin, but the commissioners and others were still proposing improvements. One suggestion, coming from an attorney for employers, was to treble compensation for injuries to children employed in violation of child labor laws, with the employer rather than the insurance company having to pay. The amendment especially intrigued Witte, for it demonstrated how with deliberate engineering potent reforms could be built into the framework of an institution. Other amendments during Witte's term as secretary provided compensation for occupational diseases as well as for injuries, and generally extended the system and liberalized benefits. Witte helped also to foster administrative procedures that followed Commons' dictum that social insurance should work to prevent the hazard and not merely to dole out compensation. In his first year as secretary the commission staff increased its systematic scrutiny of employers' accident reports to spot and eliminate specific hazardous conditions. Under his administration it also increased its co-operation with federal and state boards of vocational education, in an effort more effectively to rehabilitate workers who had suffered injury. Later, after Witte had moved to the Legislative Reference Library, he personally drafted all workmen's compensation amendments.[11] Witte's experience with workmen's compensation demonstrated that there was room for social creativity in the minute structural details of a social insurance institution, and not only in its broader conceptualization.

Witte kept his focus on structural detail even when he ventured briefly into the more abstract realm of social insurance theory. In 1930, after he had left the Industrial Commission, he undertook to reply to economists who argued that workmen's compensation was primarily a method to assign accident costs properly to industry. The system did not assign the costs effectively to industry, he argued, for workers never received benefits at the rate of 100 per cent of wages, and therefore they bore a share of the costs. Witte borrowed a phrase from E. H. Downey, author of a 1926 book on the subject, and argued that a compensation system was instead a method to achieve the "least social cost" of industrial accidents. That rationale, he argued, presented the institution in truly social terms and accorded with a 1924 decision of the United States Supreme Court that workmen's compensation was a proper use of a state's police power to promote the general welfare.[12] But Witte was not spinning theory for its own sake, nor even to be idealistic. He went on to argue that to achieve the "least social cost" lawmakers should structure compensation systems to emphasize prevention, to eliminate costly overhead and court litigation, and to benefit business as well as workers. Such immediate considerations were more profitable than trying to achieve "exact justice" or to assign with precision the responsibility for industrial accidents.[13]

Witte's preoccupation with very immediate reform goals rather than with theoretical and abstract perfection harbingered the stance he would take later, when his role in social insurance would be much greater. All of his activities as secretary of the Industrial Commission helped to prepare him for such a stance.

He dealt with industrial working conditions, women's and children's labor, employment offices and workmen's compensation, and occasionally industrial mediation—not academically, but as immediate problems requiring immediate solutions. He addressed himself to the actual working of labor law, and to improving the details of its working, rather than to ideology or to grand theories of reform.

*   *   *   *   *

In April, 1922, Witte left the Industrial Commission to become chief of Wisconsin's Legislative Reference Library. His new task preoccupied him somewhat less with administrative duties, and gave him more opportunity to engage in research. It also demanded that he develop extreme skill in the intricacies of drafting law, a skill of incalcuable value to a practical-minded reformer. Like the old job it reinforced the vein of caution in his reform outlook. In the administration of the library itself, Witte perfected the technical workings of the institution as he found it, rather than attempting to conceptualize and promote any grand new schemes. And he took great care not to offend any group in the Wisconsin legislature. His eleven years as chief were especially useful to his type of reformism because they provided an education in how to deal with legislators.

The Wisconsin Legislative Reference Library was not, despite its title, so much a library as a bureau whose purposes were to bring objective research to bear on the process of legislation, and to assure precision in the wording of laws. As such, it was in 1922 still a relatively novel institution. In 1869 the British Parliament had established a bill-drafting office that Americans eventually looked to as a model of political neutrality in its function, and late in the nineteenth century the American Bar Association began to emphasize that drafting was a task for specialists. In 1890 New York's state librarian began to develop a special research service for legislators. But it was in Wisconsin that inventive public officials combined the two functions, research and drafting, into one model legislative reference bureau.[14]

Wisconsin's services originated in 1901, when James H. Stout, a state senator and president of Wisconsin's Free Library Commission, won overwhelming approval for a bill to give his commission authority and funds to establish a reference library in the state capitol for legislators' use. The commission's secretary, Frank Hutchins, a man familiar with the New York State Library's services and a champion of new programs for his agency, was the bill's most active promoter, and perhaps its originator. According to legend a young graduate history student at Wisconsin, Charles McCarthy, also helped promote the service in 1901 by voluntarily assisting legislators with their research problems, and then offering his services to Hutchins. Without question in was McCarthy, the strong-willed man who was the library's first employee and its chief until his death in 1921, who built the agency into a law-making instrument that won attention throughout American capitals and even abroad. McCarthy energetically advertised his services to legislators, and quickly added bill drafting to the agency's original research functions. Although other states seldom built upon the exact Wisconsin pattern, by 1920 about thirty states had established agencies with one or both of the Wisconsin library's functions. Wisconsin, however, was the recognized leader.[15]

Ostensibly the Free Library Commission and the Reference Library were nonpartisan, but when the commission began looking for a successor to McCarthy, political friends of La Follette were keenly interested. So also were their opponents. The editor of the Milwaukee *Evening Sentinel* thought that the library could continue to be very useful, but warned also that it could "be a source of considerable mischief" if its chief tried "to initiate legislation or to send the state off into a field of experimentation at the expense of the taxpayers." He thought it doubtful "whether any position at the capital has a more important bearing on the work of the legislature."[16] For nearly a year after McCarthy's death the commission appointed nobody. Finally, early in 1922, progressive governor John J. Blaine began in earnest to search for a new chief. One of the Industrial Commissioners, Reuben G. Knutson, suggested Witte—albeit reluctantly, for he valued Witte highly as the commission's secretary.[17] The state's revisor of statutes, Charles Crownhart, a former chairman of the Industrial Commission whom Witte (and Blaine) admired, encouraged the choice.[18] Within a few days the Library Commission offered Witte the post, and he accepted.[19]

The progressives could not have found a man temperamentally more different from his predecessor. McCarthy had been a flamboyant and aggressive man, well suited to his role as innovator of an institution, but less well suited to overseeing its continued success. From his base in the library he had extended his hand into a host of activities, from sponsoring an excursion to Japan for the University of Wisconsin baseball team (he, of course, accompanied it) to making a futile bid, for obscure reasons, for election to the United States Senate.[20] Under him the library was strongly identified with the progressive tradition. Commons worked closely with him and in his student days Witte himself had used McCarthy's services freely for his debate and other researches.[21] McCarthy found subtle ways to lead legislators to ideas and reading material that he selected. Inevitably he had inspired and thrived upon controversy, especially the charge that his library was a "bill factory" which usurped the legislative function.[22] Witte, far more than McCarthy, was suited to the role of assuring the institution's continued success and effectiveness. He accepted the library's professed purposes of creating better-informed men and better-drafted laws as sufficiently important ends in themselves, and made little use of his position for extraneous activities. Forthright, with little taste for surreptitious maneuver and controversy, he took seriously the accepted ideal that a legislative reference service should be politically neutral.

It was not easy for the library to escape charges that it promoted partisan legislation. During each regular session of the legislature while Witte was chief, he and his library handled between 2000 and 4000 requests for drafting bills, employing up to a half-dozen attorneys as draftsmen.[23] One of the original arguments for the drafting service, in addition to the quest for technical precision in wording, was that it would free legislators from dependence on lobbyists for their bills. Champions of the service even argued that it constituted a kind of lobby for the interests of the public.[24] This argument, while ostensibly for objectivity in bill-drafting, of course had strong overtones of progressive ideology. Witte pointed out that his service did not prevent lobbyists from attempting to persuade, and even that it helped lobbyists to get reliable information. But he reiterated that it freed legislators from dependence upon the lobbyists for information and bills.[25]

Very early McCarthy had established rules of drafting that he had then cited in answer to attacks that his library promoted legislation. Only upon detailed, written, and signed instructions from a member of the legislature would a draftsman draft a bill. He would not make suggestions as to content and ideas, but only upon clerical and technical details. Nor could the library, in turn, take responsibility for the legality, constitutionality, or further handling of the bills.[26] Witte continued essentially the same rules. Perhaps because he maintained somewhat closer relations with the state's governors than had McCarthy, his agency accepted suggestions for bills not only from legislators but also from executive offices and agencies, and even from quasi-official bodies such as the County Boards Association. Yet he insisted that before such a suggestion became a bill a legislator should take it up and sponsor it. Thus he maintained the principle that the library did not manufacture legislation apart from the legislature. As a safeguard, in addition to the draftsmen's rules, he personally reviewed virtually all bills, although it meant for him a prodigious amount of work which he admitted that a better administrator might have avoided.[27] And where McCarthy had openly insisted upon his right to declare his views on controversial legislation, Witte warned his employees not to advocate, oppose, or even express opinions upon legislative proposals.[28] He recognized, with his dry humor, that he and his men had to draft many bills whose "only redeeming feature" was "that they have no chance of passage." Nevertheless, he warned his men to treat every suggestion as if it were a good one, and to attempt to fit it into the legal framework. His library, he repeatedly emphasized, was "not a bill factory but a custom order shop."[29]

Witte insisted that his custom shop concept did not reduce his service to merely passive and technical assistance. Seldom had a legislator thought through all ramifications when he suggested a bill, Witte found, nor through all the problems of fitting his proposal "into the existing governmental structure." It was therefore the duty of the draftsman to help work out "a well rounded and practical bill" through conferences with the legislator, or sometimes even by attending the caucus of the party or faction behind the measure. If the draftsman considered the proposal unconstitutional, Witte instructed him to say so, but nevertheless to proceed to draft the measure as its sponsor wished.[30] Or the draftsman might point out what existing law and proper procedure was, as Witte did, for instance, to Assemblyman John N. Kaiser, newly elected in the 1932 Democratic sweep. Kaiser favored old-age pensions legislation. Witte advised him that if he wanted a national system, the proper procedure was to propose a memorial to Congress rather than a law. If Kaiser contemplated state action, he should first acquaint himself with Wisconsin's existing old-age pensions law. Kaiser also favored higher income taxes and abolition of the real estate tax. Witte pointed out that personal property taxes yielded 65 per cent of the state's revenues, and suggested that if Kaiser meant to make up that amount without extensive change in the state's existing income tax law, he would have to propose rates that might be impossible to collect. In each case Witte requested further instructions.[31]

In giving advice such as he gave Kaiser, Witte acted consistently with his dictum that the draftsman should not decide questions of policy, but should certainly raise them. To do so intelligently, he insisted, required more than mere technical skill. It was no strange coincidence that Witte sought qualities in draftsmen that were two of his own outstanding strengths: a broad knowledge of " the structure and operation of government," and the ingenuity to imagine how a bill would actually work.[32] Each rested, characteristically, upon an attitude of intelligent realism. And the exercise of each meant a creative role in legislation, however much the demands of nonpartisanship circumscribed that creativity.

*   *   *   *   *

Witte found that strict impartiality was even more difficult in the library's other major function, investigation and research. Facility for research was Witte's outstanding strength as chief of the library. McCarthy had organized the library's research facilities with an emphasis on quick access to currently useful information. Therefore he had compiled a well-indexed collection of clippings, bulletins, exemplary laws and legislative proposals in other states and countries, and other such reference material, rather than extensive conventional library holdings. Each year Witte and his staff answered hundreds and thousands of research requests, first of all from legislators, but also from state officials, political candidates, civic, business, labor, and other groups and ordinary citizens. Some requests were brief and lightened Witte's day: please send information, an unmarried lady once wrote, as to what a girl might inherit if she married a widower in Texas with three children and he died—and similar information if she married a widower in New York with two children. Others were very extensive and highly important for pending legislation, requiring weeks of research.[33]

The emphasis upon quick collection of information to answer immediately practical questions suited Witte's own research habits and his encyclopedic facility for mastering statistics and details. Declaring that legislators would turn to hunches, prejudices, and lobbyists if confronted with too much undigested material, Witte strongly emphasized that he had not merely to guide them to information but also to summarize it into concise, usable form.[34] Often he kept his answers within the scope of an extended letter or memorandum, and even his longer reports were concise. During his dozen years as chief, he composed, with his staff's help, a hundred or more papers, briefs, and articles on a wide variety of subjects, especially taxation, labor legislation, and governmental procedure. His reports were not at all speculative or academic; they were descriptive compilations of facts and summarizations of leading issues. Even such reports took Witte very near the turbulent waters of partisan politics, however. Therefore he added to his emphasis on hard information an air of detachment and impartiality.[35] The result was a highly informative but matter-of-fact, impersonal, and passive manner of writing and of formal speaking that marked his style throughout his life, even when he dealt with controversial issues and actually advanced strong opinions.

Witte was anxious that legislators of all political persuasions use his research services; and all did, even for highly partisan purposes. Upon request he provided materials no matter what viewpoint they seemed to support. Often he furnished all the essential content of highly political speeches, or even wrote the speeches themselves, and he did so for conservatives as well as for progressives.[36] He frequently helped Republicans of the progressive faction write their political platforms, and on at least one occasion, in 1930, he drafted the platform for the state's Democrats as well.[37] He spoke with both truth and satisfaction when he observed that he was able to maintain cordial working relations with every Wisconsin governor during whose administration he served: Blaine, an ardent La Follette supporter; Fred Zimmerman, an avowed progressive but a factional opponent of Blaine; Walter Kohler, a conservative businessman-governor; La Follette's own vigorously progressive son, Philip La Follette; and a Democrat, Albert Schmedeman.[38]

Yet despite his admonitions to his staff, his style, and his help to all comers, Witte held some beliefs far too strongly to keep them buried in complete impartiality. In 1928 he did not hesitate to make a speech, in the state, advocating unemployment insurance, a constant issue before successive legislatures from 1921 until 1932. In a Labor Day speech in 1929 he openly urged workers to join labor unions, arguing that unions had benefited not only their members but the general welfare by championing reforms, by helping to achieve the great productivity for which business claimed credit, and by standing as a non-revolutionary force against radicalism.[39] Behind the scenes he participated a bit in progressive politics. In 1924, when La Follette made his third-party presidential bid, Witte helped with the legal research and other efforts necessary to put the senator's name on state ballots. After the bid failed, Witte went beyond technical help and advised national progressives not to continue with a third party. Labor unionists and socialists might quickly dominate, he warned his erstwhile politician-employer, John M. Nelson, and if they did they would destroy the progressives' effectiveness by building on class lines and by crowding out farmer support. "A real Progressive movement," he advised, "must not be too far ahead of times."[40]

Even in his official capacities he was exceptionally arduous in helping state progressives such as Governor Philip La Follette and legislative leader Alvin Reis. No doubt he worked extra hard for them because they were activists who made many demands. But his relations with them were also exceptionally warm. They were his friends, and at times he went beyond his office and offered them personal opinions on questions of policy.[41] Yet when he declared in 1932 that he was "not the Governor's [Philip La Follette's] advisor" and that "this library does not give advice or express opinions," he doubtlessly wrote, in the strictest construction, truthfully. And in a strict sense also he was correct in declaring, upon leaving his post in 1933, that he had "never made a political speech, nor have I ever suggested any bill or asked any member to vote for any measure."[42]

Witte's efforts to avoid outright partisanship helped make him sensitive to the political shoals surrounding a reformer's constructive efforts. But it was his genuine helpfulness as much as his nonpartisanship that inspired confidence in legislators. According to one assemblyman, John Schuman, everyone knew Witte was a La Follette supporter, but nobody cared. Winning the confidence of legislators, Witte declared, began with an attitude of genuine respect for their abilities. In 1914, as Nelson's secretary, he had seen a promising bill for a national legislative reference bureau lost when its promoters assumed the patronizing attitude that legislators needed academic advisers to tell them how to make law. Witte found legislators outgoing, friendly, and, contrary to stereotype, among the upper third of the population in both intelligence and character. Ever a product of the farm and the small town as well as of the university and the capitol, he moved easily among all legislators and made conscious efforts to win the confidence of all new members.[43]

The result was that Witte drew very little criticism and almost lavish praise. In 1927 one senator, Herman Severson, charged vaguely that Witte's bill-drafting service was inefficient, and recommended transferring its function to the revisor of statutes. But he got nowhere, and a *Wisconsin State Journal* writer later observed that Witte did not have "as hard a row to hoe as did his predecessor."[44] In 1929, instead of following Severson's plan, the legislators passed without dissent a resolution praising Witte for efficiency, zeal, reliability, "rare" courtesy, and "untiring and unselfish industry." Noting the library's growth "in importance and service," they recommended a commensurate raise in Witte's salary.[45] Their words, however, were more lavish than their appropriations. The *Wisconsin State Journal* observed that the legislators considered Witte worth $6000 per year but were satisfied to have the Free Library Commission raise his pay from $4750 to $5000.[46] In 1933, when Witte resigned, the legislators again praised him in almost exactly the same words—but this time added words of appreciation for the "absolute impartiality" with which he rendered "abundant service" to all members "regardless of party affiliation."[47] Less rhetorical were the private expressions of gratitude that Witte received from individual members throughout his years as chief. "I have never asked you to prepare the words of a song for me" declared Assemblyman James D. Millar appreciatively in 1929, but "when I want information I go to you."[48]

Witte's contribution in the Legislative Reference Library was to make the institution operate extremely well for its intended purposes, rather than to seek its or his own aggrandizement. He warned that a successful legislative reference bureau must ever remain in the background while it served the legislators, and cited John R. Commons' homely advice: "Don't worry about the credit. In the long run it all comes out in the wash." Witte's national reputation increased, for he frequently gave advice or even drafted bills for establishing reference services in other states. But the need to help legislators or the governor was occasion enough for him to decline speaking engagements that would have enhanced his prestige still further. When Henry Toll, director of the American Legislators' Association, offered him a position directing the development of an interstate reference bureau, he declined, and intimated disapprovingly that Toll was a "promoter type."[49] Nor did he grasp for new functions for his own institution, despite the example of Indiana, where a 1925 law gave the reference bureau broad responsibility for compiling state statistics, publishing the yearbook and the legislative journals, acting as official repository of bills, and functioning as revisor of statutes. Ideally Witte favored consolidating the statute revision function with the reference and bill-drafting services, but he made no campaign for it. In 1929 the legislature gave his agency responsibility for editing Wisconsin's informational *Blue Book,* but he warned that such functions should always remain secondary to serving the legislators. "Instead of reaching out for new activities," he declared in 1933, "a legislative reference service will do well to strive to increase and better the service it is rendering to the legislature."[50]

Witte expanded his institution's services in a few ways that he considered legitimate. He encouraged legislators to let his staff draft legislative amendments as well as the original bills. He also gave much advice on parliamentary procedures, and won a reputation among legislators for his parliamentary knowledge. He gave legislative committees vast new assistance in their investigations and in drafting their reports. Under his auspices the library became virtually the research staff for interim committees, as many as eight or ten of which conducted extensive researches between sessions each biennium. Witte frequently served as the committees' secretary, and it was especially for his interim committee work that he won repute and praise. The subjects upon which he helped to direct research and to draft reports and legislative recommendations ranged broadly, from hydro-electric power through education to a retirement system for state employees.[51] Perhaps most important for broadening his acquaintance with governmental problems was his extensive aid to a 1925–1926 interim committee on administration and taxation. The committee recommended extensive changes in the organization of the state's executive departments. But on taxation it refused to recommend lowering a controversial income tax for corporations, or to abandon Wisconsin's constitutional and traditional "pay as you go" fiscal policy.[52] Thereafter Witte maintained a strong interest in tax problems, and in 1933 and 1934, even after leaving the library, he served on another interim committee on taxation. He championed the progressive income tax, and advocated raising its rates. But he recognized that taxing high incomes could not alone yield sufficient state revenue. Nor did he ever question the wisdom of a balanced budget and "pay as you go," even when it meant cutting depression relief. Increasingly, he concluded that fiscal problems imposed severe limitations for welfare and reform.[53]

Witte continued an active interest in problems of government, especially state government, after he returned to the university in September, 1933. Throughout the 1930's he taught a seminar in "Wisconsin Economic Problems," which he broadened in 1940 and thereafter offered as "Governmental Economic Problems." From time to time he also taught a course in "Legislation" or "State Government" in the political science department, and was able to offer political science credit in many of his economics courses as well. Informally, he acted as consultant, adviser, and confidant to the Democratic governor, Albert Schmedeman, and for two terms after 1935, again to Philip La Follette. More formally, in 1933 and 1934 he helped the State Recovery

Administration formulate production codes under the National Industrial Recovery Act, and from 1935 to 1938, as a member of the State Planning Board, he helped plan Wisconsin's economic development. After his work for the national Social Security Act of 1935, he drafted a bill and helped to effect a compromise program in the Wisconsin legislature so that the state could participate in the federal welfare program. Thereafter he served as a member of a Citizens' Committee on Public Welfare, to help reorganize Wisconsin's public welfare administration. From 1937 to 1939, in keeping with one of his most persistent interests, he served very actively as a member of the Wisconsin Labor Relations Board. Nor did he confine his expertise in government procedure to the state. In 1936 he was a member of President Franklin D. Roosevelt's Committee on Administrative Management, and formulated advice for co-ordinating more effectively the numerous suggestions of administrative officials on legislation, and for closer co-operation between the executive and Congress on legislative matters.[54]

*   *   *   *   *

In 1933, at the age of forty-six, Witte returned to the University of Wisconsin to become professor of economics. It was a return to an old aspiration, and a major turning point in his life. He hoped that it would be a turn to more relaxation and family activity, and away from the grueling pace of work he had kept, especially during legislative sessions when he quite regularly worked from eight in the morning until eleven at night.[55] Yet there was no other period of his life to which Witte looked with more satisfaction, and fewer accompanying frustrations, than his years as servant of the state. He had especially enjoyed the years in the Legislative Reference Library. In it, he moved among men with whom he felt comfortable, and who gave him almost unqualified appreciation and recognition. Despite its heavy strain, the reference work had carried great rewards. There was, he noted, the "compensation which comes from being in the midst of about everything that is going on affecting state government," and there was "always something new . . . which demands all of the ingenuity and intelligence that anyone can possess. Still more important is the satisfaction of knowing that this work is distinctly worthwhile." He was confident that the legislative reference services were "helping to sustain democracy itself, to which, more than anything else, is due the progress [of] this country."[56]

On some men's lips, Witte's words might have had a trite and naive ring, or have been no more than a cynical attempt to identify with sancrosanct values. But while Witte did not carry an air of urbanity, and certainly not of affected sophistication, he was neither naive nor cynical. He accepted quite sincerely John R. Commons' ideals of public service, of sustaining democracy, and of improving its workings. So serious was he that he sometimes failed to maintain a sense of humor about his own effort, and throughout his life he continued to be an excessively compulsive worker. By the end of his years in the capitol, Witte had outgrown most of his youthful plasticity and had firmly established his ideals and habits of thought and work. His experiences during those years added to his respect for America's political and economic system, and reinforced his desire always to pursue reforms within a traditional governmental framework. Witte's state-serving experiences were highly practical, and they enhanced his inclination to direct his energies to immediate problems and politically possible solutions rather than to academic questions and grandiose goals and schemes. His efforts were in the rather limited context of state problems and state solutions. And because he was in very close touch with legislators he was ever more cautious, more sensitive to political nuances, more conscious of the fiscal and other practical problems of reform. Unconsciously he was effecting a declension of his institutional economics, for he increasingly emphasized the structure and details of economic and legal institutions, without taking time to ponder the political and economic system in its entirety as Veblen and Commons had done. It was a declension that suited the atmosphere of practical reform.

4

A Law for Labor Disputes

UNTIL 1934, WHEN HE SUDDENLY found himself among the leaders of the crusade for social insurance, Witte directed most of his reform energies toward expanding the sphere of freedom for organized labor. The challenge was how to cope with certain legal obstacles. Two of the most frequent and effective of those obstacles were the labor injunction, whereby the courts issued cease-and-desist orders against striking, boycotting, and other labor activities; and "yellow-dog" contracts, by which employers extracted from workmen promises not to engage in union activities. The yellow-dog contract and the labor injunction went hand-in-hand, for often it was on the strength of the former that judges issued the latter. Witte set himself the task of helping to break that combination. As he did, he learned more and more to skirt troublesome questions of legal doctrine, and pragmatically to argue on the basis of the laws' effects. "There is little hope for progress," he asserted in 1917, "so long as the courts [in dealing with labor] confine their attention strictly to precedents and legal theories." The problems were "economic in their nature, and should be considered from this point of view. What is needed most is information about the practical working of legal theories."[1] In the following decade and a half Witte provided that information, and helped rewrite basic legislation to change the laws' "practical working."

Beginning with his debating activities as an undergraduate, Witte's special interest was the courts' use, or alleged abuse, of injunctions in labor disputes. By the late 1920's a strategic question gradually came to the fore: Should reformers try to change the substantive law upon which judges based their injunctions, or merely the legal procedures by which they issued and enforced them? At first Witte advocated changes in substantive law. As a university senior in 1909, in his controversial commencement address, he attacked the legal doctrine of malicious conspiracy as it applied to labor disputes. According to common law, actions performed with intent to inflict injury were "malicious," and concerted action with malicious intent constituted an illegal conspiracy. By construing economic coercion and restraint of trade to be infliction of injury, courts enjoined even peaceful picketing and other nonviolent weapons that labor used, and upheld damage suits against unions for advocating boycotts of unfriendly employers' products. "The doctrine of malicious conspiracy stands in the way of industrial democracy," Witte argued in 1909. "Remove that obstacle. Adopt the principle championed by Wisconsin at the last Republican National Convention. Hold labor responsible for crime, but do not deny the right of effective combination." And "do not call the right to strike and boycott a crime." Witte had little faith in merely procedural remedies. "Let us not fall into the delusion that this problem can be solved," he warned, "by a mere correction of the procedure of the issuance of injunctions." Workmen would not achieve "real equality in the industrial struggle until it is established that such an injunction cannot be issued."[2]

Attacks on the conspiracy doctrine were nearly as old as labor's attempts to organize. More specific protests denouncing the use of injunctions and antitrust laws against labor stemmed from about 1894, the year of the historic Pullman strike, one of the earliest and most notorious cases in which courts applied both the injunction technique and antitrust laws. Some of the proposals that labor's sympathizers put forward as remedies used the procedural approach: jury trials in contempt-of-court cases to prevent judges' punishing injunction violators arbitrarily; requiring judges to serve advance notice to the party to be enjoined before issuing the injunction; and, in cases wherein judges issued temporary restraining orders without giving the enjoined party a formal hearing, a limit to the length of time the restraining order could remain in effect. Other bills, instead of pursuing such procedural approaches, used the substantive approach —proposing, for instance, that in trade disputes the courts should not consider an act done by a combination of persons (*i.e.*, a labor union) to be criminal, or in violation of antitrust laws, or subject to prevention by injunction, unless they considered the act criminal when an individual performed it. The most drastic suggestion using the substantive approach was in reply to the courts' increasing practice of issuing injunctions on the ground that the right to do business was a property right, deserving protection from interference by labor unions. In response the American Federation of Labor promoted a bill declaring specifically that the right to do business was not a property right, and therefore was not proper ground for injunctions.[3] Such were the proposals Witte studied in his formative years as a student and a protégé of Commons.

The proposals of labor and labor's sympathizers were of little avail until Congress passed the Clayton Antitrust Act of 1914. The Clayton Act included several provisions for labor, some procedural and some substantive. Procedurally, it instructed judges to specify carefully the acts and the persons they wished to enjoin, rather than to issue vague "blanket injunctions." In response to charges that injunctions were techniques for punishing offenders without fair trial, it prescribed trial by jury for labor injunction violators, when the alleged offenses were criminal and committed outside the courtroom. It provided that when a judge issued a temporary restraining order *ex parte*, on the basis of testimony from only one side, he should hold a full hearing within ten days or the order would lapse. As for changes in substantive law, the act declared human labor not to be a commodity and specifically exempted labor unions from the antitrust laws. More specifically, it declared a list of acts such as ceasing to patronize a firm, quitting work, persuading others to do likewise, and picketing to be legal, when done in a lawful and peaceful manner. American Federation of Labor President Samuel Gompers equated the Clayton Act with the federal Bill of Rights.[4]

From Witte's vantage point as secretary to Congressman John Nelson, and as investigator for the United States Industrial Relations Commission, however, Witte concluded that Congressman Edwin Webb of North Carolina and the others who framed the Act's labor provisions really wished "to please labor and yet make no change in the law."[5] He conceded that the jury-trial clause was a worthwhile innovation, but with his penchant for detail he decided that the language of other procedural provisions was ambiguous and unlikely to alter court practices significantly. As for the act's supposed changes in substantive law, Witte accurately forecast that the declaration that labor was not a commodity would not preclude injunctions to prevent interference with employers' right to do business, as labor had somehow come to expect. He thought that the exemption from antitrust laws would free labor from some extreme lawsuits such as the famous judgment against the Danbury hatters in 1908, but he doubted that it was enough really to remove labor's disability. Moreover, he pointed out, most offensive court decisions had rested not on antitrust law but on older precepts of common law. And the Clayton Act left the common law doctrine of conspiracy virtually intact.[6]

Witte drew up an extensive critique of the Clayton Act in 1914, while he worked for the Industrial Relations Commission. At that time he still emphasized the need to make changes in the substantive law governing labor combination, along the lines he had set forth in his commencement address. His recommendation to the commissioners that they support the doctrines embodied in British trades disputes law reflected that substantive approach. Both labor and employers should have full freedom to organize, Witte argued, and to achieve it the law should state explicitly that no combination of employers, combination of laborers, or trade agreement between such combinations could be considered a conspiracy or an illegal restraint of trade. British law, he pointed out, even allowed men to try to persuade others to break legal contracts, an important feature for nullifying employers' use of yellow-dog contracts against union organizers. It also allowed interference with the nonunion man's right to keep his job and the firm's right to do business. It released employer and labor associations and their officers from responsibility for illegal acts of their members. Most importantly, it denied the application of the doctrines of conspiracy and of malicious intent to labor disputes.[7]

As for conspiracy, British law declared that, in labor dispute cases, acts legal if performed by an individual were legal if performed by a combination. And as for intent, the law established the policy that the government would neither inquire into motives nor interfere in trade disputes, except to curb outright violence and threats to public order. British policy, Witte noted, removed all "taint of illegality from labor unions, employers' associations, trade agreements, and peaceable activities of both capital and labor"; and at the same time it was properly severe with violence, disorder, and other illegalities. Whereas in America almost any kind of coercion by employers was lawful but coercion by labor was not, the British law placed "labor and capital upon an exact equality. Trade unions are not favored in the law; but they are given a free hand to fight by peaceable and legitimate methods."[8]

Witte argued for the British policy on the basis of the effects he hoped it would achieve, rather than from legal doctrine. "The right of organization is valueless," he contended, "unless it is accompanied by the right to make the organization effective." Therefore "if collective bargaining is desirable," as many court decisions had asserted, "organized labor must be conceded the free use of the methods through which it can secure and maintain trade agreements." "Let the state keep 'hands off' in the struggle between labor and capital," he advised, "until either party oversteps the bounds of peace and order. Then neither party will have an unfair advantage."[9]

After he had vigorously set forth his proposals for changes in basic, substantive law, Witte went on to concur in some of the suggestions for procedural changes, such as forbidding judges to issue temporary restraining orders without first giving the party adversely affected a chance for a hearing, allowing judges to enjoin only persons who had already committed unlawful acts, and providing trial by jury in contempt cases.[10] His primary method to achieve the social results he wanted, however, was to change the substantive law to allow freedom to both capital and labor to combine and to coerce each other short of violent and criminal methods. It was a recommendation that harked back to Commons' ideas for bringing capital and labor into equilibrium.

*   *   *   *   *

In the dozen years following the Industrial Relations Commission's demise in 1915, Witte continued to study and write on the subject of labor law. The extensive reports that he and an assistant had compiled for the commission provided the beginning point for much of his activity. And he continued the research method that he had used in his commission investigations: studying not merely the cases formally described in published legal reports, but also collecting a vast body of information from newspapers, employer and labor periodicals, legislative hearings and other government records, and correspondence and interviews with protagonists in labor dispute cases.[11] Another writer, University of Chicago Professor J. Finley Christ, who bothered only with the formal legal reports, declared information on unreported cases to be "notoriously unreliable."[12] Witte, however, sought to understand not merely the legal aspects of court action in labor disputes, but also the "actual facts and results." He believed that "what the law is according to reported decisions is less important than how the law is actually administered."[13] Witte tried consciously to adopt a broad, unprejudiced perspective as he studied the "practical workings" of labor law, but he recognized that his conclusions tended to favor labor. "You know how strongly labor union I am personally in my sympathies," he wrote privately to his erstwhile employer, Congressman John M. Nelson, in 1924. It was his studies that had led him to support labor's position, he declared in 1929; he insisted that he had approached his studies from neither a pro-labor nor a pro-employer point of view.[14] Without question Witte's conclusions might have been different had he begun his studies under a teacher less sympathetic to labor than John R. Commons, but Witte tried genuinely to consider the question of labor law from the standpoint of the total public interest. "The great evil of injunctions in labor disputes," he wrote in 1922, "is not that it handicaps organized labor, but that it undermines our American institutions."[15]

Most directly harmful were the deleterious political and judicial effects of injunctions through the confusion and conflicts they caused. Witte argued that the doctrine of malicious conspiracy wrought ill because its basic idea—that acts otherwise lawful became unlawful because they allegedly were parts of organized plots—was incomprehensible to both labor and the public. Perplexed by such doctrine, labor merely grew bitter and critical of the courts. Employers then countered with similar feelings toward labor. Witte believed that judges were usually as fair as the law allowed them to be, yet he declared that sometimes even they lost all pretense of impartiality when caught in the crossfire. The conflicts drew labor into politics merely to find an injunction remedy, rather than for constructive purposes such as social reform. Employers in turn increased their lobbying. And injunctions usurped executive functions, for an injunction was virtually meaningless unless the court backed it with a force of marshals. Injunctions were prostituting and undermining respect for the courts, political harmony, and executive authority.[16]

The idea that injunctions prevented violence Witte considered quite superficial. He argued against the idea as early as his 1915 Industrial Relations Commission reports,[17] and supported his argument by citing many cases in which injunctions had apparently had the opposite effect of inciting labor to increase the level of violence. He thought that it was because of injunctions that workmen often took the attitude that one labor lawyer had expressed, namely that law was "a game in which everybody slugs. . . . I slug for labor." Although such an attitude might not be justifiable, Witte asserted, it was real, and whoever wished to make labor relations more orderly had to consider what lay behind it.[18] "Despite all the injunctions which have been issued in labor disputes," he observed in 1922, "violence is very much more common in strikes in the United States than in any other country." Injunctions had failed to minimize or settle strikes, "but on the contrary, have promoted strife between labor and capital. Their use in labor disputes constitutes one of the most serious problems demanding early solution."[19]

And beyond the violence they fomented, labor injunctions failed to achieve their other purposes. In some cases they might have been effective in bringing swift and sure justice to the lawless, but quite as often they were neither faster nor more certain than the proper remedy, criminal proceedings. Contempt cases for injunction violations could stretch into cumbersome and lengthy litigation. Witte argued that injunctions were not even effective in achieving employers' ends. In themselves they provided no added police protection for tangible property. They might severely hamper union picketing, but unions usually found other means to get their messages across to unorganized workers. And in some cases they backfired against employers, as the attempt to enjoin a boycott in the historic Bucks Stove and Range Case of 1911 had done when it provided just the publicity that the union needed. At first Witte even asserted that injunctions did not really hamper unions very much. But as the 1920's progressed and he observed that injunctions grew more and more restrictive, he changed his view. Injunctions prejudiced the public against strikers, he emphasized in 1930; they also diverted the energies of union leaders and the funds of union treasuries, undermined strikers' morale, and especially hurt weak unions and union drives for new members. Yet he continued to argue that injunctions sometimes hurt more than they helped employers.[20] Negatively, injunctions did not achieve their ostensible purposes. Positively, they undermined the stability and efficiency of American institutions.

Witte made his concern for injunctions and other court actions in labor disputes, the central thesis of his dissertation, "The Role of the Courts in Labor Disputes," which he submitted to the University of Wisconsin for his Ph.D. degree in economics in 1927. He went beyond injunctions to discuss damage suits and criminal prosecutions. He even delved into the common law and statutory principles behind the courts' actions. Yet he maintained his primary interest in "the practical results" of the courts' policies in labor disputes, and continued to argue their evil social consequences.[21]

Witte found weaknesses or at least vagueness in nearly all judicial theories that applied to labor disputes, whether the courts applied the test of illegal means, the doctrine forbidding restraint of trade, or other principles. He criticized even the mitigating doctrine that a party might rightfully interfere with trade and access to markets if he had "just cause," even though his criticism was somewhat out of spirit with Commons' defense of the doctrine of reasonableness. For courts to decide what was just cause, he argued, was to enter the realms of ethics and economics, not of facts. When he turned once more to the combined doctrines of conspiracy and of malicious intent, he found the courts' reasoning downright fallacious. Either doctrine was too weak to stand without the other, he asserted, for the judges rarely found a conspiracy without malicious intent, and rarely found malicious intent in an individual. Their central assumption—that malicious intent was significant only when backed by the power inherent in combination—was the more false because they treated great aggregations of capital in the form of corporations not as combinations but as individuals. "It is a shallow doctrine, which seeks to explain the handicap against combinations by assuming that they are dangerously powerful," Witte concluded, "and yet does not take notice of the abuse of great power by individuals and corporations."[22] His argument characterized his thought, for it cut straight through doctrines and theories, and judged only on the basis of objective social results.

More generally, Witte found legal reasoning to be so chaotic as to be almost useless. There were so many conflicting rulings and decisions that a judge inevitably had to make a subjective choice as to which he would apply. A judge might make very honest efforts, but he could hardly avoid applying his own biases. Many times his decision was really a judgment of sound public policy, to which, according to Witte, *a priori* legal reasoning did not apply. The chaos and confusion, Witte declared with a touch of charity, was "due principally to the newness of these problems." The judges were trying to apply doctrines that had been developed for quite different situations. Their mistake was not that they applied special principles to labor disputes, but rather that "they have refused to recognize that industrial disputes present special problems." And so, "in actual practice, the law does discriminate against labor, and fails to reach conduct of employers which is the fair counterpart of conduct on part of employees condemned by the courts."[23]

It was likewise with arguments as to actual results and social consequences that Witte joined the attack on yellow-dog contracts in the late 1920's. Such contracts were an old device, and as early as the 1890's a number of states, including Wisconsin, had attempted to outlaw them. But several early twentieth-century court decisions had overturned such laws. Serious consequences flowed from a 1917 United States Supreme Court decision to uphold the contracts in a case involving the Hitchman Coal and Coke Company of West Virginia. The Hitchman Company used the yellow-dog contract, backed by court injunction, not so much against its own employees who had signed the contracts, as against the United Mine Workers. The courts enjoined the union from attempting to organize the company's miners, on the ground that the union, as a third party, could not lawfully induce the men to breach the yellow-dog contracts that they had signed. With the employers' new ability to use yellow-dog contracts to induce courts to enjoin union organizers the contracts took on new effectiveness. During the 1920's management used them more and more frequently.[24] Witte argued that the courts' policy of putting the government's power behind the contracts was "most unneutral." The central issue was not so much the contracts themselves as "the attitude which the government should assume toward labor unions." He believed that "from the social point of view, . . . it is only on the assumption that labor unions are socially undesirable that yellow-dog contracts can be defended."[25] Although occasionally he delved into legal doctrine, in all his writing Witte argued most warmly and effectively when pointing to social results.

Paradoxically, the more Witte studied and wrote about the courts' role in labor disputes and its consequences, the less sure he became of what practical remedy to recommend. In the early 1920's the Supreme Court issued a series of decisions that confirmed his fears concerning the Clayton Act. The court continued to hold labor accountable under antitrust laws. It declared generally that the Clayton Act had merely set forth existing law, and had changed nothing substantively. Witte interpreted one particular decision, the 1921 case of *Truax* v. *Corrigan*, to mean that the courts would consider any special exemption for labor to be class legislation, and therefore unconstitutional.[26] He nearly lost hope that any injunction remedy stronger than the Clayton Act could survive the courts.

In Witte's own state the Wisconsin Federation of Labor pursued procedural remedies. Its counsel, Joseph Padway, drafted a bill that went beyond the Clayton Act and provided jury trial for civil as well as for criminal contempt in labor cases, and the 1923 legislature passed it. The same year the Wisconsin Federation also sponsored and won a pioneer bill requiring a full forty-eight hours' notice to the party adversely affected, before a temporary restraining order could take effect.[27] The American Federation of Labor, on the other hand, revived the substantive approach. In 1925 a vice-president of the A.F. of L., Matthew Woll, asked Witte for his comments on two bills. One proposed once more to declare that in labor cases no act that was lawful when done by an individual should be a conspiracy or a criminal offense. The other attempted to limit the power of judges to protect property by injunction to the protection only of patents, copyrights, and such "tangible property" as could be transferred from one person to the other. The latter bill would, of course, have ruled out protection of the right to do business without interference from unions. Witte discouraged both bills, believing from technical considerations that neither bill would accomplish its purpose. He was still "convinced that the remedy lies in making our law as nearly like that of the British Trades Disputes Act as possible." But, he admitted, in face of the hostility of the courts, he did not know how to administer his remedy. "My own thought has swung in recent years in the direction that no fundamental change in substantive law is obtainable at present," he advised Woll. So he encouraged Woll's organization to follow the course that Wisconsin had taken. "The best plan which can be followed at this time," he argued, "is to try to hedge in and cripple the use of injunctions in labor disputes, so as to render resort to them less frequent and less effective."[28] Such was his frame of mind when his opportunity came to help draft a national law.

In 1927 Henrik Shipstead of Minnesota introduced a bill into the United States Senate that once more tried the approach of redefining property in such a way as to prevent courts from enjoining labor union activities on the basis of a firm's "property rights" to access to customers and to do business. The Shipstead measure would have denied equity courts any jurisdiction to protect property that was not "tangible and transferable."[29] The Senate Judiciary Committee took up the bill and put it into the hands of a subcommittee consisting of three vigorously progressive politicians: George W. Norris of Nebraska, Thomas Walsh of Montana, and Wisconsin's former governor, John J. Blaine. As one source of advice, Blaine turned to Witte, who confessed that despite his years of study he was "stumped to know" what Congress should do. But he was sure that the Shipstead bill was inadequate, because employers could find ways to circumvent it. He also doubted that the courts would sustain it, since it proposed drastic change in substantive law. Meantime the subcommittee held hearings, and it too concluded that the Shipstead bill was of doubtful constitutionality and a far too simple solution to the labor injunction. So it invited four lawyers and an economist to Washington to draft a substitute. The lawyers were Felix Frankfurter and Francis B. Sayre of the Harvard Law School, Herman Oliphant of Columbia University, and Chicago labor attorney Donald E. Richberg. The economist was Witte.[30]

For three days, May 1 to 3, 1928, all of the five except Sayre met in Washington, locked themselves in a Senate committee room, and worked to shape a bill. As they discussed and reviewed past court cases they had at their disposal Witte's ample research files, which Frankfurter later declared to have been an invaluable source.[31] And they had drafts of two bills which Frankfurter and Sayre had begun to write as early as 1923, using the approach of trying to change substantive law. Samuel Gompers had reviewed one of the drafts and approved it before his death. It would have tried once more to declare a wide range of acts—such as peaceful picketing, persuasion, assembling, organizing, and the like—lawful for a labor organization. In addition it would have declared any act that was lawful for an individual to be lawful also when workmen performed it in concert. Finally, it proposed to relieve unions and their officers from liability for acts that members performed without union authorization. The other draft bill was to forbid courts to issue labor injunctions except to prevent irreparable damage to property or reasonable fear of physical harm to persons, and then only when there was no other remedy at law.[32] In addition to the two Frankfurter-Sayre drafts, the four men had at their disposal still another proposed bill, which Sayre and Oliphant had helped to draft in 1924. Its seminal idea was to attack yellow-dog contracts, not by denying the freedom to make such contracts, but by declaring them to be contrary to public policy and therefore unenforceable.[33] By the end of the third day the draftsmen reached near agreement on a tentative new bill. Thereafter Frankfurter and Oliphant, being in the East, collected some further advice from the others and drew up the completed version for the subcommittee.[34]

After three days of discussion the leading issue was how much substantive law to include in the bill. Witte stood firmly against substantive solutions, and suggested that if there had to be substantive proposals the draftsmen should put them in a separate bill. Frankfurter at first hoped that his and Sayre's substantive bills might be the basis for the new bill, but in the end he declared himself to be in "substantial accord" with Witte. "Let's see how far we can get with comprehensive adequate corrections of the procedural evils," he counseled, and "not overload" the bill "either with doubtful substantive provisions, or at all events, provisions which run counter to the deeper hostilities of the judges." Richberg, however, insisted that organized labor would never be satisfied with merely procedural remedies, and especially wanted a specific denunciation of the doctrine of conspiracy. Oliphant supported Richberg, and even Witte conceded that no bill was worth sponsoring unless labor supported it. The group consciously avoided an explicit legalization of boycotts, however, believing that such a course would arouse too much opposition. The Senate subcommittee decided that splitting the bill also was politically unwise. The final draft therefore contained substantive provisions, and a thorough attempt at procedural remedies.[35]

With the bill completed, Witte closed ranks and composed a memorandum which Frankfurter assured him would make "admirable ammunition" for congressional debates.[36] Freed from the necessity for scholarly detachment, Witte argued for the bill with all the warmth of intelligent partisanship. Nearly everyone, from the American Federation of Labor to the antilabor *Chicago Tribune*, he declared, was calling for some legislative remedy for injunction abuses. Eminent men such as former Presidents Theodore Roosevelt and William Howard Taft had warned against treating injunctions as a permanent solution to industrial warfare. Since employer groups such as the National Association of Manufacturers and the League for Industrial Rights had convinced the courts that the Clayton Act had not changed the law, the courts had assumed the "unenviable role" of helping employers force workmen to relinquish their right to organize. Their role seemed to confirm labor's charges of "judicial despotism." Witte pointed to case after case where injunctions had prevented union organizers from working, caused workers to go to jail for contempt even when a company had infiltrated the union with provocateurs, evicted workers from company-owned homes, stopped peaceful and effective picketing, and provoked violence. Yet for all his vigor, Witte did not present the new bill as grandiose remedy for every evil. Instead he emphasized cautiously that it was merely a proposal based on firm congressional authority to define the jurisdiction of federal courts, an authority that the Supreme Court could surely uphold.[37]

Having emphatically argued for the bill in general, Witte defended its specific provisions, even the substantive ones. The bill declared that since individual workers were powerless under existing economic conditions and government-fostered forms of corporate ownership, it was public policy that they should be free to organize and choose their own representatives. That, Witte argued, was nothing new. The bill went on to declare that on the basis of stated public policy, yellow-dog contracts would be unenforceable. Privately Witte was not sure that such a clause would stand up in court, but he thought it "distinctly worth trying" in order to give judges an opportunity to reconsider yellow-dog contracts in the light of their social results. In his memorandum he argued more positively that the bill's language simply attempted to protect rights to which everyone paid lip service. Yellow-dog contracts, far from being the "American Plan" that the rhetoric of employers labeled them, threatened to destroy labor unions and to allow employers unilaterally to dictate terms of employment. Witte argued that "anything more utterly contrary to the first principles of American liberty can scarcely be imagined." The bill also included language expressly legalizing specific union practices. It would make the right to strike "more than a mere paper right."[38]

Witte's true confidence was in the procedural provisions of the bill, for they hedged the use of injunctions very closely. They required a judge to hold an open hearing before he issued an injunction. He could issue it only if the hearing established that illegalities had already occurred and would continue unless enjoined, that regular law enforcement officers were unable or unwilling to protect the complainant, that "substantial and irreparable injury" to property would occur without the injunction, and that there was no other legal remedy. Even then the court could proceed only if the proposed injunction promised to injure the defendant less than it relieved the complainant. The court might issue a temporary restraining order without a prior hearing, but only on sworn testimony that it would prevent significant and otherwise unavoidable injury, and only if the complainant posted bond to cover possible damages and legal fees for the defendant. Such an order would apply for no more than five days, and the court could issue neither injunction nor restraining order if the complainant had violated any labor law, or if he had not made every reasonable effort to settle the dispute directly or through government arbitration and mediation. Witte argued that the procedural provisions would limit injunctions and restraining orders to emergency situations, and properly provide compensation when they caused damage. And they would eliminate the all-too-common practice of courts' issuing such orders "without anything to show why they were issued."[39]

Moreover the bill provided redress from unfair injunctions. Under its terms, when a court issued a labor injunction it had to file the facts and records of the case with an appellate court. And if a disputant appealed, the appellate court had to give the case precedence and speedy consideration. The bill also reiterated the Clayton Act's provision of jury trials for cases of criminal contempt committed out of court. It even went beyond the Clayton Act and provided for jury trials in all indirect criminal contempt cases, not merely labor cases. This, Witte argued, put criminal contempt on the same footing as any other criminal act, and would eliminate the shortcut of using injunctions and subsequent contempt proceedings to punish alleged crime. Removal of the shortcut would be "a most valuable check upon the abuse of injunctions." Finally, Witte praised the bill as "specific and not capable of different interpretations." The courts would have to obey it or specifically declare it to be unconstitutional. To Witte "this alone is worth a great deal more than any number of nice rhetorical phrases." He thought that the entire bill was "the most promising attack that has ever been made upon this [injunction] problem, which has agitated the country for more than thirty years."[40]

Andrew Furuseth, the saltily stubborn but sincere old president of the International Union of Seamen, did not agree. He had earlier won wide respect in labor circles for his success in winning the historic Seamen's Act of 1915 to mitigate sailors' working conditions, and for his self-acquired knowledge of Roman and Anglo-Saxon law. Arguing with colorful but imprecise references to the Kingdom of Heaven, English common law, and the Declaration of Independence, Furuseth insisted that the only remedy was the redefinition of property to exclude vague, intangible, and nontransferable property. He declared that he merely wished to restore what until relatively recent times had been the courts' definition of property. It was he who had written the Shipstead bill, and when the Norris subcommittee proposed the substitute that Witte and the four lawyers had drafted, Furuseth immediately protested.[41] Witte and the lawyers promptly agreed, in Frankfurter's words, "on a collective statement emphatically rejecting the Furuseth idea" before it could "gain lodgement in Senator Norris' mind,"[42] and thereby checked Furuseth's protest to Norris. But the old seaman had already convinced the American Federation of Labor that the solution was a radical redefinition of property. "You have got to take it wholesale and swallow it; you can't get a half a loaf on this question, it is not possible, there is no half loaf on fundamental principles," he had argued at the 1927 A.F. of L. convention, and the delegates had supported the Shipstead bill. In 1928 the Federation reiterated its position and specifically rejected the Norris subcommittee's substitute measure. Largely because of labor's intransigeance, the subcommittee bill quickly fell into almost complete dormancy.[43]

The A.F. of L. Executive Council, however, appointed a committee to study the matter. Its appointees included Woll, to whom Witte had already advocated procedural solutions, and also John P. Frey of the Moulders' Union. Early in the 1920's Frey had written a book on the labor injunction, a book that Witte had found instructive. In 1924 Frey also had helped produce the original draft of the anti-yellow-dog feature that Witte and the lawyers incorporated into the subcommittee bill. In the 1929 convention the A.F. of L. study committee supported Woll and Frey and recommended a modified version of the Norris subcommittee's bill. The convention delegates concurred, with Furuseth alone dissenting.[44] The authors of the subcommittee bill did not approve all of the A.F. of L.'s modifications, however, and once again they quickly protested. Witte personally was "inclined to go the whole way with labor, except at a few points." For strategic reasons, Witte agreed that the subcommittee should not adopt an A.F. of L. amendment to deny injunctions against workers' and consumers' boycotts, even though he believed the boycott weapon to be legitimate. Collectively, the authors concurred in Frankfurter's less pragmatic view that boycotts were questionable even in principle. The group also opposed labor's suggestion to extend jury trial to civil as well as criminal contempt cases, arguing that it, like the provision approving boycotts, would add a futile burden to the bill's chances of passage. And where the A.F. of L. wanted to go further in declaring specific acts legal, the draftsmen counseled that "it is the part of wisdom to appear careful and conservative."[45] In the end the subcommittee retained very few of the A.F. of L. modifications, not even some that the authors were willing to allow. Nevertheless, thereafter the Federation supported the bill.[46]

In June, 1930, after labor's shift, the Senate Judiciary Committee finally reported the measure out to the full Senate. But employer associations, the United States Chamber of Commerce, and the League for Industrial Rights strongly opposed the bill. The American Bar Association also disapproved it, largely because association members confused it with the original Shipstead bill. In tune with such groups, the full Judiciary Committee voted ten to seven to advise against the bill's passage. The majority report by Oregon's Senator Frederick Steiwer objected that the bill invaded state prerogatives, destroyed contracts which the courts had upheld, failed to distinguish between legal and illegal strikes, would not protect the nonunion workman, and would impose excessive procedural restrictions. Despite the fact that both Republicans and Democrats had recognized the injunction problem in their 1928 platforms, the committee majority doubted that the country needed a new anti-injunction law.[48] In 1930 the bill got no further than committee report.

The Senate's indifference left it to Wisconsin once more to pioneer the latest form of labor legislation. In 1929 Wisconsin State Senator Thomas Duncan, a Milwaukee Socialist with whom Witte was on the warmest of terms, had won passage of the first recent law in any state to make yellow-dog contracts unenforceable. In 1931 Duncan sponsored a measure that was essentially the national Senate subcommittee bill as adapted by the American Civil Liberties Union for state action. Wisconsin Federation of Labor's Padway had drafted the Wisconsin version, but Witte, who was on very friendly terms with Wisconsin's labor leaders, had participated in formulating the Federation's 1931 legislative program. Duncan's bill passed with the support of Governor Philip La Follette, giving Wisconsin a unique "labor code" against injunctions and yellow-dog contracts.[49]

By 1932, the Depression was deepening and Congress was becoming more liberal. Labor had waged a vigorous campaign in behalf of the subcommittee bill in the 1930 election. Early in February, 1932, the Senate Judiciary Committee once more reported the bill, this time with a favorable majority of eleven to five. The minority, in its report, conceded that injunction relief was imperative, and argued only that the bill went too far. The Senate approved the measure, 75–5. In the House of Representatives, where New York's Fiorello LaGuardia sponsored it, the bill passed 363–13. On March 23, 1932, President Herbert Hoover signed it, although he expressed some reservations, and the bill became law.[50] It became instantly famous as the Norris-LaGuardia Act.

*   *   *   *   *

Almost simultaneously with the passage of that landmark legislation, Witte's book, *The Government in Labor Disputes,* rolled off the press. In it Witte discussed the same material he had treated in his doctoral dissertation, but he had recast and thoroughly rewritten it, expanding the old material with up-to-date research and including a new section on a topic that in later life would be his chief interest in labor disputes legislation: the government's role as mediator and arbitrator. More fundamentally, he removed from the main body of the book all of the didacticism that had given his dissertation unity and vigor, leaving only the flat, cautious, analytical prose that was so much his style after his years in the Legislative Reference Library. At the end of the book, declaring that "it is with some hesitation that the author presents in this chapter his own views, not as the last words to be said on this subject, but at any rate, as conclusions arrived at independently after years of study," Witte offered his own recommendations. Already they were no more than a defense of existing legislation, for his program was essentially that of the Norris-LaGuardia Act. Nevertheless, it was a fortunate book for the time, for it presented with factual thoroughness both a historical understanding and a justification of the new law.[51] It may well have contributed to the act's acceptance and success.

Witte continued throughout life to comment and write about government policy in labor disputes, but never again did he play so direct a role in creating a major national labor disputes law. With the Norris-LaGuardia Act in effect, the passage of similar state legislation, and the fast-moving developments of Depression politics, the issue soon shifted from how to keep government from interfering with labor organization to how public policy might positively foster it. Early in 1934 Witte gave Senator Robert F. Wagner some advice on formulating an early version of what was to become the next major national labor disputes bill, the National Labor Relations Act of 1935. And although Wagner's notion of bringing the government into labor disputes to declare what were unfair labor practices, and to act as referee, was somewhat different from Witte's earlier "hands off" views, Witte testified strongly on the bill's behalf. He wanted a remedy for the company-dominated unions that had sprung up after passage of the 1933 National Industrial Recovery Act. During the 1920's he had argued that company unions and conventional unions should be allowed to grow side by side, in order to see which was socially more desirable. But early in the winter of 1933–1934 he helped the National Recovery Administration to deal with some company union cases, and he decided that company unions often did not truly represent the workers. He especially advised against the government's recognizing mere employee representation committees as proper bargaining agents for employees.[52]

But long before the Wagner bill came to fruition Witte had become immersed in efforts for social security, and, as passed, the act violated Witte's recommendation by recognizing the representation committees, provided employers did not control them.[53] Witte's role in the Wagner Act was in pale contrast to that in the Norris-La Guardia bill.

Witte's background of thought and study on the labor disputes problem prepared him for his decisive contribution to the Norris-LaGuardia law. As passed, the law was different from the substantive attack on the doctrine of malicious conspiracy and its replacement by the British trade disputes policy that he had espoused in the beginning. Witte's main concern, as usual, was the practical working and the social effects of the new labor law. Given his emphasis on actual results, it was easy for him to decide that the reform of substantive law was not necessary, if he and his fellow reformers could circumvent it with procedural remedies. He chose the pragmatic course, and, in contrast to substantive reforms, the conservative one. His choice was characteristic of his reform approach throughout the rest of his life, especially in the realm of social security.

5

SOCIAL SECURITY
Twisted Roots

T HE AMERICAN PEOPLE, declared President Franklin D. Roosevelt in a message to Congress on June 8, 1934, "want some safeguard against misfortunes which cannot be wholly eliminated in this man-made world of ours. . . . I am looking for a sound means which I can recommend to provide at once security against several of the great disturbing factors in life—especially those which relate to unemployment and old age."[1]

A year and a half earlier Roosevelt had swept to victory as the candidate the people hoped might dispel the darkness and insecurity of the depression years. Thereafter he and the Seventy-Third Congress had pushed through a series of emergency relief and recovery measures; but relief represented a heavy drain on public funds, and recovery came very, very slowly. On June 8 Roosevelt called for longer-term solutions, emphasizing that recovery would come only with reconstruction. Along with proposals to improve housing and to make fuller use of natural resources, he suggested "interrelated" social insurance measures to protect individual security, a goal not involving "new and strange values," but rather values that Americans had "lost in the course of our economic development and expansion." He was instituting a study of social insurance, he announced, to formulate proposals for the new Seventy-Fourth Congress the fol-

74

lowing January.[2] Before the end of July he called upon Edwin
Witte to direct the study.

Social insurance was a European invention. In the nineteenth
century governments in Europe had begun to develop the social
insurance method in order to protect industrial workers against
the economic hazards of accident, sickness, premature death, old
age, and unemployment. They built upon trade-union and other
voluntary action, and upon their systems of poor relief. In the
last two decades of the century Germany emerged as the European leader with the first comprehensive, nationwide social insurance institutions, using the principles of employer and worker contributions, state supervision and subsidization, and compulsion. Great Britain soon followed with variations that reflected her experience and disappointments with pauper relief
and workhouses, and in 1908 began giving gratuitous old-age
pensions, on the basis of need rather than of previous contributions. In 1911 she preceded even Germany with the first nationally operated, subsidized, contributory system of unemployment
insurance. By 1934 nearly all European governments and some
in the British dominions, South America, and Asia had developed a variety of state operated and subsidized social insurance institutions.[3]

In America both the states and the national government lagged
behind Europe in utilizing social insurance methods. Yet, long
before Roosevelt's endorsement and Witte's study, a relatively
small circle of reformers had been advocating social insurance
and had won some response. In 1907 the legislature of Massachusetts created the Commission on Old Age Pensions, Annuities and Insurance. In the five years beginning in 1911 nearly two-thirds of the states enacted workmen's compensation laws.
In 1913 the American Association for Labor Legislation sponsored the "First American Conference on Social Insurance."
Several American books on social insurance appeared, most
notably a 1913 volume, *Social Insurance, With Special Reference
to American Conditions*, by Isaac M. Rubinow, who was at various times an insurance company actuary, medical doctor, promi-

nent social worker, and secretary of B'nai B'rith—but always a champion of social insurance as a reform measure.[4] By World War I America had her own movement.

From the beginning of the social insurance movement Americans were of many minds. A few opposed social insurance because they thought the reform inadequate, and wanted far more revolutionary changes in American institutions.[5] A vastly greater number remained outside the social insurance circle for reasons more like those of the secretary of the Pennsylvania Self-Insurers' Association, Walter Linn, a self-proclaimed "ardent reactionary." Linn believed social insurance was akin to socialism, and insisted that when social insurance advocates swore otherwise, they were merely offering "their nostrums" under "a disguise of misrepresentation and falsehood." Noel Sargent, secretary of the National Association of Manufacturers, similarly warned in 1933 against replacing relief with unemployment insurance. He feared "individual softness and social decay," and also higher taxes that might cause industry to employ fewer people.[6] Many other Americans shared his fear that social insurance might harm individuals and society, believed that every man was already receiving his due, or were confident that existing institutions could sufficiently protect the individual.

Among those who recognized individual security as a social problem were some who advocated voluntarism rather than compulsion. Admitting in 1914 that American workers needed more social insurance, Frederick L. Hoffman, statistician for the Prudential Life Insurance Company and prominent member of the American Association for Labor Legislation, defined social insurance broadly to include private efforts, and declared that in most cases voluntary action would suffice. Reformers such as Professor Henry R. Seager of Columbia University and the Boston "people's attorney," Louis D. Brandeis, believed that where private efforts took such forms as company old-age pensions plans, employers often administered them arbitrarily, to tie workers to their companies and further subjugate them. Their proposed solution, offered before World War I, called for non-compulsory governmental insurance institutions. Samuel Gompers, on the other hand, favored company welfare plans, as against compulsory government action. Compulsory social insurance, he declared, gave government power that belonged to the workers, and would weaken their "spirit and virility." His voluntaristic solution was to win security benefits strictly through collective bargaining.[7]

Beginning about 1875, when the American Railway Express Company established an old-age pension plan for its employees, a few hundred American corporations, sometimes under union pressure, established voluntary welfare programs. Their efforts, along with trade-union benefits and governmental plans for various civil servants, provided some background of experience for social insurance institutions. Yet by 1933 barely 10 per cent of the nation's industrial workers could expect old-age pensions from their employers, and less than 1 per cent worked under the protection of unemployment insurance. The plans that existed were often actuarily and financially unsound, and they proved unreliable in the Depression.[8] With their breakdown, Gompers' successors in the American Federation of Labor, as well as employers who had experience with voluntary plans, such as General Electric president Gerard Swope and Eastman Kodak treasurer Marion Folsom, increasingly advocated compulsory government social insurance. But through the active years of the social insurance movement, most champions of voluntary action stood outside the circle of social insurance advocates. Inside the circle stood representatives of three separate traditions and schools of thought, who themselves often disagreed with increasing acrimony.

One school of social insurance advocates drew upon the ancient traditions of public relief and private charity. The earliest American settlements had adopted virtually *in toto* the Elizabethan English system of poor relief, and had firmly established the principle of public responsibility to supplement private charity. But poor relief often tended to stigmatize and degrade its recipients with "pauper oaths" and failed to differentiate between various classes of indigents. Local officials who carried the relief responsibility often added to inherent deficiencies with indifferent administration. Recognizing the abuses in the poor relief system, some reformers in the late nineteenth and early twentieth centuries emphasized amelioration through the case-work method, which looked for particular causes of poverty in the individual and his situation, and attempted to cure it through his rehabilitation.[9]

Although public as well as private welfare workers utilized the case-work method, some private charity officials seized upon its characteristics of individualism and voluntarism to advance privately supported case-work as an alternative to governmental social insurance. In 1930 Walter S. Gifford, president of the American Telephone and Telegraph Company and vice-president of the New York Charity Organization Society, declared that the state had to operate under "general rules" and therefore could not make the case-workers' careful distinctions between individuals. Gifford advocated case-work supported by private charity as "an American method of voluntary action," preferable to old-age pensions drawn from government funds. Sargent of the manufacturers' association thought that the case-work method was the proper alternative to unemployment insurance. He thought, however, that government should complement case-work with public relief.[10]

Despite the highly individualistic and voluntaristic attitudes of some relief and charity workers, some forms of social insurance, especially old-age and mothers' pensions, drew heavily on the relief and charity tradition. Social workers such as Jane Addams of Chicago's Hull House and Paul Kellogg, editor of *Survey*, championed social insurance. The welfare workers' leading organizations (*e.g.*, the National Conference of Charities and Correction, renamed the National Conference of Social Work in 1917; the American Public Welfare Association, founded in 1931; and others) provided forums for social insurance discussions and impetus for social insurance programs, especially those involving gratuitous public assistance rather than contributory insurance.[11]

A second group within the social insurance circle consisted of persons who studied foreign systems, and made themselves experts in social insurance theory and outstanding propagandists for the cause. Before World War I Isaac Rubinow became their leading figure, especially after he delivered an outstanding series of lectures at the New York School of Philanthropy in 1912, lectures which he subsequently published as *Social Insurance, With Special Reference to American Conditions.* During the 1920's, however, a younger man, Abraham Epstein, began to pre-empt Rubinow's leading role. Epstein worked for the Fraternal Order of Eagles and several Pennsylvania commissions to promote old-age pensions. He studied social insurance in Europe and wrote several outstanding books. In 1927 he organized the American Association for Old Age Security. Others, such as University of Chicago economist Paul H. Douglas, who investigated and wrote about unemployment insurance, and Mrs. Barbara Armstrong, a University of California law professor who wrote a notable 1932 book advocating a comprehensive social insurance and minimum wage program, similarly made themselves experts and propagandists, and shared a more or less common approach to social insurance.[12]

As their basic tool, the experts advocated the insurance principle of spreading the risk. Again and again they asserted that wages were too low for workers individually to meet their risks through saving. Rubinow argued further that despite its "character-building value," thrift could be a "positive vice" which might reduce the workers' expenditures below a minimal social and physiological standard. And, he deduced as early as 1904, excessive saving might induce a fall in wages.[13] The experts proposed spreading the risk not merely among workers, but also to employers and ideally to the state. Both Epstein and Rubinow favored worker contributions to distinguish social insurance from relief and the dole. But Epstein asserted that even gratuitous benefits financed entirely from the public treasury were a form of social insurance, since they distributed the risk, and Rubinow did not object to heavy subsidization. "The theory that a large national budget is of itself a dangerous thing, is one of the silli-

est superstitions of a kindergarten economics," Rubinow wrote
in 1913. "The class which needs social insurance cannot afford
it, and the class which can afford it does not need it." Social
insurance was "nothing but an effort to readjust the distribution
of the national product," perhaps not absolutely equitably, but
justly enough for "national vitality."[14]

The experts aimed at spreading the risk and redistributing
wealth because they tended to view insecurity not as myriad
individual problems, but as one problem inherent in the social
and economic structure. They had less in common with capitalists than had some charity and case workers. In 1931 Rubinow
denounced groups such as the National Association of Manufacturers, the National Industrial Council, the the "large insurance interests" for hiding their vested interests behind "gran-
diloquent slogans" that social insurance was "un-American, unconstitutional, and unnecessary." Two years later, in his book,
Insecurity, a Challenge to America, Epstein devoted a lengthy
passage to denouncing the "blind greed and stupidity of our
business leaders and their political allies," who were "blind to
stark reality and deaf to all pleas for social justice."[15] Rather
than individual solutions, the experts advocated essentially social ones.

Nevertheless, despite their far-reaching implications, the experts' solutions aimed to prevent and alleviate poverty, not to
produce basic changes in the economic system. Characteristically,
Epstein wrote in 1933 that since "the overwhelming majority
of Americans are not seriously considering the demolition of the
present social order" despite "its obvious shortcomings," he
would confine his efforts to "proposals which are within the
realm of possibility under the existing social structures."[16] The
expert-propagandists did not seek to change institutions to eliminate workers' economic hazards so much as to add new institutions to prevent the impoverishing effects of the hazards.
With insight, Gompers characterized their measures as "a patch
upon our social system."[17]

The experts' approach was in decided contrast to that of a

third group within the social insurance circle, reformers with a labor legislation orientation. Edwin Witte was personally closest to this group, for among its leaders were Paul Raushenbush and his wife Elizabeth Brandeis of the University of Wisconsin department of economics; Wisconsin Assemblyman Harold Groves; and another friend, John B. Andrews, secretary of the American Association for Labor Legislation. Although Witte's belief in redistribution of wealth was so strong that in 1932 he judged a friend's progressivism by his adherence to that principle,[18] he was also closest to the labor reformers intellectually—Raushenbush, Miss Brandeis, Groves, and Andrews had all been fellow students of John R. Commons. The labor legislation reformers, unlike the social insurance experts, did not view reform as an extraneous corrective to impose upon blind, unwilling capitalists. Rather, in keeping with Commons' concept of industrial regulation through quasi-collective-bargaining commissions, they sought changes by means of agreement among capital, labor, and public-minded reformers and officials. And they tried to design reforms basic enough to prevent the industrial causes of workers' hazards, not merely to mitigate their effects.

The labor legislationists wanted neither the palliative of relief nor the corrective social device of compulsory insurance appended to the capitalistic system. While by no means callous to workers' impoverishment, they emphasized neither the alleviation of destitution, the principle of distribution of risks, nor the redistribution of wealth as much as did the social insurance experts. Instead they sought to eliminate, or at least to mitigate, the harshness of capitalistic institutions themselves, by inducing managers to reduce the economic hazards to industrial workers. They were at once more radical than the social insurance experts—for they aimed more to alter existing economic practices and institutions—yet less radical, for they had more faith in capitalism's inherent ability to shed antisocial defects and truly serve society.

Commons stated their purposes and faith idealistically and

succinctly when, in later years, he explained: "I was trying to save Capitalism by making it good."[19]

*   *   *   *   *

In 1906 members of the American Economic Association with strong interests in labor reforms founded the American Association for Labor Legislation, to encourage study of labor law, to promote uniformity in labor legislation, and to be the American branch of the International Association for Labor Legislation. Commons was the new association's secretary and in effect its director in the formative years 1908 and 1909, and his student Andrews assumed the same roles permanently from 1910 to 1942.[20] In the early days the association was a broad, inclusive vehicle for various kinds of reformers, however, not only for those with the Wisconsin point of view. During the great campaign for workmen's compensation that began about 1911, men as diverse in their viewpoints as Andrews, Rubinow, and Hoffman of Prudential Life served together as leaders in the association's drive for reform. But about 1916 and 1917 the Association's support began to splinter—and the splintering was symptomatic of the divergencies within the social insurance movement.

The earliest major defections occurred during a campaign for health insurance, to which social insurance advocates directed their major efforts after they had won workmen's compensation for occupational injuries. General health insurance may not have been strictly labor reform, but complete workmen's compensation presented the difficulty of deciding what diseases were occupationally induced, and insurance covering all sicknesses was one solution. Therefore the association led the campaign with research, publicity, and a standard health bill for states' consideration. At first health insurance advocates were highly elated. To co-operate, the American Medical Association appointed a sympathetic committee with Rubinow as its secretary. A number of subordinate trade-union bodies defied top American Federation of Labor leadership to endorse the campaign.

And a wide variety of civic groups added support. In 1917, at the peak of interest, legislative commissions of Massachusetts, New York, and New Jersey reported favorably, six new states established study commissions, and twelve states considered variations of the bill.[21]

Then came the reaction. The association's bill included funeral benefits, and therefore threatened the sale of small-policy life insurance, or so-called "industrial insurance," for which commercial companies had found a lucrative market among workingmen. Hoffman, whose company was a leading industrial insurance carrier, resigned from the association's executive committee and denounced compulsory health insurance proponents as willfully blind to the effectiveness of private efforts. Unlike workmen's compensation, health insurance promised to add to employers' tax burdens without releasing them from any liabilities under common law, so businessmen opposed it. The campaign inevitably raised the question of reorganizing medical practice, and by 1920 grassroots pressure from doctors caused the American Medical Association to move from neutral discussion to organized opposition. In the National Civic Federation, Gompers joined his fellow members in impassioned opposition. No great popular enthusiasm developed for health insurance, and in the troubled days immediately following World War I it went down to defeat amid contradictory cries of "Made in Germany" and of "Bolshevism."[22] Its demise ushered in a lean period for social insurance in the 1920's. Faring worst were the programs designed to give benefits to the insured as a matter of right based on prior contributions, rather than gratuitously, on the basis of need. Gratuitous programs which followed more closely the methods of poor relief continued to make some slow progress.

Mothers' pensions were in the gratuitous tradition. They stemmed from charity and relief, most directly from a practice that private New York charity organizations began about 1875 of placing needy children in private homes rather than in orphanages and almshouses. "Placing-out" spread from private to public welfare practice and gradually evolved into public aid for children in their own homes. Some social workers opposed the development of "mothers' pensions," fearing that public supervision would transform this form of charity into degrading poor relief. But President Roosevelt's 1909 White House Conference on the Care of Dependent Children, and, after its formation in 1912, the United States Children's Bureau, gave impetus to the development. Mothers' pensions did not greatly offend commercial interests, and because they promised to produce useful citizens, and did not aid "ne'er-do-wells," they aroused few American antipathies. Illinois passed the first statewide mothers' pension law in 1911. By 1933 every state except South Carolina and Georgia had some such legislation. Yet in 1934 many of the laws were effective only at the option of counties, depended entirely upon county funds, excluded many people, and gave what social insurance advocates considered pitifully meager benefits. Moreover, given the financial problems of depression, many states and counties failed to provide the meager benefits called for by state laws.[23]

Another program of gratuities, old-age pensions, incited more controversy. It was a broader reform and one for the benefit of persons who, according to some social theorists, should have provided for themselves. The arguments were often verbose and inconclusive assertions regarding the pensions' effects on character, and dealing with the question of whether Americans actually could, by individual effort, hope to provide security for old age. Some practical-minded persons who were frightened by the prospect of outright pensions suggested that the proper course would be to improve existing forms of poor relief. William E. Odom, an industrial pensions adviser, accused old-age pension advocates of speciousness in their arguments that pensions were cheaper. Most aged persons needed institutional care, Odom argued, and the proposed pensions of $10 to $30 per month would not support old people in their homes. And the stigma of relief would in evitably limit the number of claimants. Charles Denby, Jr., a Philadelphia attorney active in Pennsylvania public charity administration, agreed that pensions were not economical, but conceded that industrialization had created need for broad old-age security measures. He proposed a compromise that anticipated one of the 1935 social security programs: gratuitous and regular cash aid for the genuinely needy aged, but under the euphemism old-age "assistance" rather than old-age "pensions" so that recipients would not expect benefits as a matter of social right.[24] The old-age "pensions" that states provided before 1934 were often so illiberal as to resemble older patterns of relief more than the "assistance" that Denby advocated.

The diversity among social insurance advocates was evident in in the old-age pension movement. Leading the movement were Epstein; the Fraternal Order of Eagles, which had wrestled with the problem of aiding its own aging members; and Andrews' labor legislation organization. Andrews' group never gave the old-age problem as much attention as it gave to the more strictly industrial problems of unemployment and occupational accidents. But in 1920 it drew up a model state old-age pensions bill, and in 1922 sponsored a unity conference between itself, the United Mine Workers, the Eagles, and the Pennsylvania Commission. The conferees proposed a new bill, which Andrews' group supported during the twenties, although somewhat less energetically than did the Eagles. Diversity became most clear in 1927 when Epstein formed his American Association for Old Age Security.

The fissure was partly a matter of institutional and personal rivalry. Andrews privately feared that if Epstein's organization succeeded it would take "a certain amount of financial support" from the labor legislation association. Nevertheless he and his executive committee rejected an early proposal that they hire Epstein and absorb Epstein's organization. Andrews declared that he feared disrupting his Association's good relationships with the Eagles and the United Mine Workers.[25] But the fissure also went deeper, to policy. Epstein increasingly advocated compulsory, contributory old-age insurance rather than pensions. His position reflected both the post-World War I trend in Europe and the thought of American social insurance experts. Rubinow had never accepted old-age pensions as much more than a step toward old-age insurance, and Mrs. Armstrong of the California law school believed them to be a "make-shift arrangement" of poor relief, since the laws required persons to depend if possible first upon relatives. Andrews warned that Epstein might "suddenly at some juncture come out for a contributory plan of old age pensions," which the Andrews group, the Mine Workers, and the Eagles considered unwise.[26] Increasingly, Epstein's organization became the focal point of the social insurance expert-propagandist point of view.

Reflecting his affinity with Andrews' group, Witte favored old-age pensions, but not very vociferously. Despite the fissure, he maintained a friendship with Epstein, and, with Commons, accepted what proved to be a completely figurative position as a member of Epstein's advisory council. Witte believed, as he declared in 1933, that "no man who has labored faithfully for twenty-five or thirty years. or even longer, should have to depend in old age upon the generosity of his children, or become a public charge."[27] But he was not the prime draftsman of an old-age pensions bill that Wisconsin passed in 1925 and modified thereafter; the law originated in the Eagles' model bill. In 1933, at the request of state legislators, Witte did devolop another bill, for a state system of contributory old-age insurance. It contained one unique structural feature. In keeping with the concern of labor reformers for changing industrial managers' practices, Witte's friend Raushenbush had once suggested developing an old-age pensions tax that would discourage "the premature scrapping of older workers." In his 1933 bill, Witte provided for a diminution of the employer's part of the contribution as the worker grew older.[28]

Witte's 1933 Wisconsin bill did not pass, but despite divergencies among supporters there was some progress in old-age pensions legislation elsewhere before 1934. Although official interest began with the Massachusetts study commission of 1907, not until 1923 did any state pass a law that survived in the courts. In

Edwin E. Witte (seated, center) with his parents, Emil F. Witte and Anna Yaeck Witte, and brother and sisters in about 1900. *Photo courtesy Mrs. Edwin Witte.*

Edwin Witte in 1931, as chief of the Wisconsin Legislative Reference Library. *State Historical Society of Wisconsin.*

John R. Commons and his sister Anna, photographed in 1934, just prior to the enactment
of federal social security legislation. *State
Historical Society of Wisconsin.*

President Franklin D. Roosevelt signing the
Social Security Act, August 14, 1935. *Photo
courtesy Mrs. Edwin Witte.*

Witte in about 1955, photographed in his Madison home by one of his students. *Photo courtesy Mrs. Edwin Witte.*

Chess match with a grandson, Paul Weeks, in 1959. *Photo courtesy Mrs. Edwin Witte.*

Of Edwin Witte, pictured here in 1950, Wilbur J. Cohen writes: "A complex but humble man, he always disclaimed fame for his many accomplishments. Although many people called him the Father of Social Security, he unhesitatingly gave the credit to others. He was an ordinary man in many ways, unimpressed by superficialities." *Photo courtesy Mrs. Edwin Witte.*

the 1920's ten states passed laws that the courts allowed to stand; but they were weak, and frequently were little more than enabling acts authorizing counties to provide pensions systems on their own resources. After 1929 the state laws improved. By 1934 twenty-nine states provided pensions of $15 to $30 per month, and although they frequently imposed illiberal age and residence requirements, more and more they provided some state funds and compelled counties to participate. No state, however, provided contributory annuities.[29]

Witte was much less interested in old-age security than in the hazard of unemployment, which was more certainly an industrial labor problem—and an increasingly pressing one as the Depression worsened. During a 1931 European trip as a member of a group sponsored by the Carnegie Endowment for International Peace, Witte carefully studied British unemployment insurance, but he investigated other European social insurance measures hardly at all.[30] His interest was natural, for during the lean years for social insurance in the 1920's the Wisconsin group had done more than any other to keep interest in unemployment compensation alive. From well before World War I the dean of the expert-propagandist group, Rubinow, had hoped to apply insurance principles to the unemployment hazard, but had feared unemployment insurance would be especially likely to degenerate into doles and relief.[31] The Commons group, by contrast, gradually evolved a bill not entirely based on insurance principles. Even more profoundly than with old-age security, differences in approach divided those in the social insurance circle.

To make capitalism "good," Commons hoped to force employers to feel the social costs of unemployment and hence to consider the costs before discharging workers. He believed that even bankers, investors, and financiers might be induced to consider unemployment costs before they expanded the credit that precipitated business cycles and periodic unemployment. He had seen Wisconsin's workmen's compensation law prod employers into promoting preventive "safety first" measures, and he believed new laws worked best if they were drawn on lines fa-

miliar to employers. Consequently, in 1921 Commons developed
an unemployment compensation bill on the pattern of Wisconsin's workmen's compensation law. He provided for insurance through a state-supervised but employer-operated mutual
company, which would have authority to adjust rates according
to the unemployment experience of industries and firms. Workers were to receive a dollar a day for up to thirteen weeks when
unemployed, but since he thought that workers were powerless
to reduce unemployment he did not ask them to contribute.
Commons admitted that a dollar a day was scarcely enough to
pay the worker's rent, but his defense was that he was not interested in creating a European-style "philanthropic system." His
was a "capitalistic scheme" to make efficient labor management
profitable, a plan that avoided the "socialistic and paternalistic
schemes of Europe."[32]

During the 1920's each successive Wisconsin legislature considered and rejected a version of Commons' bill. Meanwhile
Commons helped to create and administer the most extensive
and successful of the voluntary unemployment insurance systems,
that of the Chicago clothing industry. The Chicago employers
insisted that rather than pool unemployment insurance contributions, each employer should maintain separate reserve funds
and be responsible only for his own employees. Commons began
increasingly to emphasize individual employer reserves, rather
than mere adjustment of contributions, as the means to assign each employer the cost of his unemployment. In 1931 a
young Wisconsin assemblyman fresh from Commons' seminar,
Harold Groves, sponsored a bill that he, Raushenbush, and Miss
Brandeis had developed. Their basic idea was to credit each firm's
contributions to an individual account in a state-managed fund,
and then to charge against the account the benefits paid out to
workers whom the firm discharged. Firms that built up and
maintained adequate accounts by stable employment could reduce and then even discontinue contributions. With the support of Wisconsin's new Progressive governor, Philip La Follette, and after concessions to employers (*e.g.*, that responsible

firms could manage their own reserve funds, and that the bill would not take effect if enough employers acted voluntarily), the bill passed in January, 1932. Wisconsin thus adopted the first American unemployment compensation law, and the only one before 1935.[33]

With its segregation of reserves and philosophy of inducing employers to stabilize employment, the Wisconsin law conceded much to prevailing assumptions of individual responsibility and to the power of businessmen as a class in economic life. Many observers outside Wisconsin approved, including a conference of six northeastern governors that Franklin D. Roosevelt, as governor of New York, called in 1931. In February, 1932, the governors' study commission issued a report that stressed the need to prevent unemployment and recommended a plan similar to Wisconsin's. Critics, however, objected to Wisconsin's abandonment of the genuinely social device of broad pooling of risk, and in the autumn of 1932 they found a rallying point in the proposals of an Ohio commission in which Rubinow was active. Rather than stabilizing employment, the Ohio plan emphasized maximizing and assuring workers' benefits; it proposed worker contributions and pooling in one statewide fund. In the same year Paul Douglas, a participant in several official and private studies of unemployment insurance, published a book, *Standards of Unemployment Insurance*, in which he advocated a similar plan. In 1933 Epstein proposed to the New York legislature a pooled-fund bill using the English device of contributions from the public treasury, as well as from employers and workers.[34]

Epstein's action disgusted John B. Andrews, who wanted to unite unemployment compensation advocates behind his association's standard bill. His group had advocated unemployment compensation since well before World War I, and with the revival of interest about 1930 had sponsored conferences, brought various viewpoints together, and developed an "American Plan for Unemployment Reserves" for consideration by the states. Andrews subscribed to the Wisconsin concern for prevention and stabilization, and his American Plan used the device of segregated employer reserves. By May, 1933, however, the association had added amendments providing that the authorities administering unemployment compensation could order pooling if too many employer accounts ran low, and also that workers might contribute voluntarily in order to increase their benefits. Andrews hoped the modifications would make the American Plan a meeting ground between the Wisconsin and Ohio positions. Rubinow helped draft the amendments, and also hoped for rapprochement.[35]

But the two camps remained far apart. In 1933 twenty-five legislatures considered unemployment compensation bills and rejected them all. In an article entitled "Enemies of Unemployment Insurance," Epstein blamed the defeats on those who advocated segregated reserve laws. He reasoned that segregated reserves provided too little protection to workers and hence failed to arouse popular enthusiasm. Miss Brandeis observed, however, that Ohio-type bills had fared no better than Wisconsin-type. Her husband, Paul Raushenbush, stated in a 1933 article that while all unemployment compensation advocates agreed on many points, on the twin questions of employee contributions and pooling of funds "there is no practicable middle ground as yet visible."[36]

Each side clearly recognized the basic contrasts between their positions. One side spoke of "unemployment insurance"; the other was careful to speak of "unemployment reserves." Rubinow continued to declare that "unemployment insurance, being social insurance, has a specific social purpose, to relieve distress" without charity and doles: "As an insurance measure it is not called upon to express any opinion whether unemployment is preventable, and if so, how." Raushenbush maintained that the purpose of the Wisconsin law was "(a) the stimulation of more regular employment, as far as possible; and (b) the payment of unemployment benefits" to workers made idle through industry's failure or inability. He and his colleagues argued that their law attempted to do both, with proper allocation of the costs of unemployment to the companies whose production caused

it. Each side recognized that their differences involved fundamental social dogma. Raushenbush wrote that the Wisconsin
plan, "if you please, is individualism—but enlightened and modified by social responsibility"—while his wife labeled the view
that businessmen could not reduce unemployment "fatalism."
Epstein wrote that "as long as the present social structure pre-
vails, it is puerile to talk of . . . the elimination of overproduc-
tion or unemployment." In Epstein's view both employers and
workers were "the victims of the social disorganization which
is inherent in our system of production."[37]

Witte was a close and continual student of unemployment
compensation, and watched the polarization of attitudes among
its advocates with mixed feelings. At each pole he had friends.
He had helped draft Commons' original bill, and in 1931 and
1932 he gave technical assistance to Groves, the Raushenbushes,
and the La Follettes. As Andrews developed the American Plan, he
gave confidential advice on both technical and substantive details. Nevertheless, Witte's initial convictions on unemployment
insurance leaned toward those of the expert-propagandists. The
idea of prevention was perhaps not the best argument for unemployment compensation, Witte implied to Commons in 1921:
"Unemployment insurance is a method for a better distribution
of losses. Fluctuations in employment, due to business conditions, I feel, are largely beyond the control of the individual employer, and of the employers in any one state, or even of the
employers of the United States." Even after passage of the 1932
Wisconsin law he wrote privately that he was "frankly . . . very
skeptical" of its preventive value. Personally he preferred "an
unemployment insurance bill on the British model" with pooled funds and broad distribution of cost to employers, workers,
and the public. Nevertheless, in 1933 he advised Epstein that
while he thought the pooled fund "distinctly preferable," he did
"not see that the other is to be entirely condemned."[38]

Characteristically, Witte's attitude was pragmatic. He advised
American Federation of Labor President William Green against
opposing the Wisconsin plan, largely because Supreme Court

Justice Louis Brandeis and Harvard law professor Felix Frankfurter believed it much more likely than a pooled insurance system to satisfy the courts. He argued also that any system with the approval of "some of the best minds," especially of Commons and Louis Brandeis, merited serious consideration. Even in his one lone attempt to theorize about social insurance structure, his purpose was pragmatic. In 1929 he argued that labor legislators should design workmen's compensation laws to reduce the social cost of accidents to a minimum, not to assign responsibility for accidents to employers. Later he confided to Epstein that his true purpose was to develop, by implication, a sound constitutional basis for unemployment compensation and other social insurance measures.[39]

Equally characteristically, Witte tried to conciliate the various groups and factions, and to encourage experimentation. In the best Commons tradition, he suggested changes in Andrews' American Plan to make it "more palatable to employers," but also warned that "no legislation on the subject of unemployment insurance can get by in any state unless the labor unions will support it." Mediating between social insurance factions themselves, he counseled Andrews not to consider Epstein's efforts necessarily competitive with the American Plan, since there was room for all approaches. At about the same time he sent Epstein a courteous but pointed letter disapproving of schisms among unemployment insurance advocates, and warning against "witch hunting" to stamp out schemes such as segregated employer reserves. "Why should not such experiments be carried on at the same time central unemployment insurance funds are tried out in other states?" he asked.[40]

*   *   *   *   *

Witte's assumption that social insurance was a matter for state action was quite common in 1933. But increasingly the question of federal legislation was coming to the fore. Despite experience with military and civil service pensions, before 1934 the federal government did virtually nothing directly for general social insurance. Its most notable contribution was in the field of child welfare, where it provided investigations and reports, and for a time in the 1920's some subsidization, through its Children's Bureau. In 1909 Pennsylvania Congressman William B. Wilson proposed organizing the aged into an Old Home Guard to make them eligible for "military" pensions. Thereafter men such as Wisconsin's Socialist Congressman Victor L. Berger periodically introduced federal old-age pensions bills, but none of the bills succeeded. In 1927 Epstein's organization proposed that the federal government subsidize one-third of state old-age pension costs. In 1932 and 1933, embodied in a bill that Senator Clarence C. Dill of Washington and Representative William P. Connery, Jr., of Massachusetts sponsored, Epstein's idea eventually won favorable congressional committee reports, but failed to reach a floor vote. In the spring of 1934 the Dill-Connery bill was the foremost old-age security measure before Congress. It passed in the House, and had Roosevelt encouraged it, it might have passed in the Senate. Congress and Roosevelt did approve the Railroad Retirement Act, for the first time providing contributory annuities to a class of nongovernmental workers. But while he was receptive to various suggestions, Roosevelt gave no general old-age security measure his decisive support.[41]

Federal unemployment compensation bills fared little better. A 1916 resolution by a Socialist congressman from New York, Meyer London, proposed a national bill but achieved nothing. In 1928 Senator James Couzens of Michigan led a subcommittee that recommended national government action to strengthen unemployment data collection, employment exchanges, and public works planning; but it declared unemployment compensation to be a matter for voluntary and state action. In 1932 another Senate committee endorsed the idea of compulsory unemployment compensation, but concluded that at most the federal government could only grant income tax credits to employers for unemployment compensation contributions—an idea that one member, Senator Robert F. Wagner of New York, unsuccessfully introduced in several successive bills. When in November of 1932 the American Federation of Labor decisively reversed its historic position against unemployment compensation, it declared one uniform national system to be preferable but virtually impossible. Since the courts would object, the Federation declared in a report that Witte helped write, the states should separately pass measures suited to local conditions, with basic protections for unions and with other minimal standards. The 1932 Democratic national platform also favored "unemployment insurance under state laws."[42]

The man on the platform, Roosevelt, advocated state unemployment compensation. As governor of New York in 1930 he had declared that 90 per cent of unemployment was not the fault of workers and urged other governors to consider insurance as a solution. The following year he sponsored an influential conference of six governors, urged his legislature to make its own study, and vetoed a manufacturer-sponsored measure for voluntary action through commercial insurance carriers. After the 1931 legislature failed to act further, he recommended action for 1933. His industrial commissioner in New York and later Secretary of Labor, Frances Perkins, was even more intensely interested. She studied unemployment insurance, observed the British system carefully at first hand, and probably originated the insurance plank in the 1932 Democratic platform. Gradually and flexibly she moved from a position favoring a pooled-type law to tolerance for the segregated reserve plan. Early in 1934, when a new idea for federal action to prod states came to the fore, she gave her encouragement.[43]

Late in 1933 Paul Raushenbush and his wife Elizabeth Brandeis were searching for constitutional means to remove the competitive commercial disadvantage that a state allegedly would suffer if it created unemployment compensation unilaterally, and to prod the states more vigorously than could Wagner's tax-deduction proposals. In December Miss Brandeis' father, Justice Louis Brandeis, remarked that they should study the 1927 case of *Florida* v. *Mellon*, in which the Supreme Court had approved a federal tax-offset system that encouraged states to levy inheritance taxes. Raushenbush and Associate Labor Solicitor Thomas Eliot, working closely with Miss Perkins, drafted a tax-offset bill for unemployment compensation. The bill provided for a 5 per cent tax on employers' payrolls, but allowed the employer to "offset against" it—*i.e.*, to deduct from his tax payment—contributions that he made to an approved state unemployment compensation system. To be approved, the state system had to provide a minimum level of benefits, but the bill permitted either pooled or segregated reserve funds, thus avoiding the bitterest controversy dividing social insurance advocates. Senator Wagner and Representative David J. Lewis of Maryland sponsored the measure in Congress. Witte urged both Epstein and Andrews to lend support, and the Wagner-Lewis bill won praise from expert-propagandists as well as from labor legislationists. Like Andrews, Epstein testified favorably, and Paul Douglas termed it "a truly brilliant method" that constituted a first step toward state action. Rubinow also thought it "an extremely ingenious device," but he noted with dissatisfaction that it tolerated "even the weak and unsatisfactory Wisconsin law" and did not provide "really satisfactory standards." In the Seventy-Third Congress the bill never got beyond congressional committees, where it engendered a controversy as to what uniform standards the federal government should impose on states. Roosevelt stated publicly that the bill established "a suitable relation of the national government to unemployment insurance," and once expressed his hope "that the bill will be passed by Congress at this time." But he failed to give it more decisive support than he gave the Dill-Connery bill.[44]

Instead, Roosevelt hesitated. He did not wish social insurance to become a dole or a burden to the public treasury, as the Dill-Connery bill might. He listened to critics of the Wagner-Lewis bill who warned that putting huge unemployment insurance funds into the hands of the states might further dislocate the economy. Some congressmen also suspected that rather than merely approve congressional measures, he wished to win political support by proposing his own program. As early as January, 1934, he confided to Lewis that he might do nothing until he had the benefit of a thorough social insurance study. Late in the spring he apparently won explicit approval from his cabinet for such an inquiry, with pledges to support the resulting program.[45] So on June 8 he gave his message for delay and study. On June 29 he appointed Frances Perkins, Treasury Secretary Henry Morgenthau, Jr., Secretary of Agriculture Henry Wallace, Attorney General Homer S. Cummings, and Federal Emergency Relief Administrator Harry Hopkins as a "committee on economic security," responsible for the investigation.

Witte approved Roosevelt's commitment to social insurance, but disliked the delay. He refused to join a private committee to promote individual saving, because he feared it was a counter to Roosevelt's program. He believed in individual thrift and saving "both from an individual and social point of view," he advised the committee's promoter, Ray Westerfield; but he was also "a firm believer in the need for and social value of a comprehensive social insurance and compulsory health insurance" program. Roosevelt's delay of the Wagner-Lewis bill "very much disappointed" him, for he feared that while it might "'still be the final outcome,'" the bill would come too late for state legislatures to respond in their 1935 sessions. "Everybody who will have anything to do with the new national bill" should work to develop it quickly, he wrote privately, so that Congress could act on it as early as January.[46]

Witte did not know that the task would soon be his. In Washington several people were busily drawing up plans for an elaborate organization to aid the cabinet committee. They were Bryce Stewart of the Industrial Relations Counselors of New York, Meredith B. Givens of the Social Science Research Council, and Assistant Secretary of Labor Arthur Altmeyer, a Wisconsin man and Commons student who knew Witte as an old friend. Miss Perkins, chairman of the cabinet committee, had had frequent professional contacts with Witte, and she knew him as an able, honest, and practical investigator. Suddenly, on July 24, 1934, with no advance warning, Altmeyer informed

Witte that he and Miss Perkins wanted him to be executive director of their organization, heading the research staff and taking immediate charge of all investigations and studies. Within twenty-four hours Witte arranged a semester's leave of absence from the university and resigned from his largely figurative position as director of Unemployment Compensation in Wisconsin. On July 26 he arrived in Washington, accepted the new post, and took up his duties.[47]

Witte quickly decided that his task was "'primarily a work of developing a legislative program, rather than the conducting of any extensive research.'"[48] By 1934 the ideas of social insurance were old, but their advocates had become frustrated, divided, and quarrelsome through having had too much time to dream and too little opportunity to act beyond very narrow limits. Witte correctly realized that his problem was less to gather new information and generate new ideas than to find the measures that would win the broadest possible support. The assignment tested all of his powers of conciliation, for complexity and lack of clarity in the committee's organization provided ample opportunity for new misunderstandings and personality clashes. More basically, Witte had to reconcile differences of opinion regarding federal and state roles that went to the heart of constitutional theory, and settle arguments of social insurance doctrines that grew out of fundamental social and economic dogma. And always he had to do it within the narrow limits imposed by the American political, social, and economic structure, as reflected in the views of constitutional lawyers and politicians.

6

SOCIAL SECURITY
Executive Director

IN THE MOST IMPORTANT assignment of his life, Witte characteristically insisted upon pursuing economic security programs
that were immediately attainable, rather than schemes that
were grandiose or ideally perfect. "In fact, can there be security in
an insecure world?" he asked a friend rhetorically in November,
1934, with the report of the Committee on Economic Security
due at Roosevelt's desk in less than a month. Witte was "keenly
aware" that the committee could not prepare all measures needed for complete economic security in the short time between
July and December. Resigned to a less-than-perfect outcome, he
observed that "very few people will think that what we will get
is anywhere near sufficient." In order to "get something done
which will mean progress" he was "trying to keep our Committee at work within a comparatively narrow field." He hoped
his strategy would "get legislation and not merely a report."[1]

Even the pursuit of the possible, however, was a path through
conflict. Although Witte and his colleagues acted largely from
political, fiscal, and technical considerations, they could not
avoid some very fundamental decisions of social welfare policy.
Critics both inside and outside the committee disagreed with
their implicit judgments on ultimate goals and with their assessment of what was really possible. Witte pursued his "narrow field" strategy amid widespread rumors that under his lead-

ership the economic security program had, in the words of *New York Times* columnist Louis Stark, "simmered down to unemployment insurance without federal aid." Stark reported that some "social workers and experts" were saying that efforts for economic security had even retrogressed since Roosevelt's historic economic security message of June, 1934. "It has also been known," Stark reported in obvious reference to Witte, "that officials directly responsible to Secretary Perkins and who are in charge of the Committee on Economic Security" were in disagreement with leading social insurance experts.[2]

Many of the disagreements were within the Economic Security Committee's own organization, as Witte was very much aware. He was, he told Felix Frankfurter, "at a loss to know how to get through all of the maze of machinery and conflicting personal interests that are manifest down here."[3]

"The maze of machinery" was real. Observing it, *Survey* editor Paul Kellogg once sent Witte an account of a Canadian country doctor who had been called to deliver a baby. Arriving at the home, the doctor found two babies already born, and three more coming. So frail were the infants that the physician abandoned them to summon a priest for last rites. But they survived—as the Dionne quintuplets. "What with your cabinet committee, Advisory Council, technical board, staff and litter of sub-committees," Kellogg commented, "it seems to me you might take a grain of comfort in this story."[4] Kellogg's analogy was apt. Although Miss Perkins understood the broad issues of social insurance quite well, and Harry Hopkins was experienced in public welfare and relief, the cabinet committee was not composed of social insurance specialists. To provide expert information and advice, Perkins, Altmeyer, Witte, and others proceeded (from the blueprint that Altmeyer, Stewart, and Givens had prepared) to construct an elaborate organization.[5] Witte's formal task thereafter was to guide decisions upward through several organizational echelons.

At bottom, under Witte's direct supervision, was a staff of social insurance experts whom he and his associates selected from universities, foundations, business firms, and elsewhere. One echelon above the staff was the "technical board," a group of twenty administration officials and advisers with Altmeyer as their chairman. Being insiders, technical board members were more inclined than the staff to be loyal to their superiors' wishes, and sensitive to the political implications of policy recommendations. Witte served as the board's secretary, sat with its subcommittees, and constantly consulted with Altmeyer. He later declared that it was the technical board who "more than any other group" put together the social security program. Miss Perkins and her cabinet committee looked to it for advice and opinion. Witte generally shared its insiders' point of view, and encouraged it in its policy-making role. By contrast, he emphasized that the function of the staff of outside experts was not to recommend policy but to carry out the wishes of the technical board, the cabinet committee, and Roosevelt.[6] The staff's subordinate role was a source of displeasure to some experts who had strong policy opinions. Hence some of the dissatisfactions among "social workers and experts" which the *Times* reported.

To the staff and the technical board, the cabinet committee added groups of men and women to represent the public. At the outset public commentators had expressed friendly interest in the idea of economic security, but skepticism about the specific programs Roosevelt would pursue. Two days before Roosevelt's message to Congress of June 8, recommending a program for economic security, the Republican National Committee admitted that the country was backward in social legislation, and recommended government action with a "broad, liberal, and progressive" approach, not "too obstinately clinging to the past." Even the editor of the *Chicago Daily Tribune* admitted that the goals of Roosevelt's message were fine, although he believed that "American government as it existed prior to March, 1933," was capable of providing individual security, while Roosevelt was following the path of Hitler, Mussolini, Lenin, and Stalin. The *New York Herald Tribune* warned against putting reform ahead of recovery, and "fancy professional theories" ahead of "plain good times."

The *Birmingham Age Herald* saw danger in having "an eager brain truster" strike off a security program "in the wee sma' hours," and the editors of the *New York Times* decided to defer judgment until the "careful and complete plan" appeared. But the New York *Journal of Commerce* offered some criteria for judgment: the government should not make social insurance a burden on the public treasury, or pay benefits before accumulating adequate reserves, or allow unemployment insurance to be a dole. Like most newspapers, the *Journal of Commerce* professed to be friendly. It advised "conservative elements" to insist on fiscal and actuarial soundness, but not to resist social insurance.[7]

In pursuit of good public relations Witte and his colleagues evolved a combination of an advisory council of public figures, smaller bodies such as the Medical Advisory Committee to represent special interests, and one large economic security conference. Frankfurter, whom Witte consulted, warned against creating large public-relations bodies that would produce loud and disagreeable dissents, and associate *Survey* editor Beulah Amidon warned against too much Roosevelt-style "ballyhoo." Others such as Justice Brandeis and *Today* editor Raymond Moley also favored a smaller advisory council of about twelve, really to advise rather than merely to form a link with the public. Finally, Roosevelt appointed a main advisory council of twenty-three business, labor, professional, and civic leaders from lists that Altmeyer and Witte prepared. As chairman he appointed a southern liberal, University of North Carolina President Franklin D. Graham. For broader public liaison, Witte and his colleagues planned a National Conference on Economic Security, which Roosevelt agreed to sponsor on November 14, after the 1934 elections. Through a series of speeches and round-table discussions, the conference drew in many interested people otherwise excluded from the committee's councils.[8]

Witte wrote that he wanted "to give the conference the appearance, not of a meeting for launching the publicity on our program, but of giving people who are peculiarly interested in our problems an opportunity to present their view." Yet he and his fellows tried hard to keep the outsiders' views innocuously atomized. Although they invited conferees to submit ideas and criticisms individually in writing, they expressly avoided having discussion groups submit policy recommendations as groups. They showed some of the same attitude toward the advisory council, and, like the committee's internal organization, its public-relations efforts also created some conflicts of ideas and personalities.[9]

Complicating the situation was an informal pattern of decision-making that existed within the formal organization. Witte participated in both the formal and the informal. He was executive director of the staff and secretary to the technical board, the main advisory council, and the cabinet committee itself; and so, more than any other person, he tied the formal decision-making apparatus together. Most frequently it was he who outlined questions to be studied, prepared agenda, and drafted the leading reports, thus guiding formal decisions upward from the staff, through the technical board and advisory groups, and finally to the cabinet committee.[10] Informally, however, cabinet committee members depended heavily for advice on trusted subordinates in their own departments. Most important were Frances Perkins and her trusted friends in the Labor Department who had initiated the economic security study and, as Miss Perkins wrote privately, "expected to 'run the show.' " She had handpicked Altmeyer as her personal representative on economic security matters, and Assistant Labor Solicitor Thomas Eliot as the cabinet committee's counsel. When Witte arrived the Labor Department insiders took him into their confidence, and together the four discussed all important procedural and policy questions. Witte's young protégé and aide, Wilbur Cohen, later observed that a decision was "ninety-eight per cent won" if Perkins, Altmeyer, and Witte agreed upon it.[11] The informal arrangement was of course very natural. But it, too, was a cause of frustration to staff persons and outside experts who coveted a voice in policy-making.

Witte's position cast him as something of a broker between the various formal, informal, and conflicting groups, so that he felt deeply the tensions of personalities and ideas that no organization could have fully avoided. But he also had the satisfaction of being more than a mere technician or executive, for he helped chart the actual policy decisions. His technique was not to press personal policy opinions upon his superiors, for he saw himself primarily as head "staff man," working for Miss Perkins. Rather, both before the formal bodies and in the inner discussions, he employed his unique ability to delineate issues and evaluate alternatives analytically, critically, and carefully, and to synthesize ideas into practicable proposals. The competence and unobtrusiveness with which he made his presentations won him deep respect among cabinet committee members. Their confidence in his judgment helped in turn to bring them to consensus on key issues. That role, and a similar role he later played in educating and convincing congressmen and senators, were his most crucial contributions to social security.[12]

* * * * *

From August until well into November the Economic Security Committee's most pressing problem was to define broad guidelines and limits of its task. One question was whether Witte and his colleagues should design social insurance with the focus mainly on the individual's problem of security, or try specifically to use it as a tool to refashion the total economy. With their focus on the total economy they might try to design it to achieve recovery and control, perhaps a a channel for Keynesian-style deficit spending. By 1935 there was in the Treasury Department a small group of Keynesian economists who advanced a view of social insurance primarily in terms of fund flows and occasions for planned deficits.[13]

Roosevelt's own instructions did not encourage such bold use of social insurance. Both before and after the President's June 8 message General Motors president John J. Raskob and his fellow-members of the Department of Commerce Business Advisory and Planning Council insisted that the federal government should take custody of all social insurance reserve funds, presumably to prevent their investment from exaggerating business cycles. Roosevelt stipulated federal custody of the funds in his June 8 message, and also expressed hope that his various reconstruction programs would speed recovery. But he also suggested financing social insurance through payroll contributions rather than general taxation, which tended to preclude a bold use of social insurance for control and counter-cyclical spending. In private conferences with Miss Perkins, Altmeyer, and Witte, Roosevelt recognized the necessity of providing assistance funds gratuitously from the general treasury for those already dependent or approaching dependency. But he reiterated his preference for financing permanent programs through contributions, in order to be cautious fiscally.[14]

Like Roosevelt, Witte and most members of the technical board were not impressed with Keynesian economic doctrines. Witte criticized them as too abstract, and scarcely grasped the idea that deficit spending might increase the nation's total wealth. He believed that some governmental contribution for social welfare was desirable, but that relief expenditures had already strained the general treasury almost to its limit. Large increases in welfare expenditures, therefore, had to come from current taxation. From his experience with the Wisconsin legislative committee earlier in 1934, he concluded that taxpayers were in an even more disgruntled mood than the unemployed.[15] Acting on his preconceptions and the observation that the New Deal had other programs for recovery, Witte suggested at the outset that recovery programs lay "largely outside" the committee's task. The technical board, which included Alvin Hansen, a Keynesian economist who had studied the probable effects of unemployment reserve funds upon the total economy, added with a slight shift in emphasis that all proposals "must be weighed in the light of their effects upon economic recovery." At least dimly recognizing the potentially deflationary effects of payroll contributions and accumulated reserves, Witte and his colleagues eventually decided not to introduce old-age insurance contributions very rapidly, and they sponsored a study of the proper handling of reserves. The technical board agreed with Witte, however, that their major concern was not total economic effects, but simply "the protection of the individual against dependency and distress."[16]

Throughout, Witte and the others answered the largest economic question more by default than by squarely facing the issue. They confined their consideration of total economic effects almost entirely to a double negative: security programs should not be unsound fiscally. The final security program did include numerous gratuitous assistance and grant-in-aid measures that incidentally involved injecting large sums from the national treasury into the economy. But the major long-term programs—unemployment and old-age insurance—were contributory and largely self-supporting. The focus of Witte and his fellows on the individual and his security was a reasonable delimitation of their task, very much in the social insurance tradition, and politically realistic. But it was more cautious than innovative, and Keynesian dissenters saw an opportunity lost.[17]

A second broad policy question was how much to emphasize social insurance as opposed to gratuitous relief and other approaches to social welfare. Paradoxically, the relief approach was a favorite of both social welfare liberals and fiscal conservatives. The liberals saw in it opportunity for more generous benefits than social insurance on actuarial principles could promise. The conservatives saw opportunity to keep social welfare payments temporary and at the lowest possible maintenance levels. From a middle position, Witte and the technical board recognized early that "economic security is a much broader concept than social insurance,"[18] and included relief in their studies.

At the outset Witte suggested that in addition to social insurance, the committee had the alternatives of an "annuity" approach, involving compulsory individual savings, perhaps with some contributions from employers and government; a "guaranteed employment" approach, using public works and aids to private employment; and the relief or "maintenance" approach, emphasizing satisfaction of emergency needs. Social insurance alone could not guarantee complete security, Witte concluded. In his eclectic way, he suggested combining features of all the approaches, and especially emphasized the immediate need for emergency relief. For a brief moment in August, however, Witte considered completely abandoning the insurance solution in favor of the relief approach. Edith Abbott, editor of *Social Service Review*, insisted that insurance was costly but nevertheless failed to relieve those already unemployed. She favored instead free grants of cash, euphemistically labeled "aid," "allowances," and "assistance," rather than "relief." "I strongly feel," Witte advised Altmeyer, "that there is a good deal to what Miss Abbott says."[19] But he soon returned to the idea of a combination of social insurance and relief measures.

Until well into December, Hopkins and Roosevelt considered combining a work-relief bill with the permanent economic security measure, and were dissuaded only when Budget Director Daniel Bell objected that it would cause a bitter fight among congressional committees.[20] The leading advocates of a work relief bill were officials in Hopkins' Federal Emergency Relief Administration, who had seen Roosevelt cut off their Civilian Works Administration in April for fiscal reasons. In August they eagerly furnished quarters to Witte's staff and, since Hopkins was in Europe, even installed Witte at Hopkins' personal desk. Eventually, however, they found more direct lines to Roosevelt's interest, and developed their work-relief bill separately from the economic security program.[21] Their loss of interest in Witte's work demonstrated the ambivalent attitude of the relief and welfare tradition toward social insurance. For his part, Witte reciprocated with equivocal feelings towards work relief. He believed that it was quite necessary in the current emergency, but emphasized its limited application: it should be given only to persons who were genuinely employable, and only for work on projects of permanent value. Ultimately, he declared in October, the solution for unemployment was more private employment plus unemployment insurance.[22]

Moreover, the cabinet committee decided that unemployment insurance must not, to use the words of a November speech that Witte wrote for Roosevelt, "become a dole through the mingling of insurance and relief." At first Witte and his colleagues considered the English practice of extending unemployment benefits with general treasury funds in periods of prolonged unemployment, but by October the technical board advised against it.[23] Their superiors concurred. The final security program included "assistance" for various classes of unemployables, but kept work relief separate from insurance, and made no provision for gratuitous or "extended" unemployment benefits. Significantly, the government did not commit itself to permanent promises of relief for the employable. Instead, it established an American tradition of careful distinction between social insurance and relief, and a bias in social security away from the relief and towards the social insurance method.

A third broad question, arousing far sharper antagonism than either the issue of making social insurance an instrument for total economic control or that of social insurance versus relief, was the question of which programs to recommend immediately to Congress. In his June 8 message Roosevelt had mentioned specifically only the problems of unemployment and old age, but had hinted at a broader, more comprehensive program of social insurance. During June, Altmeyer and Givens outlined a very broad set of social welfare problems, and a White House statement on June 29 promised studies of "unemployment compensation, old age pensions, workmen's compensation, health insurance, mothers' pensions, maternity benefits, and insurance against the special hazards of self-employment in small business and agriculture."[24]

Witte gradually learned that a commitment to study was not a commitment to act, and that the real question was one of priorities and the timing of separate social insurance measures. In his first enthusiastic days in Washington Witte drafted a speech for Roosevelt declaring boldly that "the time is ripe for a comprehensive program for economic security. As I envisioned this, it is broader than any of the categories of social insurance," and "should afford protection in all contingencies involving loss of earnings" whether by workers, farmers, or the self-employed. Roosevelt omitted Witte's brave words.[25] Yet Witte continued to toy with the concept of one unified system of insurance not divided into the traditional social insurance categories, to pay benefits for all involuntary interruptions of earnings. The technical board thought the idea worth exploring, but, like the cabinet committee, inclined much more to the idea of separate systems for separate risks, begun at different times. They doubted that Congress, even if favorable to a very broad program, would want all parts to begin operating at once. From the very beginning Miss Perkins had tended to divide her committee's goals into immediate and long-range.[26] From about October 1 the practical question was not Witte's vision of one unified system, but rather which programs to recommend first, and when.

Top priority for unemployment compensation was never in doubt. Hopkins once encouraged Roosevelt to abandon it entirely in favor of a program of public works and guaranteed employment, but because unemployment insurance was the favorite of Miss Perkins and her Labor Department group, it survived.[27] Nor was there much conflict over including a subsidy for state aid to dependent children and for a variety of other child and maternal health and welfare services. The technical board once suggested that such aids were among the types of residual relief best left to local effort, but Miss Perkins and Witte encouraged their consideration. The committee left the matter to the Children's Bureau for study, and in the end approved in substance the measures that the bureau's acting director, Katherine Lenroot, and her aide, Dr. Martha Elliott, recommended.[28] The programs around which controversies arose concerning priorities and inclusion were old age security and health insurance.

By mid-November, angry champions of old-age insurance suspected that Witte was undermining their efforts. In the beginning the committee had authorized a study of contributory old-age annuities. Staff members Barbara Armstrong of the University of California Law School and J. Douglas Brown of Princeton University, along with technical board member Murray Latimer, chairman of the Railroad Retirement Board, began enthusiastically to plan a contributory old-age insurance system. Late in September, the technical board advised that a different type of program, based on grants to states for gratuitous pensions to the needy aged, was even more important. Early in October Witte reported that old-age security was "very much in the foreground."[29] But he saw dark clouds on the old-age security horizon.

Witte noted that public interest in old-age pensions was high, but he believed it represented false hopes. By late 1934, some thirty-six organizations were agitating for old-age pensions. Chief among them was the group gathered around the California physician Francis E. Townsend, who for nearly a year had been preaching the twin doctrines of cheer for the aged and new life for the nation's economy. Townsend believed that the government should levy a heavy sales or transactions tax, and then distribute the money in pensions, perhaps as large as $150 or $200 per month, to anyone sixty or over who promised to spend it immediately. Townsendism spread rapidly by means of a great promotional campaign, complete with plans for organizing "THE BIGGEST MASS MEETING EVER HELD IN ALL THE WORLD," and pleas for everyone except the widow with her mite to "give A DOLLAR or AS MANY DOLLARS AS POSSIBLE." Witte considered Townsend's proposal flatly impossible, since it would penalize economic activity and divert half the national income to ten million elderly people. To him it was cruel fraud perpetrated upon the aged poor. He pointed accusingly to the Townsend organizers' appeals for funds, tried to induce postal authorities to halt Townsend's use of the mails, and was disappointed to learn that the Post Office had already investigated and found no illegality. With Townsend followers flooding Roosevelt and the committee with petitions at such a rate that it took a half-dozen of Witte's typists merely to mail his form replies, Witte felt "no end of concern." He was sure that by arousing false hopes the Townsendites were undermining the possibility of a sound program of old-age security.[30]

His conviction led to events that angered advocates of old-age insurance and embarrassed Roosevelt. In August Witte had conferred with the President and found him apparently favorable to old-age security measures.[31] But by November, when he drafted a crucial speech for Roosevelt to deliver at the National Conference on Economic Security, Witte suggested an ambiguous stance. He emphasized the seriousness of the old-age hazard and the eventual need for genuine old-age insurance, but also the impossibility of "solving all our problems at once." Specifically, Witte wrote for Roosevelt: "I do not know whether this is the time for any federal legislation on old age security. Organizations promoting fantastic schemes have aroused hopes that cannot possibly be fulfilled, and have greatly increased the difficulties of getting sound legislation." But, Witte concluded more optimistically, "I still hope that we may still be able to give the aged something better than impossible promises—that we can work out a program that is both sound and just to the aged." Witte submitted his draft to Roosevelt via Frances Perkins. Roosevelt edited it extensively, and what was left seemed to shatter all optimism for immediate action. "I still hope," he finally declared, "that in time we may be able to provide security for the aged,—a sound and uniform system which will provide true security."[32]

"In time." The words set off what Washington columnist Arthur Krock termed "The Mystery of the President's Speech, or Does the English Language Mean Anything." Reporters, especially of the Associated Press, interpreted them as a death knell for immediate old-age security measures. Roosevelt's words were the occasion for columnist Louis Stark's front-page revelations of the dissatisfaction of "social workers and experts" with chopping "the entire social security program down to one subject for early enactment—unemployment insurance." Hurriedly Miss Perkins called newsmen in and informed them that their interpretation was wrong. She hedged on specifics, but finally led them to expect some old-age security program. Witte quickly (but still ambiguously) informed National Conference guests that Roosevelt "most decidedly" had not killed old-age security legislation. Rather, he was "very much interested"—but undecided. Krock, claiming information from "reliable friends of Witte," reported that Miss Perkins scolded Witte. But he correctly defended Witte on the ground that Miss Perkins had approved the speech and that Roosevelt had surely rewritten it. Witte later denied the scolding, but admitted that the episode was very "unfortunate."[33]

Latimer, Brown, and Mrs. Armstrong interpreted the speech to mean indefinite delay for their nationwide system of contributory annuities, and they blamed Witte. Witte continued to insist that he and other insiders had not lost hope for some old-age security program, and many years later Altmeyer recalled that the insiders' real aim had been to dampen public enthusiasm and expectations for excessive old-age pensions, not to kill all old-age security proposals. Witte's and Altmeyer's explanations were consistent with Witte's unfortunately worded draft. But shortly before Roosevelt's speech, Latimer, Brown, and Mrs. Armstrong had participated in a technical board discussion that dwelt on the difficulties of old-age security programs. They knew further that Witte had grave doubts about the constitutionality and administrative feasibility of a national insurance system such as they were planning. They concluded that Witte was responsible for Roosevelt's apparent threat to delay. In response, Latimer leaked word of the issues at stake to columnist Stark, emphasizing that contributory insurance would eventually reduce the expense of gratuitous old-age pensions. Stark publicly aired the issues on November 17.[34]

Whether or not Latimer's information was decisive, Latimer, Mrs. Armstrong, and Brown won their case. On November 22, New York Mayor Fiorello LaGuardia made public a letter from Roosevelt asserting that "undoubtedly" the new Congress would consider old-age pensions. Curiously, the letter was dated November 13, the day before Roosevelt's speech.[35] After some further resolution of technical issues, Witte joined the champions of old-age insurance in recommending a broad old-age security program that included both gratuitous aids to the needy aged and gradual introduction of a nationwide system of contributory insurance. Altmeyer later recalled that it was the idea that contributory annuities would gradually make the gratuitous aids unnecessary, dramatically illustrated with graphs and curves by the authors of the insurance plan, that convinced the cabinet committee to accept national, contributory old-age insurance. On November 27, only thirteen days after Roosevelt had said "in time" and twelve days after Stark had criticized the committee's timidity and limited vision, the cabinet committee approved the program.[36]

Witte and his colleagues approached health insurance even more gingerly than old-age security. Roosevelt had not specified it in his June 8 message. Important people, from insiders such as Miss Perkins, Altmeyer, Witte, and Hopkins to outsiders such as Frankfurter, Brandeis, and even social insurance zealots such as Abraham Epstein and Isaac Rubinow, advocated giving priority to unemployment insurance and old-age security. Yet the committee engaged Edgar L. Sydenstricker, chief statistician of the Public Health Department and researcher for the Milbank Memorial Fund, and his Milbank associate, I. S. Falk, to study health insurance. Immediately the editor of the *Journal of the American Medical Association*, Dr. Morris Fishbein, complained that Sydenstricker and Falk did not represent the medical profession.[37]

Despite a barrage of protests to Roosevelt from doctors and local medical associations, Witte began to entertain optimism. In September he was "unsure that health insurance is out of the question" and in October he observed that even the officials of the American Medical Association may have had "some change of heart." Witte had somewhat pacified them by promising to appoint a truly representative Medical Advisory Committee. When he, Sydenstricker, and Roosevelt's physician, Ross McIntyre, selected the members, Witte worked to include practicing physicians and staunch opponents of health insurance such as A.M.A. president Walter Bierring, as well as ardent champions such as Dr. Michael Davis of the Julius Rosenwald Fund. The security committee promised to respect doctors' concerns, and granted the medical advisers' request to delay their report until March 1, well beyond the date that Roosevelt would present the main security bill to Congress. For a time there was co-operation. The medical advisers quickly approved extension of public health services, which the cabinet committee then recommended in its main report. Meantime, two representatives of the A.M.A.'s Bureau of Medical Economics, Roscoe G. Leland and Algie M. Simons, worked with Sydenstricker and Falk to develop a preliminary health insurance plan. "Speaking of miracles," *Survey* editor Kellogg complimented Witte on December 31, "Sydenstricker and you have certainly done a deft job in enlisting and holding collaboration in the medical field."[38]

Witte's optimism, however, was already ebbing, for even amid the co-operation there were signs of conflict. Witte had made no compromise in principle, for in December he spoke of the "crying need" for "better distribution of the cost of illness in low income groups," and declared that the health insurance question "cannot be decided by the profession alone." Sharp conflict had broken out when the Medical Advisory Committee first met in mid-November. Harvey Cushing of the Yale Medical School, a committee member, father-in-law of Roosevelt's son, and close friend of the President, complained to Witte of the A.M.A.'s being "manoeuvered into the position of being obstructionists which is not at all justified." To quell the conflict, Cushing asked Witte to "get the Milbank people to soft-pedal their propaganda" and advised Sydenstricker to keep health-insurance advocates "off the grass for the time being." At the same time he pleaded with Olin West, the association's general manager, to stop propagandizing against health insurance, and warned Bierring not to split the association over the issue. His efforts were more for quietude than constructive conciliation, and Witte later concluded that the doctors' brief show of co-operation had been chiefly to hold their own organization together. After a new Medical Advisory Committee meeting in

January, Cushing himself became resentful. Sydenstricker tried
to limit initial discussion of health insurance to technical details, and Cushing complained directly to Roosevelt that he had
tried to squelch discussion of basic principles.[39]

In the end, with his eye on the politically possible, Witte helped
to end immediate hope for health insurance. Publication of
the Security Committee's main report and bill in mid-January
set off a new round of American Medical Association attacks, for
the report and bill discussed the principles of compulsory health
insurance and made cursory reference to further study. Sydenstricker, who did not want to see Roosevelt "licked by a group
of doctors," still wanted "a strong unequivocal stand on health
insurance." He complained that "we are paying entirely too
much attention to this group of reactionary physicians." In
March the cabinet committee decided to recommend Sydenstricker's plan for a federal offset tax to stimulate state health
insurance. But Witte intervened, fearing that it might jeopar-
dize the main security bill. Through McIntyre he inquired and
got the report that Roosevelt did not wish to endanger the main
bill, and he then persuaded the cabinet committee to await
Roosevelt's approval. The decision meant indefinite delay, and
the health insurance battle was lost.[40]

Witte's action was one more retreat from the bold, broad program that he had contemplated in his first days in Washington.
But it was quite in keeping with his philosophy of pursuing the
feasible and his strategy of concentrating on a "comparatively
narrow field."

The fourth and most troublesome question of broad policy
was that of the proper balance between state and national action.
More than rejection of a broad view of total economic effects,
than the social insurance versus relief issue, and even than the
question of what programs to recommend immediately, the question of state versus national action pitted Witte against Stark's
"experts." Once more, Roosevelt had not given an entirely clear
directive. In his June 8 message he had alluded to social insurance "national in scope," and to the national government's

constitutional duty "to promote the general welfare." But he had also advocated "a maximum of cooperation between States and the Federal Government," and suggested that the states carry "a large portion of the cost of management." From conversations with Roosevelt, Latimer believed that the President was receptive to centrally administered, national insurance. But in 1932 Roosevelt had promised unemployment insurance "under state laws," and in conference with Labor Department insiders, including Witte, he revealed a preference for state administration with federal encouragement.[41]

With his background in state government, Witte's initial and continuing bias was to be skeptical of both the wisdom and the constitutionality of national administration. When he arrived in Washington on July 26 he assumed that the national government could do little more for social insurance than to stimulate state action through devices such as the Wagner-Lewis offset tax. Then he dined with Latimer, who impressed upon him the difficulties of state-by-state old-age insurance, and he began to treat the question more openly. For a brief time he reasoned that before he and his colleagues could proceed someone had to decide whether a national insurance system was constitutional. His early contacts, however, were chiefly with a few Labor Department insiders, who also tended to favor state administration. Very soon he concluded that "a nationally administered social insurance system does not seem to be in contemplation."[42] But as the committee collected staff and advice, the question proved to be very much open, and very troublesome.

There were prestigious and vociferous spokesmen on both sides of the question. On the side of state administration with federal stimulus, a leading spokesman within the committee organization was Eliot. As co-author of the Wagner-Lewis bill he continued to favor the tax offset device, and as committee counsel he produced constitutional arguments for his point of view. Outside, Justice Brandeis and Professor Frankfurter also preferred state administration on principle, although they recommended some standards in federal law to assure adequate state systems.

Frankfurter's initial advice was to put "economics and statesmanship" before "sterile constitutional questions," to judge measures on their intrinsic merits and not to assume that "because a law may be constitutional therefore it is wise." Later, however, when Eliot asked his opinion of national administration of unemployment insurance, he warned strongly that the courts might reject it as regulation of intrastate commerce. Frankfurter "was so strongly opposed" to national administration, Eliot reported, "that he did not approach the problem in a very judicial way." From another quarter, a subcommittee of the Business Planning and Advisory Council also favored state rather than national administration.[43]

On the side opposing state administration were other prestigious spokesmen. Within the committee organization, staff member Mrs. Armstrong (herself a professor of law), and technical board member Alexander Holtzoff (who met with the cabinet committee as Attorney General Cummings' proxy), matched Eliot's opposing briefs with constitutional arguments in favor of national administration. Advisory Council chairman Graham, staff member Bryce Stewart, and others concurred. Outside, constitutional lawyer Erwin Griswold, a former assistant to the Attorney General, believed that the court might uphold a national system on the basis of the government's taxing and spending powers, if insurance taxes and benefit appropriations were kept carefully separated. From another perspective, Mayor LaGuardia advised Witte that the state was a dying unit for administration, and that the State of New York would merely use control of unemployment insurance to carry tax money out of his city.[44] In the face of the conflicting counsels, the technical board deliberately decided to consider national as well as state administration.

The question was far less troublesome for old-age security than for unemployment insurance. Virtually everyone accepted state administration of free pensions to the needy aged, later termed "old-age assistance," even with federal subsidies. As for contributory old-age insurance, Eliot tried at first to apply a tax offset with state administration, and Witte ran into sharp conflicts, especially with Mrs. Armstrong, because he continued to doubt the constitutionality of a national system. But as early as September the technical board decided that national administration was preferable for old-age insurance. Mrs. Armstrong, Latimer, and Brown planned a national system, and built defenses for it on such grounds as the actuarial soundness of distributing the risk broadly and the interstate character of the labor market, with its high mobility of workers between states during their long period of contribution. By November Witte agreed that their plan included security guarantees that "would be impossible in any but a straight national system." With little hope that the courts would approve, he joined in recommending the measure. The cabinet committee concurred.[45]

The national versus state question erupted most hotly over unemployment compensation, where controversies were already deepest. Witte was sharply at odds with most of his staff. His leading staff members assigned to studying unemployment compensation, Bryce Stewart and University of Minnesota professor Merrill Murray, vigorously favored exclusively national action. Others not specifically assigned to unemployment compensation, such as Mrs. Armstrong and Mrs. Burns, vociferously supported their view. Stewart very early outlined a national plan for the technical board to consider. Witte, on the other hand, believed that Roosevelt had ruled out any purely national system of unemployment insurance. He based his belief on his interpretation of Roosevelt's June 8 references to federal-state co-operation, and on the President's further remarks at a conference that he had attended in August. He allowed Stewart's plan a hearing, but he himself recommended state administration. His personal influence was more important for this than for any other important specific policy decision.[46]

The technical board vacillated, and thus kept the tension between Witte and his staff alive. About October 1 the board's subcommittee on unemployment insurance, whose chairman was Hansen, unanimously recommended a national system. The full board supported the recommendation, but warned the cabinet committee to satisfy itself of the system's constitutionality before advocating it publicly. By early November Hansen's subcommittee decided that constitutional and other practical difficulties made a bold national system impossible at that time. The subcommittee unanimously reversed its former decision, although still agreeing that one uniform national system of unemployment insurance was theoretically preferable to separate state systems. But the larger board did not endorse the subcommittee's reversal. Instead, it laid the difficult decision before the cabinet committee, with a report outlining the alternatives and the issues. Witte drafted the report, as he did virtually all major reports, and the technical board edited and amplified it. It suggested three major alternatives.[47]

One alternative was a fully national system that would completely ignore the states as administrative units. Witte and the technical board emphasized that such a system would be most effective if the cabinet committee wanted to create stringent national standards. But by the same token it would force the committee to make sharply controversial decisions. A national system promised the advantages of uniformity in unemployment compensation and easy protection of workers who moved interstate. The technical board argued that national administrators would be more efficient and honest than state officials, although Witte had doubts. Witte and the board pointed out that with a national system the committee could, if it chose, create a huge, nationwide pool of risks, and thus provide maximum protection to workers in industries and areas with exceptionally high unemployment. In fact, the committee could hardly escape the old issue of broad pooling versus individual employer reserves, as well as other divisive questions such as employment stabilization devices and employee contributions. In creating a national system it could not avoid controversial stands, whereas some sort of federal-state system would leave such questions to the states. And finally, if the courts objected and set federal unemployment compensation law aside, the national system would crumble. But a federal-state plan might leave in its wake state-administered systems that could continue to operate.[48]

Witte and the technical board suggested two federal-state plans as alternatives. One was the time-honored Wagner-Lewis offset tax proposal—the favorite, the technical board reported, of Witte and of Hansen's subcommittee. The other was a "subsidy" or "grant-in-aid" plan. The subsidy plan had emerged from a technical board discussion late in October, and champions of strong national action such as Stewart and Mrs. Armstrong had taken it up as a halfway house to outright national administration. Under the plan the federal government would collect a payroll tax and distribute the money to the states which operated unemployment compensation systems. It would not withdraw, as the Wagner-Lewis plan proposed, to let the states collect as well as distribute benefit money. Witte and the technical board pointed out that the subsidy plan held greater possibilities than the Wagner-Lewis tax for national control, and also for holding back some money for a nationwide pooling of risk. But once again, the possibility of national control would probably enmesh the security committee in highly controversial decisions, which by the Wagner-Lewis method they could easily leave to the states. And of the three plans, the Wagner-Lewis scheme would most likely leave state unemployment insurance systems intact if the courts invalidated the federal law. Witte also presented what was to him surely an important consideration, that the Wagner-Lewis device would fare best in Congress. The technical board deleted that argument, but warned that either the straight national or the subsidy system might bring great pressure on Congress to subsidize unemployment insurance gratuitously from general treasury funds.[49]

On November 9, at the urging of the technical board, the cabinet committee deliberated on the question of national versus federal-state administration of unemployment insurance. Before it was the report outlining the three alternatives, and advocates for both national and federal-state systems. Stewart led the argument for a straight national plan. But the committee chose to recommend federal-state collaboration, and expressed a tentative preference for the Wagner-Lewis over the subsidy method. Roosevelt endorsed the federal-state approach, and Witte wrote it into his draft of Roosevelt's National Conference speech. "I am still of the opinion expressed in my message of June eighth," declared Roosevelt on November 14, essentially in Witte's words, that unemployment insurance "should be a co-operative federal-state undertaking." The federal government should encourage state action and handle the reserve funds, but "for the administration of insurance benefits the states are the most logical units." There was room for differences in methods, differences "impossible under an exclusively national system."[50] The committee's decision and Roosevelt's speech were important turning points in the battles between champions of national and of state administration. But they did not lay the issue to rest, as Witte hoped they would.

The day following Roosevelt's National Conference speech, Stewart presided over a meeting of unemployment insurance specialists who let Witte know that the issue was not dead. In private, Witte was patronizing. "I expect that you will probably get very little out of them," he had advised Stewart. "Since there are so many people, however, who think that they are experts on unemployment, . . . we should give them a chance to talk to us privately." Instead of the individual, private conferences that Witte apparently intended, Stewart gathered group opinions in a roundtable discussion. The group included not merely would-be experts, but men as prominent as Rubinow, Douglas, Raushenbush, and Andrews. Nearly all were National Conference guests from outside the committee organization; they were not content to express merely individual, atomized opinions, as Witte hoped. Stewart explained the conference ground rules: that discussion groups were informal and without authority to make collective recommendations. Nevertheless he allowed the group to prevail upon him to transmit minutes to Witte and the cabinet committee, including the results of straw ballots on important issues. On the national versus state administration issue, he advised them that Roosevelt's speech had apparently precluded a straight national plan. Yet the discussion turned in favor of such a plan. Stewart found that thirteen favored purely national action, against only three favoring federal-state.[51]

Moreover, the national versus state control issue survived in a campaign for the subsidy type of plan, against which the cabinet committee had made only a tentative decision. Stewart transmitted the minutes of his rump session to the newly functioning Advisory Council, who then led a campaign, very troublesome to Witte, for the subsidy proposal. And Stark of the *New York Times* took the issues to the public in a front-page account of Stewart's supposedly confidential roundtable meeting. Very probably he did not get his story directly from Stewart, but from Abraham Epstein, who had not attended the discussion. He reported erroneously that the "subsidy" option would involve gratuitous government contributions from general tax revenues, the kind of subsidy that Epstein favored.[52] Stark added his revelations to the public furor that arose because Roosevelt had seemed to suggest that there would be no immediate old-age security program. It was one more evidence of the dissatisfaction of "social workers and experts" with Witte and the committee.

The antagonisms merely strengthened Witte's antipathy for national forms of social welfare administration, and for centralized government. It was on November 19, on the heels of Roosevelt's speech and the ensuing public criticisms, that Witte complained to Frankfurter of the "maze of machinery and conflicting personal interests" in Washington. Witte was accustomed to working in "a much less complex state government." Out of his element and overworked, Witte felt the personal conflicts more deeply than he probably should have. Frictions in the machinery exacerbated the conflicts. On November 22 Stewart and Murray complained that the technical board's subgroups and the cabinet committee procrastinated on essential policy decisions, reversed decisions already made, and ignored each other's decisions. Their complaints were largely justified. But most fundamentally, the national versus state administration conflicts involved disagreements on constitutional dogma. "Yes," Frankfurter replied, "the Federal Gov't is *too big* for most things. . . . Don't let the doctrinaires and those who know not the problems of national administration and control have their own way."[53]

Witte was caught up in one of the fundamental tensions of the Roosevelt administration, and indeed of the American constitution. The question of national versus state forms of social welfare administration was more troublesome than any of the other three major guideline decisions. Neither rejection of social insurance for total economic control, nor the adoption of a social insurance more than a relief approach, nor determination of which programs to include immediately divided opinions so sharply. Witte and his colleagues steered through the conflicts pragmatically. For old-age insurance they chose national administration. For unemployment insurance they chose federal-state collaboration.

As they settled rather uncertainly upon their major policies, Witte and his associates turned increasingly to more highly technical problems. Sometimes even technical decisions implicitly involved profound questions of social and economic policy. And for ultimate success in social welfare, care in technical detail was just as important as theoretically correct determination of the broadest guidelines. Witte worried especially that technical blunders might leave social security open to political attack.

The security committee could not entirely escape the old technical issue of segregated versus pooled reserves for unemployment compensation, largely because the issue involved broad social considerations. On the side of segregated reserves was the concern for perfecting the capitalistic wage system by making employment stabilization profitable to the employer, and the concept that an employer was responsible primarily for protecting only his own employees. On the side of pooling was the concern for guaranteeing maximum benefits to the worker, and the concept that social responsibility for the unemployed was as broad as the nation's economic system.[54] Not only did persons such as the Raushenbushes on the one hand and Rubinow, Epstein, and Douglas on the other remain unreconciled; management and labor also lined up on opposite sides. Employers preferred to concern themselves only with their own or their own industries' employees through segregated funds. Labor sought the added protection of broad pooling of risk. No doubt the administration could ignore labor or management and still force a measure through Congress, Witte declared publicly in December; but he feared "the violent opposition of either group is likely to mean trouble hereafter."[55]

Within the committee organization there was ambivalence, and therefore an attempt partly to bypass and partly to compromise the segregation-versus-pooling issue. Roosevelt, attuned to the Business Advisory Council, continued to emphasize stabilization. Frances Perkins, with her social work background, still favored broad pooling but tolerated experimentation with plant reserves. Altmeyer and Witte had each accepted the Wisconsin law but with reservations about its extreme lack of pooling, and had tried to select a neutral staff. The technical board subcommittee decided to recommend the Wagner-Lewis tax offset device partly to allow openness and experimentation with each method. The cabinet committee tentatively concurred on November 9 after Witte and the technical board pointed out, among other considerations, that the Wagner-Lewis device permitted it to evade the segregation versus pooling issue. The committee also chose compromise. It endorsed an Altmeyer suggestion that the federal government require states to pool one-third of the money for which they got credit against the offset tax. Witte reflected the committee's spirit of evasion and compromise when he declared in December that he was "so anxious to get unemployment compensation started" that he was "willing to accept any measure that will give us action *now*."[56] The Wagner-Lewis plan with a clause demanding partial pooling was the committee's tentative solution.

After November 9 those who wanted to guarantee high levels of benefits to the worker increasingly placed their hopes in the subsidy plan. Technically, the quarrel between subsidy plan and tax offset advocates was merely over which government should collect unemployment insurance taxes, federal or state. But behind the technical quarrel stood the twin principles of guaranteeing adequate benefits and stronger national control. Advocates of the subsidy plan assumed that they could translate stronger national control into higher benefit standards.

In late November Witte, still believing that the tax offset device was safest politically, was "not at all" in favor of the subsidy system. But the issue would not die. Concurring with Witte were the most important insiders—Altmeyer, Eliot, and Hansen's subcommittee. But staff members such as Stewart and Mrs. Armstrong who had first favored a straight national plan became strong champions of the subsidy arrangement. Even more troublesome was the fact that the committee's difficult public relations groups took up the cause. One of the straw votes that Stewart took among unemployment insurance experts on November 15 favored the subsidy over the offset tax, nine to four. Even worse, the committee's main Advisory Council chose to back the subsidy plan. It appointed *Survey* editor Kellogg, a strong advocate of both high benefits and strong national action, as vice-chairman of the full council and of its unemployment subcommittee.[57]

Much of the agitation for the subsidy plan centered around Stewart, whom Witte increasingly distrusted. The Advisory Council sought the advice of Stewart and Mrs. Armstrong far more avidly than that of the technical board, and Stewart obliged with extensive arguments for the subsidy plan. The cabinet committee got reports that Stewart was also trying to convince council members individually. One evening Witte inadvertently walked in on a "caucus" of Stewart with employer members of the council. Although he might have seized the opportunity to debate with Stewart on the spot, Witte exited as soon (and as graciously) as possible. The next day, to the surprise of columnist Stark, the five employer members joined with American Federation of Labor President William Green, Council Chairman Graham, Kellogg, and New York settlement worker Helen Hall in the Advisory Council to form a small nine-to-seven majority favoring the subsidy plan. The Advisory Council action was supposedly confidential, but Stark got the information and reported the vote as a setback for the security committee. Witte blamed Stewart for the leak, and thereafter his distrust of Stewart was complete. To him, Stewart's actions were clearly insubordinate, offensive to his sensitive loyalty to Roosevelt, to the cabinet committee, and to the team effort to produce a workable program.[58] Stewart, on the other hand, had little sense of subordination to Witte. He was a recognized unemployment insurance expert and consultant. Before Witte had arrived in Washington, he had helped Altmeyer plan the committee's organization.[59] Frustrated by the subordinate role Witte expected of staff members, he apparently decided to bypass formal organizational lines if necessary to win what he considered desirable goals. In the end the cabinet committee reconsidered both the national administration and the subsidy plans. But sensing opposition from Congress, it once more rejected the programs Stewart favored.[60]

Against the committee's wishes, the Advisory Council submitted an official final report in which it supported the subsidy plan. The report demonstrated the difficulties of Witte and his colleagues with their public liaison efforts. At the outset Miss Perkins had informed the council that the committee did not expect a final report. She had also asked for either unanimous decisions or merely individual dissents. Nevertheless, the council produced a final report, and when it failed to stipulate unemployment payroll taxes higher than 3 per cent and benefits longer than the fifteen weeks that the cabinet committee contemplated, Kellogg led dissidents to produce a minority report as well. The cabinet committee refused for a time to make public either of the uninvited reports, although by early February the contents were so widely known that Witte decided to publish them. Kellogg complained of the suppression, and privately took the case for the subsidy system and higher benefits to the President.[61]

Roosevelt, however, had already had Undersecretary of Agriculture Rexford Tugwell surreptitiously investigate the subsidy plan, and possessed a copy of Stewart's argument for it. He rejected Kellogg's effort, observing that "it is a matter of finance and we cannot eat the whole cake at one meal."[62] Witte and his colleagues had won Roosevelt's backing for their more cautious unemployment compensation program under a tax offset law.

Old-age insurance presented somewhat different technical problems—problems which revealed how unwilling Roosevelt was to engage in deficit financing for social insurance, and how reluctant he was to place financial responsibility for social insurance on the general public through subsidies from the general treasury. He intervened, and a program which his own technicians had carefully constructed was suddenly wrenched and reshaped in his own hands, and the hands of a dissenting cabinet member.

In planning for old-age insurance, the committee faced two especially troublesome questions. One was whether to use a reserve system for financing old-age annuities; the other was whether to introduce an element of gratuity into a system basically conceived on actuarial insurance principles, in order to give workers who would soon retire larger annuities than their brief contributions would earn. Several of the committee's actuarial experts, including M. Albert Linton of Provident Mutual Life Insurance Company and W. Rulon Williamson of Travelers' Insurance Company, favored a plan they euphemistically termed "pay-as-you-go." Their plan was frankly to mix gratuitous old-age assistance with contributory old-age insurance, and to pay for both from current contributions and eventually large government subsidies.[63] Such a plan would avoid all reserve financing. The extreme opposite of their plan would have been to accumulate contributions from workers and their employers and invest them as a full reserve, and then pay workers only such benefits as their contributions earned actuarially. But a full reserve plan would have provided almost nothing to workers already near retirement except the separate system of old-age assistance for the impoverished. And it would have put reserve funds estimated at fifty to sixty billion dollars in the government's hands, which virtually everyone thought was fiscally and economically unsound.

Rather than accept the actuaries' complete mixing of relief and social insurance, staff and technical board members worked out a compromise. They proposed to keep the old-age insurance and assistance systems separate, but to give some extra insurance credits gratuitously to older workers to increase initial annuities. Their plan was to introduce payroll taxes slowly to soften the shock to the economy, and after five years gradually to begin paying annuities. Young workers would eventually receive benefits calculated as if the system operated fully on actuarial principles. In fact, however, the system would accumulate not a full actuarial reserve, but only a partial contingency reserve of about ten billion dollars. At first Witte feared putting reserve funds in government hands and inclined toward "pay-as-you-go" financing. Nevertheless, in November, under pressure of the public furor for old-age insurance following Roosevelt's National Conference speech, he joined his staff in recommending that the technical board consider the compromise plan. Eventually, the plan's chief architect, Latimer convinced him that at least a contingency reserve was desirable.[64]

The problem with the compromise plan was that it called for some eventual subsidies from the general treasury, mostly to provide funds that a full reserve would have collected in interest, and also to pay for the gratuitous benefits to workers who retired in the early years of the system. Despite this problem, the technical board and the cabinet committee, understanding that the contributory plan would eventually eliminate the burden of old-age assistance on the treasury, approved. On December 24 Miss Perkins, Hopkins, and Witte explained the system orally to Roosevelt, and Witte thought the President also understood the subsidies and concurred. On January 5 George C. Haas of the Treasury Department warned Treasury Secretary

Morgenthau of the subsidies. Morgenthau had been participating in the committee's work through subordinates, and had neither a clear grasp of the issues nor a positive counterproposal. Yet he objected, declaring that he would show the committee "the bad curves" and "it's up to somebody else to say whether they want to do it." Despite his objections, Miss Perkins persuaded him to sign the committee report with the compromise system intact. The report went on to Roosevelt, the White House staff released publicity on it, and Roosevelt arranged to transmit it to Congress on January 17.[65]

Suddenly, on January 16, Miss Perkins summoned Witte to the White House. Roosevelt, perhaps with Morgenthau's help, had detected the projected deficit and subsidies. He asked Witte if there was an error, and Witte explained that there was not. Since it was too late to construct a new plan, Roosevelt instructed Witte and Miss Perkins to change the report in a manner to indicate uncertainty as to the wisdom of the plan's tax and benefit schedules. The committee made the changes, and afterward Witte, Altmeyer, Eliot, Latimer, Haas, and others worked out new schedules to make contributions rise faster and reach a higher plateau, and to lower initial unearned benefits. Roosevelt approved, and the committee offered the change as the Morgenthau Amendment. Although it meant projecting a reserve fund of nearly fifty billion dollars, Congress also approved.[66] But the prospect of such huge sums at the government's disposal brought much political criticism in the late 1930's.[67] Roosevelt's unwillingness to allow even small public contributions to old-age insurance and his tampering with a carefully constructed mechanism very nearly discredited the entire concept of a genuine old-age insurance system.

*   *   *   *   *

On January 17 the committee's report went to Roosevelt in its final form. Various committee members and their subordinates had aired doubts and objections in the final stages, but after some redrafting and persuasion from Miss Perkins and Witte, all members had signed.[68] The report emphasized the importance of well-planned public works employment for the long-term employed, but left specific work-relief legislation to the separate work-relief bill. For protection during short-term unemployment, it recommended unemployment compensation, suggesting that 1 per cent of payroll taxes be pooled, but otherwise approved either segregation or pooling of reserve funds. It favored the tax offset type of law allowing considerable state autonomy, except for crucial requirements that all money credited against the offset tax go for unemployment compensation and that states require companies to have relatively high reserves before allowing them to reduce contributions. For the aged it recommended furnishing half the money for state pensions of up to $30 per month to the needy, a compulsory system of contributory insurance, and voluntary contributory annuities for those left out of the compulsory system. It proposed one-third subsidies for state and local aid to dependent children, plus federal assistance to states for a variety of child health and welfare measures. It suggested expenditures to improve national, state, and local efforts for public health, and discussed the principles of health insurance without recommending it. Finally, the report recognized that its program left "residual" classes of dependents, and advocated state and local responsibility for them, hopefully through "public assistance" rather than old forms of poor relief.[69]

The security committee's program reached only for what was politically possible. It did not pursue doctrinal purity, nor embody great, new, original ideas, nor even probe the extreme limits of what Congress and the public might approve. Witte and his colleagues were reformers who wished to improve life in America, but they did not attempt fundamentally to change the economic and social order. Neither did they pursue one narrow reform doctrine, either a Commons-style attempt to make social responsibility profitable to capitalism's managers, or a more radical effort for a massive redistribution of wealth. They consciously circumvented controversial issues of social welfare doctrine whenever possible. Ultimately they preferred compulsory, contributory, pooled insurance, and they were conservatively careful not to mix gratuitous relief and contributory insurance freely in the same institution. But they allowed segregated unemployment reserve funds, and recommended quasi-relief measures. They made most of their decisions not on the basis of social welfare doctrine, but on constitutional, political, fiscal, and other technical (though important) considerations.

Witte helped to shape the committee's approach, in keeping with his own pragmatism and circumspection on social questions. He was eclectic, and willing to listen to divergent points of view, at least for a time. He had some fixed preferences, most notably for balanced budgets and state forms of administration, but they were so imbedded in his thinking that he scarcely recognized them as doctrinal positions. He also believed in wide latitude for experimentation, scarcely recognizing that social experiments seldom remain experimental, but quickly become permanent, established institutions. Above all, he was more concerned with technical perfection than with doctrine. His grasp of technical issues was absolutely necessary to the committee's work. And he achieved his original goal: not "just another investigation,"[70] but a defensible legislative program.

Witte's and the committee's defiance of doctrine, subordination of their research staff, and attempts to keep outside criticism distant and atomized, brought criticism. Three days after Roosevelt publicized the committee program, Stark once more reported in the *New York Times* the unhappiness of "social insurance experts." Espousing views remarkably like Epstein's, Stark's unnamed experts complained that the committee had produced a "debacle." It had not advocated national government leadership, nor planned to redistribute wealth through subsidies from the general treasury. Only the gratuitous old-age assistance program was worthwhile. Stark also told of the committee's refusal to consult important social insurance experts, and its treating its own advisory council as "window dressing." And he revealed that there had been "heated arguments" between Witte and the committee staff. The staff experts had complained "that they were being 'directed,' the direction coming from Edwin C. [*sic*] Witte, secretary [*sic*] of the committee," Stark reported, ignoring Witte's actual title of executive director.[71]

One advisory council member, Grace Abbott, however, commended Witte for "patient, persistent education of one group after another" in favor of her favorite program, child welfare. Even Kellogg, who was often in conflict with Witte, credited him with working "mightily to bring a coherent and rounded program through," despite the "ten-ring circus on your hands." Stark's reports were not broadly representative. Yet they reflected tensions that Witte himself felt deeply. "I have never thought of myself as an executive," he confided to his old friend Saposs late in August, "and at times I wonder why I ever let myself be persuaded to come down here." By November he told another friend of being "so terribly crowded in my work," and expressed doubt that anyone could persuade him to stay in Washington very long. "I have been very discouraged," he confided to Frankfurter, as he complained of the "maze of machinery and conflicting personal interests."[72]

Even while discouraged, however, he detected that "we are making some progress." In later years, after social security was well established, Witte declared that "of nothing I have done am I more reasonably satisfied than of the work I was privileged to do as Executive Director of the President's Committee on Economic Security."[73] But in 1934, in his role as midwife, he felt keenly every threat to the newly delivered program. Nor would his sensitivity decrease in 1935, when he would fully expose his committee's progeny to Congress and the public.

7

SOCIAL SECURITY
Advocate

IN THE LEGISLATIVE COMBAT that inevitably began when Roosevelt proposed his new economic security program on January 17, 1935, Witte fought to protect the measure that he had worked so hard to bring into existence. The economic security committee had prepared a bill to accompany its report. Senator Wagner, Representative Lewis, and House Ways and Means Committee chairman Robert L. Doughton of North Carolina quickly introduced the social security bill in Congress. More than any other person, Witte undertook to educate congressmen about the program, first as the administration's prime witness at the public hearings of the House Ways and Means and the Senate Finance committees, and then as a consultant. Although he returned to his post at the University of Wisconsin on a half-time basis in February, he attended all of the committees' executive sessions during the ensuing months, was on the floor of the Senate at the invitation of Senator Robert M. La Follette, Jr., during debates in June, and then advised legislators at the joint House-Senate conferences called to resolve differences between the two houses' versions of the bill.[1] Between appearances he prepared numerous arguments and briefs. He worked to explain the bill's logic, to clarify its details, and to anticipate objections and proposals for amendment. By emphasizing the conservative tone of the bill he tried to convince legislators that it represented a sound and workable program.

As a witness before the legislators Witte was quick with encyclopedic facts and reasoned explanations, but was not stubbornly argumentative.[2] He presented himself as a specialist and performed the role with great competence, but characteristically without arrogance. After the leading Republican member of the House Committee, Allen Treadway of Massachusetts, thundered that the economic security committee retained too few "practical business people" and too many "theorists," "brain trusters," and "college professors," Witte even requested that the legislators not address him as "professor" or "doctor." "Our purpose primarily is to give you information," he assured the legislators, and encouraged them to make any changes they thought necessary for wisdom and constitutionality. "This," a subdued Treadway said, "is a much more liberal expression than we have had in connection with any legislative proposals before us in the last Congress." Witte's attitude was in keeping with Miss Perkins' assurance that although her committee had consulted experts, it was not experts but Congress and the President who decided social insurance policy. It also reflected long experience with legislators, and went a long way toward winning their confidence. Treadway testified that he detected forthright honesty merely by looking at Witte's face. Murray Latimer, after attending many of the committee's executive sessions, decided that Witte's practical appeal to the men of Congress was decisive in convincing them to take the bold and uncertain step to launch the program.[3] No other contribution by Witte, except the remarkable way in which he had assembled and synthesized proposals to create the program initially, was so crucial for social security.

Witte was, of course, defending a program in which he believed. He avoided polemicism, yet his logic always led to the measures that he and his colleagues had proposed. The economic security bill was "not the last word on the subject," he conceded, but it was "a long stride forward," well "adapted to our American conditions and traditions," and built upon principles that both major political parties had endorsed. It would be costly but not excessively so, since it was largely self-sustaining and would greatly lessen future needs for outright relief. For many years the government could, if it wished, finance the most costly feature, old-age assistance, by borrowing from old-age insurance reserves. Old-age assistance, insurance, and voluntary annuities together formed one well-rounded and relatively economical program of security for the aged. For the unemployed, self-sustaining state systems would provide temporary benefits for enough time that many would never need relief. The children's welfare program presented new costs to the federal government, he admitted, but it was consistent with previous federal action during the 1920's under the Sheppard-Towner Act. The preventive health provisions also represented new expenditures, but they built upon the existing public health program, and were "most certainly not" an attempt to introduce socialized medicine.[4]

At first the climate for Witte's persuasions seemed propitious. Roosevelt's January 17 message proved that the President was indeed an "authentic liberal," declared the *Richmond Times-Dispatch*, for he had invested governments, employers, and workers "with a high degree of social responsibility" by his "comprehensive and well-articulated program." Other newspapers noted what even the apprehensive *New York Herald Tribune* called the "many evidences of intelligent care in the drafting of the scheme." But their greatest praise was for Roosevelt's caution, especially the warning he had expressed against "permanently discrediting" economic security efforts by attempting too ambitious a program without adequate experience. The editor of the New York *Journal of Commerce* surveyed Roosevelt's proposals and decided that they honored "most of the principles recognized as indispensible for a sound social insurance program." The editor of the *New York Times* thought that perhaps workers should contribute more and the government should not sell voluntary annuities. But he found cause for general satisfaction since the new institutions would in the main be self-supporting, moderately priced compared to relief, in harmony with sound national credit and states' rights, and not too burdensome upon industry and recovery. The prices of stocks continued upward with Roosevelt's announcement, and even the *Chicago Daily Tribune* chose not to attack the program squarely. A *Tribune* writer explained that "we've got used to big money now and this social safety thing that is going to cost 218½ million just makes us yawn."[5]

Underlying many editors' encouraging remarks was a deep conservatism, however. Abhorrence of Townsendism explained many of the remarks. The *Boston Evening Transcript*, while lamenting that social security "outlaws all our traditional ideas of thrift" and individual responsibility, conceded that Roosevelt's program had some merit if it forestalled "the unsound and ruinous Townsend Plan." Although the editor of the *Chicago Daily Tribune* pointed to Dr. Townsend as an explanation of why the administration bill was "slapped together in considerable haste," most editors used Townsendism in the bill's favor. "In contrast with proposals of a similar tenor that are having wide circulation and support, the President's program is conservative," declared the *St. Louis Globe-Democrat*. Yet the editors advised Roosevelt to proceed slowly. Ignoring Roosevelt's call for quick action before state legislatures adjourned, the *Globe-Democrat* editor declared that the bill was not urgent inasmuch as it offered nothing for those already unemployed. The *New York Times* even contended that Roosevelt had not necessarily asked Congress to pass the entire program at once.[6]

Witte believed that the program was very urgent, but he agreed with the editors about the danger of the Townsendites; indeed his anxiety was such that his measured, analytical style barely concealed it. Congressional mail bags were full of Townsendite letters. Witte's student and aide, Wilbur Cohen, looked upon them philosophically, finding their plan "more radical than that of the Socialists and more conservative than the program of the United States Chamber of Commerce; ergo," he decided, "it is a true outgrowth of American conditions." Cohen even thought that the Townsendites helped make "the average person consider

the broader problems involved in economic theory, that is, purchasing power, production and consumption," and that "very
practically" they "encouraged the movement for larger old age
pensions grants." But Witte never viewed Townsendism with
the same good humor. The value of raising broad theoretical
questions did not impress him, although he argued theoretically
that the cumulative burden of Townsend's proposed 2 per cent
tax on all financial transactions would simply bring the economic
system to a halt.[7]

As a practical matter, he did not greatly fear the Townsend
proposal itself, especially after the House of Representatives
voted it down in April by 206–56. Rather he feared the influence it might have generally to cause the aged to demand extravagant gratuitous pensions, regardless of need. He found
practically all legislators agreeing that a Townsend system would
wreck the nation's economy. Yet many were afraid to vote
against it, even if they voted for the administration bill, lest
they anger their aged constituents. With his ingrained sympathy
for legislators' concerns, Witte would not concede that the
Townsend movement helped the cause of social security, even
though he recognized that somehow old-age security had become
the most popular part of the program. He predicted in mid-
April that Congress could hardly fail to pass some old-age assistance measure in 1935; but he later declared that it was "doubtful whether the Townsend movement helped or hindered the
cause of old age security." It was, in his view, an effect, not a
cause.[8]

Witte gave equally short shrift to the other leading radical
measure, the Workers Unemployment and Social Insurance Bill.
This brief proposal, completely undeveloped in the technical
sense, called upon the Secretary of Labor immediately to set up
systems of unemployment and other social insurances, including
benefits for those already unemployed. The beneficiaries—workers and farmers—were to control the systems, collecting the money
from taxes on gifts, inheritances, and incomes of over $5000.
Minnesota Farmer-Labor Representative Ernest Lundeen had in-

troduced it in the House of Representatives in February, 1934, but had failed to get it reported from the House Labor Committee. The Committee on Economic Security had given it no serious attention. In March of 1935, however, the Labor Committee reported it to the House—partly, Witte believed, from pique at not having won jurisdiction over the economic security bill. To the legislators, Witte stressed the Lundeen bill's technical inadequacy and the fallaciousness of the data marshalled by its supporters. He admitted that some union bodies, a score of city councils, and the Montana legislature had supported it, but he emphasized that communists were giving it the most vehement support and even claiming its authorship. With almost unWittean pungency he dismissed it as "excellent propaganda for the 'front line trenches' in the battle for communism" but a bill that offered nothing but "meaningless promises" for workers.[9]

Witte's argument was valid on technical grounds, but it concealed the fact that had he and his colleagues and Roosevelt chosen to support the bill's radical principle, they could have worked out the technical details. His emphasis on the measure's subversive support similarly obscured the main issue: whether the country did not need a radical redistribution of wealth, more consumption, and less capitalization. His attack was completely in character with his own technical and nontheoretical approach to legislative problems, and was undoubtedly the strongest possible argument to present to congressmen. Inadvertently, however, it revealed how limited was his and his colleagues' conception of social insurance as a measure for basic economic reform.

Witte also continued to differ with more orthodox social insurance experts and propagandists. Sometimes the disputes echoed the question of redistribution of wealth; more often they were the noise of the old debates that persisted inside and outside the President's committee, over pooled versus segregated reserve funds, and over national or "subsidy" versus tax offset types of unemployment insurance law. The dean of social insurance propagandists, Isaac M. Rubinow, kept a discreet silence before the legislative committees about his reservations concerning the administration bill.[10] But dissident staff members such as Stewart, Brown, Mrs. Armstrong, and Eveline Burns, and advisory council members such as chairman Graham, Kellogg, American Federation of Labor president Green, and Helen Hall of New York's Henry Street Settlement, carried the quarrel into the legislative chambers. From outside Witte's organization, Epstein, Douglas, and other professors, liberal editors, social workers, and labor leaders added to the dissent. A year earlier, in the spring of 1934, the principal critics had united around the Wagner-Lewis offset bill for unemployment compensation. But as Roosevelt's program made victory for social insurance seem much closer, the dissenters had become increasingly confident that the victory could be for bolder measures.[11] Witte, by contrast, was profoundly pessimistic. He had worked prodigiously to put together a coalition of measures, and he felt it to be very insecure. To him, dissent was both a severe irritation and a dangerous threat.

Increasingly, the largest pebble in Witte's shoe was Abraham Epstein. Superficially the two men's differences were highly personal. Witte could fight stubbornly for a position once he was convinced or a decision had been properly made. Often his final position bore little resemblance to his beginning assumptions; yet he remained the investigator and technician who arrived at positions by mediating between ideas and then argued for them in guarded understatements. Epstein's efforts for social insurance, by contrast, had more and more taken the form of forceful overstatements by a dogmatic crusader and propagandist.[12]

Witte and his staff had taken care to consult with Epstein on the subject upon which his credentials were soundest, old-age security, and had included him as a speaker at the November conference. Because of his dogmatism, however, they had quite deliberately kept him out of their inner councils. Epstein felt the exclusion very keenly. Before the House Committee he at first pronounced the entire bill to be "the most outstanding and courageous program that has ever been attempted in the history of the world." But later he complained of the committee's failure to consult him on unemployment insurance, and attacked the unemployment insurance provisions. Witte attributed Epstein's sudden vehemence to embarrassing questions that Lewis asked him, and to an unfortunate attempt by the House Committee to limit his testimony to five minutes, a ruling which Witte protested in a note to the chairman, and which the committee reversed. He appealed to Epstein to "make it more clear that you differ from the [economic security] Committee only with regard to methods."[13] Witte was partly correct in considering Epstein's objections personal and methodological; but he did not fully appreciate that they also went deeper, to the ideological differences within the historical social insurance movement.

Epstein had given his advice to the economic security committee, particularly in an *American Mercury* article of October, 1934, and quite apparently in Louis Stark's attacks. But the committee had ignored two of his emphatic precepts: the utter depravity of the Wisconsin plan for unemployment compensation, and the need to subsidize social insurance from the general treasury in order to redistribute wealth. The government should have provided for extended unemployment insurance benefits at its own expense, Epstein wrote, because "in social insurance it is legitimate to integrate relief and insurance in one plan."[14] Before the House Committee, Epstein endorsed "one hundred per cent" the administration bill's old-age security provisions, which did involve subsidization and quasi-relief for old-age assistance. But he sharply criticized the unemployment insurance provisions as contrary to the advice of experts. Witte privately replied that Hansen and Leiserson of the technical board, who had approved the provisions, were certainly experts, and asked Epstein to correct his testimony where it was "a little askew." But Epstein was even more vehement a few days later before the Senate Committee, and ridiculed every Wisconsin-style effort to promote employment stabilization as a "panacea" in the same class with Townsend's. "Everybody seems to have abdicated thinking" on the unemployment insurance question, he complained.[15]

In fact, Epstein's own thinking did not appear entirely clear. The subsidy plan he offered as a substitute curiously provided that industries and even separate companies operating interstate could maintain the hated separate reserve funds, if they guaranteed high enough benefits. His proposals resembled recommendations for a subsidy plan that the Business Advisory Council later made to Roosevelt—recommendations that Witte learned Stewart had prepared. Witte believed that the Council offered them "in the interests of the very large employers," and argued that "we should get ready to fight . . . to the limit." Epstein's inconsistency made it very difficult for Witte to appreciate that his opposition had its roots in legitimate policy questions as well as in mere personal pique.[16]

Under the auspices of Epstein's American Association for Social Security, twenty-four of the most prominent advocates of unemployment insurance urged the Senate Finance Committee to adopt some "subsidy" arrangement. They emphasized that the American economy was not divided along state lines, and declared that in contrast to a tax offset law the subsidy method would create fewer administrative difficulties and make it possible to guarantee uniformly high standards. Douglas, apparently contemplating pooling of risks even across state lines, testified independently that the subsidy method was imperative in order to maintain high benefits in states with high rates of unemployment. Mrs. Burns asserted that since the tax offset provisions would allow employers who built up adequate segregated reserves to reduce their contributions, a state could disingenuously save its employers great expense by providing very low benefits to workers. "Experimentation in the absence of standards," she predicted, would "almost inevitably" be at the workers' expense.[17]

In his debating style, Witte sought to counter his opponents' arguments. Opportunity for experimentation he presented as a point in the tax-offset plan's favor: the plan would equalize unemployment compensation costs, but still allow flexibility and efficiency of administration. He assured members of Congress and the public that the tax offset provisions demanded the necessary minimum standards, especially administration through employment offices and guarantee that every dollar of contribution would actually go towards unemployment compensation. Although he avoided much explicit reference to the subsidy plan in his congressional testimony, publicly he reiterated that its supporters greatly exaggerated its differences from the tax offset measure. "Subsidy," he declared, was a misnomer, since the plan contemplated no contributions from the general treasury. Had the economic security committee considered unemployment insurance a form of relief, he argued, it might have provided a real subsidy. But the committee had considered it only the "front line of defense." Its companion measure, the four-billion-dollar public works bill, provided real aid to the unemployed. (Actually, the works bill was a temporary measure and not a permanent means of redistributing wealth, but Witte chose to ignore that fact.) [18]

Witte could not fully counter the arguments of critics of unemployment reserve funds. He continued to make no claims of superiority for either pooled or segregated funds. Instead he emphasized that it would be unwise to incur the wrath of employers by outlawing the segregated funds which they almost universally favored, and that the bill was a compromise measure that gave states freedom of action. Pooled funds, like separate funds, could become depleted, he noted further. He never quite met the argument that broad distribution of risk would make the pooled funds safer.[19] Neither did he meet Mrs. Burns' objection that segregated reserves might become a device merely to lower both contributions and benefits, an objection that later proved to have much substance, if benefits were measured as percentage of weekly wages.[20]

Although at a crucial later time labor spokesmen made it clear to senators that they wanted the administration's bill passed, William Green of the American Federation of Labor testified extensively in favor of the subsidy system, compulsory pooling, and

the futility of state experimentation. He also urged unemployment insurance contribution rates of 5 per cent rather than the
bill's 3 per cent of payroll. To Miss Hall and to Kellogg, the 5
per cent rate was even more important than the question of the
Wagner-Lewis versus the subsidy plan. Kellogg editorialized in
The Survey against the bill's mere "Fifteen Weeks and Insecurity" of benefits, and told the legislators that the primary question was: "What is a decent level that we should stand for as
Americans to cover this risk of unemployment?" The question
"Where do you get the money to pay for it?" was, he said, "secondary." For Witte the level of contribution and benefits was largely a matter of practical judgment rather than "abstract theories."
He also pointed out that it was a question of whether unemployment compensation was to be a program for long term or merely
temporary unemployment, and that states were free to provide
higher benefits if they wished.[21]

Why, Witte asked Kellogg, did the dissenters not devote their
energies to influencing state legislation instead of "loading the
federal bill with standards" that would delay both federal and
state laws? "Many members of Congress seem to think that we
have altogether too many standards. I wish that some of you . . .
would give us some help to hold the standards we have." But,
he observed despairingly, "the liberalists are generally individu-
alists" whom one could not expect to unite in a solid front. He
did not believe that the "high-brow supporters of social insurance" had much direct political influence, yet they gave politically powerful opponents occasion to say that social insurance
supporters were confused and disagreed among themselves. Consequently he complained that they were "sabotaging" the measure with their criticisms. Against Epstein his charge was justified. Epstein professed that he did not wish to be accused of
"preventing the passage of the bill." Yet he testified that if unemployment insurance passed unchanged he would "fight and
fight to repeal it for the next couple of years."[22]

But against a dissenter such as Kellogg, whom Witte bluntly
accused of "bitterly fighting this bill," Witte mistook criticism

for opposition. Both Kellogg's testimony and his editorials made his essential support clear. Witte's deep irritation stemmed largely from his pessimism about the bill's chances, but the clash was also over articles of faith. To Witte, "the assumed vast superiority of federal over state action" seemed "debatable." The advocates of national action always assumed that Congress would legislate the particular standards they desired, he believed; but he doubted that Congress' standards would necessarily be higher than those of state legislatures.[23] Witte's faith was still deeply rooted in the state progressivism of Wisconsin.

The radicals, especially the Townsendites, frightened Witte. The dissenting social insurance advocates vexed him. But it was people of more conservative bent who were established in positions of power to oppose the bill. During the formulation of the program, Roosevelt, and Witte as representative of Roosevelt's committee, had been careful to consult the sort of business leaders who made up the Commerce Department's Business and Advisory Council. Witte had won infinitely warmer personal respect for his work from a man such as General Electric's president, Gerard Swope, than from some professional social insurance experts and advocates. The committee's failure particularly to recommend a national system for unemployment insurance was, declared George Soule, editor of *The New Republic*, just one more evidence that the Roosevelt administration "has always been too timid in the face of the opposition of employers." Nevertheless, Roosevelt's caution by no means assured support of all defenders of "sound" traditions. "In Congress," Witte wrote late in January, "our principal battle is with the Conservatives and I am not at all sure what we may be able to save."[24]

The counsels from the business community were by no means monolithically hostile. Two days before Roosevelt announced his program, the National Retail Dry Goods Association recommended measures that were in some respects even more liberal. "The interest of the retailer," explained the association's chairman, Samuel Reyburn, "is the interest of the consumer." Reyburn testified generally in favor of Roosevelt's bill, declaring that social insurance principles were "as old as Adam and Joseph," and that it was time Americans became "less self-centered, more aware that what is for the good of the whole group is, in the end, better for each individual." Eastman Kodak treasurer Marion Folsom, a member of the Business Advisory Council and an adviser to the economic security committee, also assured legislators of his general support, even though he had many specific criticisms of the bill. His company already provided its employers with both unemployment benefits and old-age pensions, and Folsom impressed the congressmen with his knowledge and experience. Latimer, observing him closely, decided that he was the one witness who shared with Witte the distinction of profoundly influencing the legislators to believe that a social insurance program was practicable.[25]

Henry I. Harriman, president until May of the United States Chamber of Commerce, also gave qualified support. Along with persons close to the Business Advisory Council he led a vigorous opposition movement when, just as he was leaving office, the Chamber repudiated his position in a general break with Roosevelt's economic policies. The Chamber endorsed social insurance in principle but opposed its immediate passage. Both its factionalism and its official doubletalk were symptomatic of businessmen's ambiguous stance. In congressional testimony even James Emery, general counsel of the National Association of Manufacturers, observed the ritual of noting that his association had "general sympathy" for the bill's objectives. But then Emery launched into an argument that social security taxes would merely increase unemployment, and recommended only temporary legislation to relieve those actually indigent.[26]

Despite the ambiguities of their positions, the amorphous group of conservative critics frequently agreed on several points of opposition. As members of the economic security advisory council, Swope, Standard Oil of New Jersey president Walter Teagle, and Philadelphia businessman Morris Leeds had joined with the other employer members and with Roosevelt's confidant Raymond Moley to recommend employee contributions for unemployment insurance. In April, Swope, Teagle, and Leeds were a majority of a committee of the Business Advisory Council that once more urged such contributions in a report to Roosevelt. The Retail Dry Goods Association, the *New York Times,* the New York *Journal of Commerce,* and other similar voices friendly to unemployment insurance strongly concurred in their position. The same committee, with Folsom joining in, also attacked the Morgenthau Amendment's plan of large old-age insurance reserves, a position with even more enthusiastic support in conservative councils. Harper Sibley, the new president of the Chamber of Commerce, warned that the government would not be able to invest the reserves "or keep them out of political hands." Life insurance company executives similarly warned against "huge reserves in a political system." Provident Mutual's president M. Albert Linton, who had been the economic security committee's leading actuarial consultant, expressed a sentiment prevailing among even friendly conservatives when he suggested that Congress might be wise to pass old-age assistance, but to leave old-age insurance for "more mature considerations."[27]

The idea of splitting the social security program into separate bills was a favorite among advocates of caution. They frequently coupled it with advice to delay action. Early in February Witte declared that "the game of the opponents is very apparent": to put the matter off, hopefully until a more conservative tide, by delaying action until state legislatures, who would have to create the actual unemployment compensation systems under the tax offset law, had adjourned. A day earlier the American Liberty League had attacked the bill's omnibus character and declared that there was no need for haste, since the bill was in no way an emergency measure and no part would take effect before 1936. In May the Chamber of Commerce urged delay of the whole program, ostensibly for further study until another session of Congress. The *New York Times* disagreed, but a month later reiterated its own argument that each part would get more careful consideration if the bill were divided, and urged postponement and expert re-examination of old-age insurance.[28]

"Our only hope for carrying the whole program," Witte wrote privately in January, "is a strong stand by the President to coerce the southern Democrats into lying." Yet he continued his own crucial efforts to convince congressional conservatives that the administration program was a practical one for which they could vote. He assured a group of Minneapolis businessmen on April 18 that business spokesmen could combine with radicals and defeat the bill, but warned that if they did they would soon regret the shortness of their vision. Social legislation would soon come, he predicted, and the real question was whether it would be "destructive," instead of the "conservative, although forward looking" program of the administration. The day following, the House of Representatives passed its rewritten Social Security Bill, with Roosevelt's entire omnibus program substantially intact, by a vote of 372–33. But even so phenomenal a vote, which probably reflected the power of the Ways and Means Committee more than the popularity of the bill, did not relieve Witte's anxieties. As the scene of deliberation moved from the House to the Senate, he noted "increased opposition from business interests" and "very strong opposition on part of influential southern senators against any action." He feared that conservatives and reactionaries would either block the entire bill, or emasculate it and pass only gratuitous old-age assistance.[29]

Witte continued his persuasion at every opportunity. At one point, apparently in an effort to save what he still considered most important, he even agreed to prepare an argument against old-age insurance for Senator William King of Utah to use in the Senate Committee, if King would vote for unemployment insurance. Ironically, another senator called on Witte to answer "King's" argument extemporaneously. Witte did so, frankly acknowledging the difficulties of old-age insurance, but emphasizing that the alternative was probably some modified Townsend plan. Immediately thereafter the committee chairman, Senator Pat Harrison of Mississippi, called for the vote on old-age insurance. Every member whom Witte had considered doubtful voted for it. Witte had expected a close vote, but it passed with a comfortable majority. The Senate committee likewise retained all other essential programs in the bill. Witte then helped the committee write its report, just as he had done earlier for the majority of the House committee. Witte's assistant, Joseph P. Harris, exulted that "we are all feeling very good about the Senate Finance Committee's action. Mr. Witte made a wonderful statement on Friday just before final action was taken and undoubtedly swung several votes." It was "the finest speech I have ever heard him make," declared Assistant Treasury Secretary Josephine Roche. She believed it "saved the contributory old-age insurance program."[30]

On June 19 the Senate passed its version of the bill by a lopsided vote of 77–6. After his long period of anxiety, however, Witte always believed that the congressional votes in no way reflected the degree of danger the bill had faced. He attributed its passage primarily to timely intervention by Roosevelt, and to skillful legislative management, particularly by Chairman Harrison. No doubt his observations had much substance. Although at first Roosevelt had declined to pressure Congress, beginning in March and April he had repeatedly intervened, insisting that the bill's congressional managers keep it intact, and calling publicly for its passage.[31] But Witte, having labored so hard, and feeling so keenly a burden of responsibility for the bill, may also have been somewhat too pessimistic. Just as with the dissenting social insurance advocates, very probably he interpreted too many of the conservatives' doubts and criticisms as adamant opposition.

In its course through Congress the bill underwent several important changes which made it more acceptable to conservatives. The House committee thoroughly rewrote the old-age insurance titles. Although the committee did not meet the fundamental objection of those who opposed compulsory insurance and favored only quasi-relief for those actually indigent, the revisions undermined their arguments that a national insurance system was unconstitutional. By carefully severing the technical connections between payroll taxes collected under Title VIII and benefits

given under Title II, the committee strengthened the argument
that Congress was not legislating an insurance system, but two
separate systems, one of taxes and another of annuities. Even
then the House Committee approved Titles II and VIII only
after a deal eliminating the provisions for voluntary annuities.
To Witte the voluntary annuities rounded out the old-age security provisions for those technically excluded from the compulsory
system. But to others, voluntary annuities appeared to be an
assault on private enterprise even more menacing than compulsory insurance. The Senate committee restored the voluntary
annuities by one vote—mostly for bargaining purposes, Witte believed. But on the Senate floor Augustine Lonergan of Hartford,
Connecticut, led opposition that quickly defeated them.[32]

Congress made Title I, which provided the 50 per cent subsidy for state pensions to the needy aged, more acceptable to conservatives by removing essential standards the federal government might demand. Senator Harry F. Byrd of Virginia flailed
away at a requirement that the pensions provide a "reasonable
subsistence compatible with decency and health." The requirement, he declared, would give a federal administrative official
"supreme power to deny a sovereign State of the Union any
benefits" unless the state bowed to his dictation. Witte rejoined
that the requirement was reasonable, but he could not deny that
the bill implied some regulation. Southern congressmen "feared
that someone in Washington would dictate how much of a pension they should pay to the negroes," Witte wrote privately in
May, and a month later the outspoken Senator Huey Long of
Louisiana, who favored free pensions for all the aged, openly
raised the race issue to criticize selection according to need. Who
most needed pensions in the South? Long asked rhetorically in
the Senate. "It is the colored man. How many colored people
do you think would get on one of these select lists? Let's be
frank about this business. I am possibly the only Southern Senator here who can be frank about it."[33]

Part of Byrd's objection, Witte learned, rested on a misinterpretation. Byrd and many other southerners mistakenly thought that the $15-per-month upper limit on federal pension grants meant that the states had to contribute a full $15 and give each pensioner the full $30 per month. Witte's solution was to remove the upper limit. The change, he believed, would make clear the southerners' freedom to give lower pensions. In addition it would undermine the arguments of Townsendites in the West who criticized the $30 limit as too low, and make the bill more popular in urban areas where the cost of living created need for higher pensions. But rather than liberalize, Congress removed the "reasonable subsistence" requirement. It also removed a stipulation that states choose their pension administrators by the merit system, a provision which Witte considered most important and which, through a report he prepared for Miss Perkins, he had encouraged Roosevelt to try to save.[34]

It was Congress' penchant for removing such standards that made Witte view the dissenting social insurance advocates' insistence upon added federal regulations in unemployment insurance as irrelevant, and as a practical matter treasonable. In the end Congress made the unemployment compensation titles more conducive even than the original bill to the indivdual employer reserves that businessmen favored almost universally, and that most of the dissenters so much abhorred. But the House version would have ruled out any segregation of the reserves into individual funds. Witte complained that the House Committee favored "the suggestions of [American Federation of Labor] President Green and of social workers like Kellogg and Epstein." In fact, however, the committee never considered the dissenters' subsidy scheme. Instead it responded to objections from several committee members that the unemployment compensation tax would not be uniform (and hence perhaps not constitutional) if it allowed offset credits for contributions that firms, by building adequate reserves through stabilizing employment, avoided actually paying. Although normally much impressed with constitutional arguments, Witte protested that "this change will make the bill very distasteful to all employers and will wreck the Wisconsin law."[35] He urged that the Senate restore clear permission for the segregated reserves.

"The real issue," Witte advised Senator La Follette, "is one of freedom of state action." Earlier he had written that "I have tried to look at this entire question without particularly considering Wisconsin." But he advised La Follette that unless Congress restored permission for the segregated reserves, "Wisconsin will have to scrap its unemployment compensation law . . . and begin all over again."[36]

Witte or someone who thought much as he thought prepared a brief for Senator La Follette to use in favor of the law. It argued that "for Congress to penalize those who have pioneered because, forsooth, what they have done does not please some theorists, is a gross injustice and would have a most retarding effect upon all pioneering toward social progress." Witte urged restoration of the company reserves as a "necessary" amendment in a report to Roosevelt that he outlined for Miss Perkins. His appeal fitted Roosevelt's own strong concern that unemployment compensation provide an incentive for stabilization. La Follette led a Senate committee move to restore individual reserve and stabilization credit provisions, succeeded easily, and the Senate retained the provisions in its bill as passed on June 19. In the joint Senate-House conference that began ten days later to work out the differences with the House bill of April 19, House spokesmen capitulated. The final bill even omitted the requirement that 1 per cent of the payroll (one-third of the tax offset contribution) be pooled.[37] Most businessmen preferred contributing only to their own firm's fund. A few others who had begun voluntary unemployment benefit plans, and the state of Wisconsin, had a vested interest in individual reserves. Witte's personal concern, however, was primarily his deeply rooted predilection for states' rights and state action in social legislation.

One further amendment sponsored by vested and conservative interests failed, but it delayed conference agreement and dragged out final passage of the bill until August. H. Walter Forster, a Philadelphia insurance broker, led a movement to exempt employees of companies with private annuity plans from the compulsory old-age insurance, and attempted to persuade even Perkins, Altmeyer, and Witte. Senator Champ Clark of Missouri led a successful fight in the Senate for the amendment. Roosevelt and his forces strongly opposed the measure as one that would weaken the protection of the exempted employees and load the government system with the poorest risks. Witte believed that the amendment threatened the bill's constitutionality as well, and declared in April that "I shall fight this to the end." With his usual strategic flexibility, however, he also advised administration forces to have in reserve a substitute version of the amendment with stringent regulation.[38]

By July 6, with the fight over the Clark amendment at a stalemate in the conference committee, Witte sailed for a two-month vacation in Europe. "I feel guilty running away before the Social Security Act has finally been disposed of," he confessed, but "the issues at stake are really political and no quantity of arguments that I can produce can have any possible effect." Comforted by his political realism, he and Mrs. Witte made the tourists' rounds of art and ruins, observed the political emotionalism in Germany and Italy, took some time to inquire about social insurance developments under Hitler, and watched Witte become "brown as a berry" and surprise himself "at how good a walker I still am." Ironically, the man who had with great labor and technical skill attended the birth of American social security, and then strategically and persuasively fought for its survival, was far from the scene in his moment of victory. Early in August, as he thirsted for some news of the bill's fate, he received a cryptic message: BILL PASSED CLARK AMENDMENT OUT. The conference committee had finally agreed to refer the Clark Amendment to a joint study commisssion.[39] On August 14, 1935, Roosevelt signed the Social Security Bill into law.

It was a victory for Witte, for the law represented essentially the program whose formulation he had directed. There were changes other than the lowering of old-age security standards and the restoration of completely segregated unemployment compensation reserves. Congress adopted the Morgenthau Amendment. It exempted large groups of agricultural, domestic, and nonprofit institutional workers from the contributory insurance titles. It raised from four to eight employees the basis for exempting employers from unemployment compensation, with the general effect of putting heavier loads upon gratuitous old-age assistance and general relief. It lowered limits on aid to children, but added aid for the blind and for vocational rehabilitation of the disabled. It removed some administrative authority from the Federal Emergency Relief Administration, gave it to the Social Security Board, and then, despite insiders' opposition, made the Board independent of the Department of Labor. But despite the changes, the general outlines of the new welfare program were as the economic security committee had recommended.[40]

*   *   *   *   *

Fourteen long and, for Witte, extremely tedious and laborious months had passed between promise and passage. Yet the Social Security Act emerged amid accusations of haste and with an air of tentativeness. "Congress rushed the measure through with very little opportunity for either legislators or outside experts to perfect it," declared the usually friendly *Journal of Commerce.* The legislation was "experimental," according to the *Washington Post,* and its revision would begin almost immediately. Congress should reconsider in a session "'less driven than this,'" advised the *San Francisco Chronicle,* for while "the aims of the bill are high, . . . the measure is not well worked out." The bill's objectives were "now generally accepted by enlightened opinion," agreed the *New York Times,* but the new measure threatened to produce huge old-age insurance reserves, failed to make employees contribute for unemployment insurance, and suffered from questions of constitutionality and from other "crudities." The *Times* suggested "quiet, dispassionate study and mature amendment now that "a social security measure is assured, and haste is no longer necessary."[41]

Witte, however, argued that specialists, advisers, and Congress had already given the act most thorough consideration. Congress had not created old-age insurance in haste, but had merely chosen to act upon its own judgment, rather than follow overwhelming public demand or the advice of experts. It had done its duty and "acted wisely," he declared, even though it had "departed widely" from his own preferences. Witte was "not satisfied with many parts of the bill," but he believed that it was "a beginning along the right lines." He doubted that Congress would have passed any security measure soon if not in 1935, and felt "fortunate to get even as much as we did." It was, at least, "something upon which we can build in the future."[42]

Although his direct influence over the development of social security declined sharply with the passage of the bill, Witte continued as an apologist and advocate for the new system of public welfare. Especially in the first several years he saw the primary task as defense of gains already made, rather than planning bold new steps for the future. He thought he sensed "a rising tide of extreme conservatism" late in 1935, so he continued to try to assure businessmen and other conservatives that the act was not "an extreme or revolutionary measure." Radicals had much more cause for criticism than conservatives, he told the Wisconsin Chamber of Commerce in November, for the act interfered only minimally with states' rights and presented no sudden and tremendous new tax burden. Its taxes would not come until 1937, and then only gradually. When they came they would represent costs that industry had to bear in one way or another. To the American Mining Congress he stressed at great length his most emphatic argument, the necessity of meeting persistent radical demands for almost unlimited benefits gratuitously paid from general taxes. He continued to take the Townsend Plan very seriously, partly because he thought it was "being used by big business interests as a means of splitting the natural Administration support." He denounced it at every opportunity, except that he refused to debate Townsendites and thereby to "be drawn into a position where quacks who are interested only in a financial rake-off at the expense of the old people can make me appear as an opponent of old age pensions." After Roosevelt's 1936 election victory his fear that the Townsend agitation would result in some system of universal, gratuitous pensions receded for a time. It rose again briefly about 1940 as Republican candidates frequently endorsed universal pensions, and as a group of Keynesians within the government, led by Marriner Eccles of the Treasury Department, urged universal pensions upon Roosevelt as a spending device.[43]

Witte continued to have his disagreements with the "small group of 'specialists' " connected with Epstein's organization. They "regard any departure from the European models [of social insurance] to be treasonable," he wrote, and "believe that everything should emanate from Washington." In 1936 Mrs. Burns and Douglas published books in which they paid their respects to the act as a historic step forward, but then cogently criticized its low administrative and benefit standards and its general failure to face squarely the question of whether state programs and programs entirely financed from payroll contributions could ever greatly add to workers' ultimate security. Being themselves polemicists who were trying to change political attitudes, the authors did not weigh carefully whether Congress would have approved their bolder approach either in 1935 or in 1936, although they did express optimism about judges' attitudes. Witte encouraged James Thompson, vice-president of McGraw-Hill Book Company, to publish their books, declaring that their views were "well worth considering." But he still believed that they were "fighting the legislation" and that they provided ammunition for those who had no intention of following their recommendations and would use their constitutional questions and their criticisms of the act's inadequacies as arguments against it.[44]

Witte was much less tolerant towards Epstein. In December, 1935, Epstein wrote in *Harper's Magazine* of "Our Social Insecurity Act," and in 1936 he added a chapter on the act's failures to a new edition of his 1933 book, *Insecurity: A Challenge to America*. His criticisms were multitudinous, but his fundamental

objections were still the autonomy left to states in unemployment insurance, and the failure to redistribute the "infinite"
profits of capitalists through contributions to social security from
general taxes. The act, he charged, merely robbed "poor Paul
for impoverished Peter." When Epstein and his friends called
a small conference in New York early in 1936 to reconsider unemployment insurance, Witte quickly dismissed the group's proposals as irrelevant. Their case for a national system was "theoretically . . . quite sound," he admitted, but Congress would not
approve national administration, nor would it have "the slight-
est chance" in the Supreme Court. Their concurrent case for
a "subsidy" system was also "an extremely theoretical approach
to the very practical question." It would be "innocent amuse-
ment," Witte declared, "if Epstein would but lay off active opposition."[45]

Witte was upset when Epstein did not hesitate to attack the
act even before a conservative audience, such as the National
Industrial Conference Board. He noted that reactionaries frequently found Epstein highly quotable. In mid-1936 he concluded that the Committee on Economic Security had failed in
1935 by not vigorously refuting Epstein and similar dissenters.
"These highbrow critics should still be shown up in the light
of trying to sabotage the program," he decided. So he used a
review of the new edition of Epstein's book publicly to discredit
his antagonist. Epstein had "done much for social insurance
and, undoubtedly, still sincerely wants to advance its cause,"
Witte wrote. But unfortunately he had become "a tragic figure"
whose criticisms of the act very often conflicted with his own
past statements.[46] While Witte was correct on minor points, he
failed to note that Epstein had been consistent in his most fundamental demand—that social insurance, as an economic equalizer,
should provide a radical corrective to capitalism.

Aside from fundamentals, Epstein also charged that the act
was a "perfect labyrinth of constitutional and administrative puz-
zles." But as it began to function, the new law proved to be
at least administrable, and was successful in stimulating state

legislation for unemployment compensation. It also proved to be consitutional, for in May, 1937, the United States Supreme Court upheld both its unemployment insurance and its old-age annuity provisions. Paradoxically, however, Witte recognized that the act's success did not necessarily represent a victory for his own point of view. Even "a federal unemployment insurance system might now be sustained," he confessed in September, 1937. "I am not certain in my own mind where the balance lies between advantages and disadvantages." About 1940, after social security had survived its first crucial years, mutual friends arranged a personal reconciliation between Epstein and Witte. But there was little reconciliation of the two men's ideas and approaches.[47]

In addition to his role as public apologist for the Social Security Act, Witte began late in 1935 to serve the new Social Security Board as consultant, whenever his university duties allowed. Chiefly he investigated and gave opinions on specific questions of policy, but he also acted as a private gadfly to encourage the Board to take initiative in building good relations with state administrators. "It is just as far from Washington to Madison as it is from Madison to Washington," he protested. He thought that too many of the Board's major appointments were going to "easterners whose knowledge of the country is bounded by the Hudson," and to "social workers" who were unsympathetic with the act and inexperienced in public administration.[48]

Whatever their validity, his charges carried a touch of irony, for despite a promise of much more than his university salary he had himself refused a high position with the Board, declaring that he had had "all of the administrative experience I want." His Washington experience had offered almost constant frustration and discouragement. "It has been a long struggle, . . ." he wrote in June of 1935. "Personally I feel pretty tired of it all." Upon leaving for Europe he declared that "I am definitely through with Washington, and am not going to be pulled down there again." Witte's roots were in Wisconsin and his entire outlook and manner of life suited Madison far better than Washington. His Washington experience merely reinforced his predilections, for even before he left Madison in July of 1934 he determined to return and follow through with his 1933 decision to link his career to the university.[49]

By choosing Wisconsin and the academic life Witte very largely relinquished direct influence on the subsequent development of social security. People still frequently honored him as the "Father of Social Security," but he declined even that title, pointing out that many people had co-operated to create the Social Security Act. His friend Arthur Altmeyer, who became a member of the new Social Security Board and more than any other person guided social security's early development, also declined the title. "I have been called the 'father of social security,'" Altmeyer once remarked, "but what really happened was that I was the man on whose doorstep Ed Witte left the bastard."[50]

Whether his offspring was legitimate or not, Witte was devoted to it, as he proved in the years from 1937 to 1939, when it underwent trauma, diagnosis, and major surgery.

8

SOCIAL SECURITY
Adviser

"**M**Y STRONGEST HOPE is that the Social Security Act will remain unchanged in major features until it can really have a trial," wrote Witte to Russell L. Greenman of the United States Chamber of Commerce in March of 1937.[1] Two months later Witte's words, offered in reply to an attack by the Chamber on the reserve and other features of old-age insurance, took on new meaning. In May the Social Security Board appointed him a member of a new advisory council to consider overhauling the old-age insurance system. Until Congress extensively amended the Social Security Act in 1939, Witte found himself vigorously defending what he considered the essential principles of the 1934–1935 security program. The council's discussions exposed a strong strain of individualism in Witte's assumptions and premises, as well as in the premises and assumptions of the 1935 social security law.

The 1936 presidential campaign had heightened a public controversy that finally led to the appointment of the new advisory council. From the time that the social security bill was before Congress in 1935, critics had questioned the wisdom of planning to accumulate an estimated $47 billion in United States Treasury securities as an old-age reserve fund. But in 1936 the Democrats defended their act, declaring that they had laid the foundation of security and would erect on it "a structure of economic security for all our people." The Republicans agreed that "society has an obligation to promote the security of the people" against unemployment and old age, but charged that the 1935 act was "unworkable" and denied too many people protection.[2]

"The so-called reserve fund estimated at $47,000,000,000 for old age insurance is no reserve at all," the Republicans argued in their campaign platform, "because the fund will contain nothing but the government's promise to pay, while the taxes collected in the guise of premiums will be wasted by the government in reckless and extravagant political schemes." The Republicans professed that every American citizen sixty-five or older should receive enough supplementary income to protect him from want and that the federal government should help finance such aid. But they asserted that a "pay-as-you-go policy, which requires of each generation the support of the aged and the determination of what is just and adequate," rather than reserve financing, was the proper method. And they declared that the money should come from "a direct tax, widely distributed," since "all will benefit and all should contribute." Republicans, asserted presidential candidate Alfred Landon, would have the federal government do its duty for security, but in full recognition that there could be no security amid "mounting debts and increasing taxes."[3]

On September 26, in his major campaign speech on social security, Landon raised two issues that might have elevated the partisan discussion to the high level of social principles: individual versus social responsibility, and contributory insurance versus quasi-relief assistance. The Democrats assumed that "the stern management of a paternal government" must force people to provide for themselves, he declared, while Republicans recognized that in an industrial society some people could not provide for themselves and society had to come to their aid. He suggested that Republicans might therefore abandon the contributory old-age annuity system and rely entirely upon the old-age assistance method. Unfortunately, however, the principles Landon raised soon got lost in confusion, and in murky political exchanges. Landon failed to spell just what the nature of the Republicans' "direct taxes, widely distributed" might be, nor did he explain the conditions under which his party proposed to give assistance to the aged. He hinted darkly of workers having to wear identification tags around their necks; while pro-Republican employers began putting workers' pay in envelopes printed with warnings that payroll deductions would soon begin and there was "NO guarantee" that workers would ever receive benefits. Roosevelt hardly dispelled the confusion. He replied that the warnings were "below the level of decent citizenship," and invited those who would not trust their social security funds to their government to find a country with a better government.[4]

Because of the confusion, Roosevelt's overwhelming 1936 election victory hardly represented a specific public decision on social security, beyond vindication of cautious federal action. Shortly after the election, officials of the American Federation of Labor called for an end to payroll taxes. On the other hand, several Republican members of Congress—Senators Arthur Vandenberg of Michigan and John Townsend of Delaware, and Representatives Daniel Reed of New York and Thomas Jenkins of Ohio—introduced a resolution that ignored their party's campaign promise to end payroll deductions and called merely for keeping the taxes at a level low enough to prevent an excessive old-age reserve fund. Most of the act's "mistakes and weaknesses" stemmed from its "full reserve" financing provisions, declared the legislators. The projected reserve fund was "a positive menace to free institutions and to sound finance," and "a perpetual invitation to the maintenance of an extravagant public debt." Reserve financing required needlessly high payroll tax increases in the early years, and put the burden of debt retirement on the lowest incomes. And the reserve was "unnecessary in a compulsory, tax-supported system."[5]

Witte admitted that some changes in the old-age insurance system might be in order, but he preferred to wait a while. For the present, he argued, it was "far more important to get the old age security program into full operation than to perfect it in details." The government had to educate people about the program and against the idea of universal free pensions. And until May, 1937, when the Supreme Court upheld the social security law, Witte argued that it was more necessary to develop constitutional defenses than to correct the law's every detail. Critics, he believed, were giving far too much attention to the alleged danger of large reserves many years hence. In fact, he argued repeatedly, Congress had written neither mandatory reserves nor any other theory of financing into the law; it had merely authorized future Congresses to appropriate annual sums for old-age annuities in amounts no larger than those necessary to maintain an actuarially calculated reserve fund. Should the fund grow to excess and become burdensome, a future Congress could simply choose not to appropriate the money, with absolutely no change in the law.[6]

Nevertheless Witte was willing even to contemplate some changes in old-age annuity financing. He did not adamantly oppose increasing early annuities, even though it would upset the self-sustained financing plan of the Morgenthau Amendment. Let those who feared accumulating a large reserve fund argue for liberalization of initial benefits rather than for lowering of taxes, he challenged. Or, he advised Altmeyer, he was willing to follow suggestions that benefits begin earlier, in 1938 rather than in 1942, provided that Roosevelt and the Congress understood clearly that it would create a deficit in the system. "Immediate payment of benefits would greatly increase the popularity of the measure," he reasoned. Therefore he could accept the risk of a deficit. Even lowering payroll taxes would be "O.K. provided that you actually increase income taxes *now*," rather than later, when actual disbursements would begin to exceed collections, as "pay-as-you-go" proposals implied. "Pay-as-you-go," Witte argued, was a complete misnomer; for any system that did not put assets in reserve at the time that liabilities were actually accruing in the form of promises of future benefits did not truly pay-as-you-go.[7]

But "pay-as-you-go" was the Republicans' chief concern. Their lawmakers who raised the issues in Congress did not propose to abandon contributory insurance and substitute gratuitous assistance. Instead, they proposed even to extend payroll taxes and annuities to excluded groups, such as farm and domestic workers. As for their criticisms of social security financing, the Senate, at Vandenberg's request, referred their resolution to its Finance Committee. The Committee in turn directed Vandenberg, Chairman Harrison of Mississippi, and Byrd of Virginia to work with the Social Security Board in selecting an advisory council.[8]

The advisory council as it emerged included people with various approaches and concerns. Among them was Mrs. Theresa McMahon of the University of Washington, who usually agreed with Witte but offered an added dash of feminine acerbity. Gerald Morgan, of Hyde Park, New York, was chief spokesman for adding permanent disability benefits. Another member, Jay Iglauer, president of Cleveland's Halle Brothers Company, was most concerned that the government put the reserve fund into custody of trustees who would invest it in "productive" enterprises, rather than in government expenditures that he assumed were not productive. The chairman of the council was J. Douglas Brown of Princeton University, who had helped to construct the original old-age insurance plan only to see Roosevelt and Congress distort it with the Morgenthau Amendment plan of financing and with exclusion of agricultural and domestic workers. Brown had been concerned with developing more rational patterns of benefits and coverage and with the fiscal effects of the reserve funds. As chairman, however, he acted primarily as broker for the ideas of other members.[9] Among the most liberal of those members was the Keynesian economist Alvin Hansen, who saw in social security the opportunity for anti-depression deficit spending. Among the most conservative and insistent was M. Albert Linton, president of the Provident Mutual Life Insurance Company, who favored pay-as-you-go.

Witte's essential position on old-age insurance was still that which he had held in 1934, the individualistic view, that social security was primarily a mechanism by which each man provided for his own future. He had maintained that view continuously. While the Republicans were attacking payroll taxes in 1936, Witte argued that "in our economic system it is desirable that employees should as far as possible provide for their own old age." As for the alternative of financing through progressive income taxes, Witte wrote that he was "a strong believer in income taxes," but that "all of us realize their limitation." Even a 100 per cent tax on upper incomes would not cover the cost. Payroll taxes were equitable, Witte argued, since all workers would get benefits larger than they could have bought commercially with their contributions, and since unlike income taxes they exacted no contributions from workers whom the system excluded for administrative reasons.[10] Witte's central consideration was that each man get a return for his contribution. Out of the same individualistic consideration he defended the reserve system of financing. Providing reserves against the liabilities as they accrued, actuarial-fashion, was the best way to guarantee the annuitant's future benefits. To Witte, assuring the individual his promised benefits was the crux of the question.

*   *   *   *   *

As the advisory council discussions got underway late in 1937, Witte knew that his individualistic approach was under sharp attack. From the Right came the assaults of Linton and several men from outside the council. From the Left came those of Alvin Hansen and others who thought more or less as he did. Curiously, from Witte's point of view, Left and Right converged; for both dissented from his concepts of sound social security financing.

Linton, on the council, was Witte's chief antagonist. As early as 1934, when he was actuarial consultant for the Committee on Economic Security, he had argued for a system combining old-age insurance and old-age assistance into one pay-as-you-go system; but the committee had rejected his plan. Thereupon he became a leading public critic of the old-age insurance titles, and after the Morgenthau Amendment raised the prospect of a large reserve fund, he openly opposed passage of the annuity system. He was an active Republican, and Witte understood that he had acted as consultant to Landon and chief adviser to Senator Vandenberg on social security matters. Indeed, Witte tended to view him as chief spokesmen for a cluster of critics with ulterior motives: Republicans, business interests, publisher William Randolph Hearst, a group of sixty life-insurance company presidents whose support Vandenberg cited as he asked for changes in the act, and Vandenberg himself, who had originally voted against inclusion of the old-age insurance titles. Witte conceded that he might be "misjudging Mr. Linton," but he had doubts as to the sincerity of Linton's "professions that he wants the Social Security program to succeed."[11]

Actually Linton never renounced the idea of at least using the contributory principle for old-age security. And he claimed to "yield to no one" in his desire "to see a practicable solution worked out" to the old age insurance problem. But he did object to a large reserve fund. His opposition rested on highly traditional assumptions regarding government finance, plus an undercurrent of mistrust for government officials, legislators, and the people. Throughout the depression, even in the recession of 1937–1938, Linton warned against inflation and called for a balanced budget. His most strenuous criticism of the reserve fund was that, invested as the law required in government securities, it made government borrowing and deficit spending far too convenient. He did not want the Treasury to be able to borrow "irrespective of market conditions" and without "the appraisal of the financial community." And he feared that the people, not understanding actuarial principles, would demand that the government give the fund away as benefits; to expect Congress to resist such demands, he argued, was in "the realm of dreams." Ostensibly it was such fears, more than the threat of direct government competition in the fields of insurance and investment, that led the insurance company president to oppose the 1935 provisions for old-age insurance. Prestigious spokesmen such as Folsom of Eastman Kodak within the council, and the *New York Times,* the United States Chamber of Commerce, and many others on the outside, shared his general fear and his pay-as-you-go views.[12]

Linton proposed to solve the problem with a paradox: to prevent irresponsible raids on the public treasury he would preclude the accumulation of a large reserve fund partly by raiding the treasury (partly also by retarding payroll tax increases); to prevent the giving of unreasonable benefits he would increase unearned benefits to the first annuitants who retired under the system. The 1935 system provided for paying such annuitants $17 per month beginning in 1942, already more than their brief contributions could earn. Linton argued for increasing their benefits, to equalize them with old-age assistance grants that might go as high as $60 for man and wife, and to forestall dissatisfaction that might lead to demands for even higher benefits. Even Folsom saw the paradox, and argued that it was hardly "conservative" to increase benefits and lower payroll taxes simultaneously. But Linton argued that the government could not conservatively promise larger future benefits than it was willing to pay currently. And that argument he rested on a sound principle of logic: that each generation had necessarily to support the aged of its own time, and therefore could not really commit any distant generation to a specified level of old-age support.[13]

As his concept of each generation caring for its aged—rather than each individual caring for his old age—suggested, Linton approached the question with a genuinely social point of view. In 1938 he led the social security policy deliberations of the Republican National Committee; and no doubt that committee expressed the personal convictions of Linton—a Quaker businessman—when it spoke of "social stewardship" and "giving to the weaker members of society responsible protection against those hazards for which they have no responsibility and which they cannot control." Though social security cost billions, Linton wrote, if the taxes went to "support a system that will confer worth-while social benefits, the country can well afford to pay them." To him social insurance was a system to which people contributed "and thereby acquire, as it were, a claim upon society to receive support when old age arrives." It was not like individual saving, nor like commercial life insurance, a system whereby each man provided for himself. The error of the 1935 act, he insisted, was that it rested too much on private life insurance principles, too little on genuinely *social* insurance principles.[14]

Witte, starting from the individualistic premise, tried to checkmate Linton's logic at every point. To the dire predictions of an unwieldy reserve fund Witte replied that apparently the original actuarial assumptions were already proving wrong and that a large reserve fund would never materialize: it was a fiction of projection. Moreover, if there were a fund, having the government borrow from it rather than from private investors would be a way to divert interest payments to social welfare, thus providing a government contribution to social security with no increase in over-all government expenditure. As for the danger of enabling the government to borrow without "the appraisal of the financial community," Witte remarked wryly that "coming from the section of the country I do, I see nothing dangerous" in the government's being "independent of Wall Street." And to Linton's argument that modest increases in the early annuities would forestall further irresponsible demands, Witte argued that the increases would be irresponsibility's "entering wedge."[15]

Worst of all, in Witte's view, Linton would give the unearned increases by undermining the certainty and adequacy of benefits to those currently young, those who would earn their benefits by contributing throughout their working lives. Witte was still thinking in individualistic terms. He sometimes conceded that in actuality the aged individual had somehow to depend upon society for his support, for he recognized that current real benefits came from current real production. Still he thought than an insurance institution based on the reserves principle gave "old people a definite claim upon a portion of current income." And he doubted that either Congress or the people would accept any arrangement that did not assure workers equity for their contributions.[16]

The notion of equity was one to which Reinhard Hohaus, assistant actuary of the Metropolitan Life Insurance Company, objected in a presentation to the council. Hohaus insisted that the consideration should be adequacy, not equity. Like Linton, he advocated raising initial benefits, adding benefits for surviving widows, possibly reducing tax rates, and reducing promises of later benefits so as not to increase the total social insurance load. Such a program would provide benefits based on adequacy, he implied, in contrast to the 1935 act's emphasis on equity. Hohaus, like some other critics, frequently spoke as if the old-age assistance titles, which were based on adequacy, did not exist. Nevertheless, his chief argument rested on what was a valid distinction between private and compulsory insurance. Private, voluntary insurance had necessarily to treat each contributor more or less equitably, he argued; otherwise new contributors would no longer join the system. But social insurance could compel persons to join the system and contribute. Therefore it "views society as a whole, and deals with the individual only in so far as he constitutes one small element of that great, and more important whole."[17] No statement could have been more at odds with Witte's individualistic concepts.

W. Rulon Williamson, who like Linton had served as an actuary for the Committee on Economic Security in 1934, detected most clearly the extent to which Witte's thinking was tied to the individualistic concepts of private, especially ordinary life, insurance. In 1934 Williamson had joined Linton in favoring pay-as-you-go, and in 1935 he had given a thoughtful address to the American Management Association in which he developed the distinctions between private and social insurance. In 1938 he was an actuary for the Social Security Board, and as such was in constant touch with the advisory council, and through extensive correspondence in personal touch with Witte. Williamson objected most strenuously to a principle that Witte emphasized, that every individual contributor should receive at least the equivalent of his contributions with interest, even if, as the 1935 act provided, he "received" it in the form of death benefits to his survivors. And like Linton, he advocated increasing the unearned initial benefits.[18]

The fallacy of Witte's approach, Williamson declared in private correspondence, was insistence upon "a banking rather than an insurance basis." The 1935 annuity plan was "not sufficiently *insurance*." Instead it was "advance banking to a very large extent for future insurance." Hence the reserve fund. By insurance without a banking element, Williamson had in mind the pattern of term or group insurance, which forewent all savings features and merely spread the risk of the social group at a given point in time. That, more nearly than ordinary life insurance with its equity feature, was the proper model for social insurance, he suggested.[19]

Witte, however, rejected Williamson's analysis. Such a restricted definition of insurance ignored what Americans had learned to expect of insurance, he argued: "Insurance might be a better institution, if it did not include the savings element, but it does include the savings element."[20] Witte's thought was fully perpendicular to that of men such as Linton, Hohaus, and Williamson. However conservative fiscally, such men viewed the economic risk of old age as one to be socialized, to be spread laterally throughout society; Witte clung to the view that it was the responsibility of the individual, to be carried forward, through time.

Because Linton and those of his general views thought in large terms of social responsibility, general social policy, and fund flows rather than of the individual and his problem of security, their thinking coincided at some points with that of men such as Alvin Hansen. Frequently sharing Hansen's assumptions was Paul Douglas; although Douglas, instead of emphasizing the opportunity for deficit spending, directed his liberal emphasis more to financing through progressive taxes and to extending old-age insurance to the entire population. A labor member of the council, Philip Murray of the United Mine Workers, expressed concurrence from a less theoretical stance when he proposed that social security reserves be invested in such job-creating enterprises as construction of public housing. (Most labor members of the council, however, were absent so often that Witte considered their apathy "a real obstacle" to "a more liberal program.") Outside the council Epstein and others such as John T. Flynn, a neo-muckraking writer and a director of Epstein's organization, wanted a system whereby the government would contribute to social insurance directly, along pay-as-you-go lines, rather than through reserves and interest. Ironically, despite his earlier vitriol against businessmen, Epstein agreed with Linton on almost every specific recommendation. So did Hansen, leading Witte to think that the Keynesian spoke "like an extreme reactionary."[21]

In reality Hansen spoke quite differently from Linton. Linton suggested that the government might have to reduce future benefits already promised in the 1935 act. He argued that society could probably never afford to spend more than 10 per cent of payroll for old-age insurance, at least if it wished to provide additional new programs, such as disability and health benefits. Hansen, however, declared that he wished to read Linton's plan in the other direction: that a growing economy could provide higher early benefits and also sustain the later ones. He thought it inexcusable to reduce promises already made. And while he was willing to rest assurance of future benefits on "the good faith of the Government" rather than on a circuitous system of reserve accounting, he arrived at his rejection of reserve funds by a route quite different from Linton's. Whereas Linton viewed the reserve account as something separate from general treasury funds and an unfortunate influence for a treasury deficit, Hansen considered it to be a part of the government's total fiscal activity and too rigid an influence in the direction of an over-all government surplus. Hansen noted that in the recession year 1937 the government had exacerbated the deflation by extracting money from the economy, since its receipts had exceeded expenditures by $400 million. Without $500 million collected as social security taxes, it would instead have added a countercyclical $100 million.[22]

Witte accepted Hansen's arguments hardly more than Linton's. He frequently made the point that the government after all returned the excess social security receipts when it borrowed and spent them, especially for grants-in-aid for old-age assistance. Replying to Hansen, he protested further that in depressions it would disburse even greater sums as unemployment relief. But he failed to convince Hansen, who insisted that the government would spend for such purposes regardless of the social security taxes, and that the taxes simply nullified the stimulating effects. Nor did Hansen see the problem merely as one of additions to and substractions from the private sector; he argued further that during the period of their accumulation reserve funds tended to displace opportunity for private investment. And they did so even in depressions, when too many investment funds already lay idle. Hansen was indeed, in his own words, "very sympathetic to Mr. Linton's proposal"—but from premises quite opposite from Linton's.[23]

From the fiscal Right of Witte and from his fiscal Left came criticisms of social security based on more social, less individualistic emphases than Witte's. But each emphasis, whether it was Linton's ideal of stewardship, Hohaus' concern for adequacy, Williamson's emulation of group insurance, or Hansen's vision of deficit spending as an antidote to depression, pointed in the direction of gratuitous benefits. And to Witte gratuitous benefits always posed twin dangers. One was Townsendism. Townsendism, Witte wrote in 1938, was still "the real menace to the Social Security Act." And, he protested to Hohaus, "once the concept is abandoned that the old age insurance system must be self-supporting and that the benefits should be, at least approximately, in proportion to taxes paid," the inevitable result would be adoption of a "financially and socially undesirable . . . modified Townsend Plan."[24]

The other danger was that gratuitous benefits might regress toward the pitiful and degrading "poor relief" of history. Linton drew support from some quarters, such as the National Association of Manufacturers outside the council and Curtis Publishing Company president Walter Fuller inside it, which seemed scarcely able to see beyond social security taxes to the benefits.[25] Linton's own insistence that society should probably reduce promised old-age benefits in order to stay within his 10-per-cent-of-payroll figure made the danger seem even more imminent. Also ominous to Witte was the prominent role that political partisans and representatives of vested interests played in the criticism. To be sure, he allowed his opponents' connections to blind him to the possible compatibility of interestedness and sincerity. But very probably it was true that the Metropolitan Life Insurance Company was not acting merely as a disinterested benefactor when it subsidized Epstein's organization, and when it maintained a social security information bureau for men such as Henry Hazlitt, editorial writer for the *New York Times*, to visit and use.[26]

"It is my conviction," declared Witte in 1938, "that the conservative groups which have assailed the old age insurance system are playing with fire." For "strangely, both the Left and the Right are making substantially the same arguments" and "radicals of all stripes want the benefits increased."[27] The ironic convergence of vested business interests, Townsendites, Epstein, and supporters of Norman Thomas created a confusing babel of voices. Sometimes it deafened Witte to the intrinsic force of some of Linton's arguments, and even to the arguments of a disinterested fellow-academician such as Hansen. He did not hear in them the principle of broadened social responsibility. Instead, he quite understandably heard the aberrations of the social responsibility doctrine—Townsendism and subsistence relief. It was against the aberrations, not the social principle itself, that he sought to maintain individual responsibility and equity.

"All my life I have been a compromiser," Witte declared in his major statement to the council. He did not unalterably oppose all changes in the law. He continued to be open to the idea of advancing the beginning of old-age benefit payments, and although he did not find much reason for increasing early annuities he was "quite willing to go along" with that change if the additional benefits went to widows and children, who most needed them. He also favored extending benefits to the permanently disabled, but in face of an unsympathetic council majority he was willing to make them more a bargaining point than a program. Swope of General Electric, also on the council, suggested further changes. Among other, more technical amendments, he proposed extending old-age insurance coverage to employees of banks and of nonprofit institutions, and, if it were administratively possible, to agricultural and domestic workers. For those who still remained excluded, Swope wished to revive the stillborn system of voluntary annuities. Witte expressed hearty approval of Swope's suggestions.[28]

Even more strongly, however, he advised his fellow councilors not to pressure for changes until experience had clearly shown a need for them. If the council opened fundamental questions, he argued, Congress very likely would seize upon the occasion to act, but to act quite differently from the council's recommendations. Senator Vandenberg had already shown his contempt by introducing a bill to lower social security taxes without waiting for the council's recommendations. Privately Witte revealed that his opposition to change was partly tactical. "The most active members" of the council were "pronouncedly anti-administration in their views," he declared, and he wanted to do more than to "badger them," although "that gives me a certain amount of pleasure." His strategy was to divert their opposition from a merely destructive attack into support for an acceptable benefit plan: "I want the anti-administration men of the Council to be solidly committed to this plan before I reluctantly accept it as a compromise." But on some points his opposition was genuine. "If the benefits are increased as contemplated," he argued, "any tax reduction would be outrageous." He "unalterably opposed" lowering taxes even though he was sure that the big business-insurance company coalition which had been attacking the reserves "will not be satisfied unless they get a tax reduction." He was "fighting to the end any surrender on fundamental principles."[29]

One principle for which he fought was that the council should condemn neither the method of financing nor the government's handling of the funds. Because of the indifference of labor members, Witte was almost the lone nonemployer voice on the council's interim committee, which acted as a steering group. Early in the deliberations of the council and the interim committee he pressed for a statement assuring the public that the government was handling the old-age insurance funds entirely legally, and by investing them in government securities was investing them the safest way possible. Linton objected that the statement would imply approval of the reserve system. For a time Linton's view prevailed. But in April, 1938, Witte extracted from the council a pronouncement which he had drafted. Although it declared that other ways of financing might prove better, the statement assured the public that regardless of different views on financing, the council members believed that the 1935 provisions for investment involved neither misuse of nor danger to the money.[30]

Thereafter Brown proposed a recommendation that referred to avoiding "excessive reserves." Witte immediately assured Brown that he would fight "to the drop of a hat" any statement "that implies that the Republicans have been correct." With the threat of a dissenting report he foiled Brown's recommendation. The whole tenor of the council's final report suggested a reduction of reserve funds, and it mentioned only a "reasonable contingency fund." But when Brown, in an early draft, made its implication explicit by stating that under the new benefit schedules the reserve fund "can and should" be kept lower, Witte once again threatened to submit a dissent "stating as vigorously as I can my objections to the unsound policy endorsed in the three little words 'can and should'. . . . If the dominant group insists upon its pound of flesh," he explained, "the rest of us should at least tell the public what is happening." Once more he won his point, and in its final report the council avoided criticism of past reserve policy and stated merely that under the new schedules the reserve fund "will" be lower.[31]

A second principle upon which Witte insisted was that whatever its theory of financing, the government should keep before the public a clear concept of the future obligations and costs that promises of benefits implied. Public commentators almost universally assumed that old-age insurance reserves were the fund created by a residue of contributions in excess of disbursements, and should appear as solid assets on the credit side of the old-age insurance ledger. Witte, however, argued that the reserves were merely a device to show the accruing liabilities of the insurance system and to inform Congress what appropriations were needed to meet those liabilities. While he and almost everyone else continued to speak quite confusedly and unclearly as to what the reserves actually represented, he more and more spoke as if they appeared on the debit side of the ledger. Therefore he emphasized that benefit increases would not reduce but increase the reserves. More clearly, he argued that "to merely appropriate enough money to the old age reserve account to meet current disbursements, without even disclosing to the people how much the accruing liabilities are, is fundamentally dishonest bookkeeping." His argument did not save the reserve "fund," but it did contribute to preserving a concept of reserve "liability." In the end the council agreed that "sound presentation of the government's financial position requires full recognition of the obligations implied in the entire old age security program." It recommended, therefore, that "treasury reports should annually estimate the load of future benefits and the probable product of the associated tax program."[32]

As a third principle, Witte insisted that the government should not merely acknowledge liability, but should plan definitely to meet its liabilities with a fully financed system. Folsom and sometimes Linton assumed that when benefit disbursements under pay-as-you-go approached mature levels and exceeded payroll tax collections, the government would meet the operating deficit from general funds. Witte dismissed their forecast as nothing more than a "pious expression of hope." He argued that if the government intended to make direct contributions, rather than contribute by means of interest on the reserve fund, it should make its commitment immediately and back that commitment with at least token contributions. Consequently he began advocating an immediate program of tripartite financing —by government, employers, and workers.[33] So long as reserve fund securities were accumulating, government contributions would have amounted to little more than earmarking future general revenues for old-age insurance purposes without even the equity rationale that lay behind earmarking on the basis of payroll taxes. But that fact bothered Witte not at all. Even though contributing was only a bookkeeping transaction, he argued, it created a financial commitment that future Congresses and Presidents could not avoid except by explicit act. In the end the council recommended that there be no immediate change in contribution schedules until after further experience and study, to be reported no later than 1942. "When tax provisions are amended," it added, the principle of equal tripartite contributions "should be definitely set forth in law." But the councilors stopped short of recommending that the government actually begin to contribute at that time.[34]

In the end the advisory council severely compromised Witte's fundamental principles of financing, but to its other proposals he could very largely accede. By December, 1937, the group recommended, in addition to several technical amendments, inclusion of seamen, workers in private, nonprofit institutions, and employees of national banks. At the same time it declared that coverage of farm and domestic workers was "socially desirable" and should take effect, if administratively possible, by January 1, 1940. In its final report a year later it suggested study of means to include even the self-employed and other excluded groups. The council also advocated advancing the beginning of benefit payments by two years (to January 1, 1940) and increasing early benefits. Part of the increase was to take the form of adding benefits for dependents of living annuitants and survivors of deceased ones. With an adequate system of survivors' protection, it advised, death benefits should be severely limited. As one means partly to pay for new and increased benefits, the council recommended that unless increase in national income made it unnecessary the government should reduce benefits promised to unmarried annuitants. Such reduction would not violate the "principle of individual equity," the council hastened to add, since all single persons could still receive benefits equal to their own contributions with interest. The council drew back from advocating disability benefits, declaring merely that they were "socially desirable" but that the council was of a divided mind as to their immediate feasibility. Despite lack of disability provisions and the council's objectionable financial doctrines, Witte agreed sufficiently with the over-all report to join the other members in unanimously signing it on December 10, 1938.[35]

*   *   *   *   *

In 1939, when the issues moved into the halls of Congress, all of Witte's arguments and compromises to ward off attacks against the reserve system proved largely futile. In late March, even as Witte was testifying before the House Ways and Means Committee against reducing taxes, insiders in the Roosevelt administration and a few outside experts were debating the issue. In the conferences Altmeyer and Brown opposed social security tax reduction, but Marriner Eccles disagreed. Eccles was chairman of the Federal Reserve Board of Governors and had been attributing the 1937–1938 recession to social security taxes and insufficient government and private spending. He had support from other "spending boys," as Witte termed them, including his subordinate Lauchlin Currie, Hansen, and relief administrator Hopkins. Treasury Secretary Morgenthau vacillated, but seemed anxious to appease business with a tax reduction, and a few days after the conferences testified that he favored a reserve fund no larger than the equivalent of three to five years' benefit payments. On the same day Roosevelt himself stated publicly that he considered large reserves unnecessary.[36]

The administration shift gave Witte "a sinking feeling about the future of old age insurance." He conceded that it was perhaps an astute move politically, to force the opposition either to halt attacks on social security or to move to one or another untenable extreme—either reactionary opposition, or support of the Townsendites. He also sympathized with what he understood to be the administration's ulterior motive—to win business support for its defense program. But he felt despair when he pondered Morgenthau's implication that it was necessary to plan only several years ahead in social security financing, and the uncertainty that "all or substantially all workers will get at least their own money back with interest." "What really makes me boil," he wrote, was that the undermining of younger workers' security would come partly through measures that would relieve companies writing group insurance of much of the burden of paying benefits to workers who were already old. "Mr. Linton must feel very happy these days," he declared, adding that Linton was "an honest man who serves very well the interests" of his own group. "I do not begrudge him his victory," Witte concluded. But he wished that it would have borne the label of a Linton-Vandenberg victory, instead of administration sanction.[37]

After his first emotional moments, however, Witte gave the proposed amendments highly qualified support. The bill delayed any step-up in payroll taxes from 1940 until 1943, and made absolutely no commitment of even eventual government contributions. It put the reserve fund into the care of trustees, and except for requiring actuarial statements, directed them to report annually on the prospective financial status of the system for only five years in advance. But since Witte saw no chance of maintaining the 1935 provisions, he decided that the bill was better than an explicit commitment to pay-as-you-go. Witte testified further against tax reduction, but indicated "that the revision of the benefit schedule was a distinct improvement."

He could swallow a great deal, he wrote, to get dependents' and survivors' allowances and the advancement in benefit payment to 1940 that the bill provided. He also believed that there was still serious danger that the government would have to abandon the contributory principle for Townsend-style, universal, gratuitous pensions unless it won businessmen's support for the act, which he hoped that the amendments might win.[38]

Later Witte questioned the wisdom even of his qualified endorsement, doubting that it would placate the businessmen and fearing that Republicans and Townsendites would merely shift their attacks to the new inequities. He was particularly incensed that the new provisions violated equity by taxing but not guaranteeing return benefits to persons who worked only intermittently in covered employment—persons frequently in low income brackets—while they gave early windfall benefits to many who needed gratuities far less. The amendments' shift primarily to average wages rather than total accumulated wages as a basis for calculating benefits abandoned the principle of individual saving as well as of equity. Despite his reservations and later doubts, however, at the crucial moment before the Senate Finance Committee, Witte testified for the bill's enactment. On August 10, 1939, the amendments became law.[39]

Old-age insurance was still contributory insurance, but Witte and those who thought as he did had failed to keep the contributory principle tied to their concepts of equity and fiscal soundness. Perhaps he would have been more effective, and have done greater service to the cause of social security, had he devoted his vigor and tenacity to achieving universal old-age insurance coverage. His concept of equity was vulnerable from a social point of view. His premises as to financing extended far into an uncertain future, and hence were fully as hypothetical and questionable as economic arguments that he himself rejected as "too theoretical." They included assumptions regarding monetary stability and limits to government credit that one future cataclysm—such as World War II—could largely nullify. The difficulties that European countries, especially Germany, had

had maintaining benefits during periods of financial instability had deeply impressed Witte. He pointed to inflation as the cause of Germany's increase in contribution rates and decrease in benefits in 1933 and 1934. Somehow he overlooked the point that against inflation, reserve funds were scarcely a safeguard.[40] Even with economic stability, the mechanisms he advocated could not reduce the future real burden of old-age support, but could at best merely shift it somewhat among various groups in future society.

In contrast to the equity and financing arguments, the only meritorious argument against extending coverage at least to all persons of insecurely low incomes was that of administrative difficulties. As Altmeyer emphasized, the opponents' very arguments for spreading the old-age security burden throughout society rather than throughout time gave eminence to arguments for universal coverage. Witte recognized the relationship, but used it more to argue for equity than to insist on broad inclusion. Only after 1939, when Congress had failed to include significantly large new groups, limited even further the coverage of agricultural workers, and made the system even more inequitable by destroying all benefit returns to some who contributed only occasionally, did Witte give an address entitled "Extension of Coverage—The Vitally Necessary Next Step in Old Age Insurance."[41]

Witte cared less that a social insurance mechanism be universally applied than that it be operationally dependable for the individual contributor. "The real question" that abandoning reserves posed, said Witte in 1936, was "whether the younger workers will get their promised benefits in full." There was grave danger, he warned his fellow councilors in 1938, that rather than appropriating general funds, future Congresses would increase payroll taxes or lower benefits, as Germany had done and as Linton sometimes contemplated.[42] When Witte, pitted against the paradoxical combination of "spending boys," fiscal conservatives, and others, could not win commitment to the principles of individual savings and equity to secure younger workers' benefits, he worked at least to assure the quality of the government's promise to pay. Therefore he insisted that the government explicitly estimate its accruing liabilities and express its promise with an immediate appropriation. Even if the contribution amounted only to bookkeeping, he believed that such a gilt-edged security transaction within the Treasury created a more certain promise and therefore more dependable insurance than did mere legislation of a benefit schedule.

For assuring promised benefits, the alternative to a formal mechanism such as a reserve fund in Treasury accounts ultimately lay in the popular acceptance of social security, an acceptance that might ensue from broader coverage and from educating the people to the logic of the social approach to economic security. Witte's former student and aide, Wilbur Cohen, concluded from his constant contact with congressional committees in 1939 that "Republicans, as well as Democrats, accept the principle of social security and realize that there is no possibility of turning backward."[43] But Witte, as always, looked on the pessimistic side and remained cautious. He feared the aberration of a fully social approach, a demand for excessive gratuitous benefits. He continued to put his faith in mechanical safeguards, declaring that "the more the insurance features of the Old Age and Survivors' Insurance system are stressed, the less likelihood is there of abuses."[44] He was less concerned that the social welfare mechanism apply universally than that it be self-validating and reliable, with the least element of governmental caprice. He was not a social worker. He was an engineer of social welfare institutions.

Witte approached unemployment insurance with the same concern for building a well-functioning mechanism. In the doctrinal battles that continued to rage after passage of the 1935 Social Security Act until well into the 1940's, Witte advocated pooled funds with "experience rating." Experience rating was the practice of varying the employer's contribution rate according to his employment record, a device that Commons had embodied in his original 1921 bill. Witte thought that his position was more than merely a convenient compromise between Wisconsin's "crude method" of adjusting rates through individual employer reserve accounts on the one hand, and the "State responsibility approach" embodied in pooled funds with flat contribution rates on the other. To him, experience rating was a mechanism with inherent merit. He repeated the old Wisconsin argument that experience rating could induce employers to eliminate some unemployment. But he argued that, contrary to his opponents' interpretation, the more important purpose of experience rating was to apply the old insurance practice of adjusting the rate to the risk, whatever the cause of the risk or the possibility of reducing it. Allocation of an increased share of the cost of unemployment to the firms, industries, and products that caused it appealed not only to his concept of sound market economics, but also to his sense of equity.[45]

Witte built an argument for the justice and constitutionality of experience rating from the results of a 1936 Wisconsin Industrial Commission study which he directed, and which concluded that employers frequently tried deliberately to keep their unemployed workers attached to the firm by continuing their fringe benefits and by promising them preference when rehiring. The victim of short-term unemployment usually returned to his old employer after a period of drawing unemployment benefits. Experience rating, Witte argued, would properly charge the employer the cost of maintaining his reserve labor force. For the chronically unemployed who did not fit his pattern, Witte advocated measures such as vocational rehabilitation and continued relief. He specified that the government should keep relief carefully separate from unemployment insurance.[46] In unemployment insurance, as in old-age insurance, Witte was more concerned with mechanical reliability, insurance principles, and equitability than with universal application.

Witte's ideas for unemployment insurance were, as he recognized, consistent with economic individualism.[47] But he did not carry individualism to excess. In old-age insurance he emphasized individual responsibility because he could hold no particular economic institution responsible for the cost of aging. But in unemployment insurance he placed claims for the economic burden of unemployment upon the employing firm more than upon the individual victim. To the degree that his emphasis was individualistic, it represented economic individualism, not a moralistic individualism. He could agree with the statement that people "ought to make" their own provisions for old age, he declared in 1949; and he believed that "to the fullest extent possible, consistent with the basic concepts of a civilized Christian society," social security contemplated that "the individual and the family must be made responsible." But he argued that it was unrealistic merely to declare what people ought to do, in the face of the many social and economic difficulties confronting individual effort.[48] In unemployment insurance, Witte did not appeal to a personal sense of stewardship or social morality in the employer. Rather, he appealed to the employer's function within the economy.

Witte did not attempt to make social welfare dependent upon individual character and altruism, or even upon a governmental sense of social responsibility. He rejected the "State responsibility approach," which he believed stemmed from the relief tradition and by 1943 had become the "dominant Washington-New York view."[49] Just as the authors of the United States Constitution sought to base the concept of the general welfare not upon benevolence and morality either of rulers or of the people, but upon political education and loyalty of the people, so the success of social security rested upon the general contributory principle and upon public education and acceptance, more than upon any more exact and particular mechanism or financial transaction that Witte or anyone else could design.

After the culmination in 1939 of his largely futile struggle for his doctrines, Witte felt that he was "persona non grata with many people concerned with the Washington end of Social Security," and was no longer of much influence. His withdrawal was, however, partly a result of his own decisions. Late in 1939 the Social Security Board offered him the first chairmanship of its new Board of Review for old-age insurance. But once again he declined a Washington administrative position and a salary increase in order to continue his university career.[50] From 1940 until the early 1950's he served as a member of the Federal Advisory Committee on Employment Security, but it was not a highly demanding or crucial position. Witte continued his interest in social security not primarily as a protagonist, but as a commentator from the sidelines, a guardian of principles that he considered most sound.

9

SOCIAL SECURITY
Keeper of the Faith

"I HAVE SOMETHING of a missionary zeal for social security," declared Witte in 1957, "and strongly believe that much more attention needs to be given the subject than it is receiving from Americans."[1] To the end of his life, Witte was the kind of economist who felt his greatest enthusiasm when working with "practical problems of current interest," especially that of security.[2] By habit and temperament, however, Witte was actually more the debater than the missionary. He addressed his appeals not to the unbelieving but to the heretics within the church, and his utterances were less calls to salvation than warnings against false doctrines. "I am particularly concerned because there is such hazy thinking about social security and what may properly be expected from it," he declared in 1944. However much his message sounded like a jeremiad he had not lost faith in social security, he hastened to add; but he did see trends that he viewed "with alarm."[3]

As usual, the heresies were frequently old ones, played by a new cast. With seeming assurances of support for the latest version of the Townsend Plan, the Republicans won the public support of Dr. Townsend for their 1940 presidential campaign. The Democrats in turn promised "early realization of a minimum pension for all who have reached the age of retirement." The Democratic plank was characteristically ambiguous, but Witte

saw in the words "minimum pension *for all*" the familiar specter
of universal free pensions. The vision disturbed him, and not
him alone. A fellow economist, Frank C. Dickinson of the University of Illinois, decided that apparently for aged voters there
was no middle ground between individual and social responsibility. "The doctrine of social responsibility is coming home
to roost—and we don't like the fowl," Dickinson declared. He
proposed a maximum voting age to protect society against Townsendism and "votocracy."[4]

Witte was neither so pessimistic nor so harsh with the aged.
He continued to hope that improvements in and use of the
contributory system and the means test might yet prove a viable
middle way. For the free pension agitation he blamed "well-
to-do conservatives" who had "talked so much about the 'economy of abundance' that the masses . . . are asking for what they
believe to be their share." Also to blame were politicians who
ran "on such an incongruous jumble of promises as 'reduced
expenditures, a balanced budget, and the Townsend Plan.'"
Not least he blamed "even reputable economists [who] see the
solution of all or most of our problems in increased government
spending." He understood that presidential assistant Lauchlin
Currie had written the Democratic plank, with the support of
other insiders who had influenced Roosevelt to accept the prospect of deficits in the 1939 amendments. Eventually, as war
production provided jobs and income to the aged, Witte's fear
of the political power of outright Townsendism declined. Be-
latedly, he even conceded that Townsend's notions of sharing
government handouts equally, and his desire to make everyone
prosperous through controlling money, fitted several basic American beliefs. But the "Baby Townsend Plan" of Currie and the
Keynesian "'spend-lend' crowd" continued to disturb him.[5]

The Baby Townsend planners proposed a system of minimal
flat pensions to all aged persons from general tax sources, without necessarily destroying the superstructure of additional contributory annuities. They saw in the basic pensions a potent device for fiscal control. Presumably the pensions would put money

into the hands of people who would spend it, and also create a steady flow of funds through the Treasury that would assist the government's use of strategic taxation to control the economy. Witte admitted that their pensions, being universal and equal, had a democratic appeal, and that they provided one answer to inequities in the 1939 amendments. He conceded even that universal flat pensions would prevent old-age assistance from seeming to go only to ne'er-do-wells—although rather inconsistently he also argued that they might undermine "motives for work and enterprise." Specifically, however, he questioned the planners' theoretical premises. He believed that practical experience indicated that even very old people tended to save for their further "old age," so that much of the money would reappear not in the economy but only in their estates. He argued further that "American experience suggests that it is easy to increase governmental expenditures when business tends downward, but most difficult to increase taxes when inflation looms." Congress' utterly illogical freezing of social security tax rates at a low level throughout the entire inflationary decade of the 1940's bore witness to his assertion.[6]

With a kind of inadvertent theorizing of his own, Witte raised objections based on his own social security and fiscal premises. He believed that social security already helped to keep up spending during recessions and to smooth business cycles, but that "maintaining purchasing power is not the objective of social security." It was rather "only an incidental effect and one that can only be partially realized." The Keynesian method might lead to "uncontrollable costs," since the government could much more easily increase gratuities than lower them. Even if the basic pensions remained at a level such as the $8 or $10 per month that Frederic Dewhurst of the Twentieth Century Fund was suggesting in 1941, perhaps 60 per cent would go to people who did not need them. Such pensions would represent a great waste of public money. Witte, who always retained marks of the Depression-induced psychology of scarcity, never developed great faith that society might receive its return value and even an increase of total wealth through public spending and economic planning. He was quite sympathetic with the general objectives of the economic theorists and planners, he declared in 1942, but he doubted that they could forecast business fluctuations well enough to be of much value. Much later, in 1958, he admitted that the Keynesians' social security policy was "very attractive." To have social security contribute toward the maintenance of a high-level and stable economy would be "an added advantage," if it could continue to "fulfill its basic purpose of providing a minimum necessary income" during "the personal economic hazards of life." But he still insisted that "subordinating social security to general economic policies seems dangerous." To treat it primarily as a question of fiscal policy, and to be "concerned only with its effects upon the total economy, completely distorts its true purposes."[7]

Witte continued to see heresy and perversion of social security when, especially in the postwar period, the watchword of economic planners who thought in terms of the total economy increasingly became the slogan of "full employment." Full employment was a method to prevent dependency, and just as he had resisted too much emphasis on prevention by his fellow Wisconsin institutionalists, he resisted its overemphasis again. He refused to define full employment as a goal of social security, as did many Europeans and some Americans. "Social security," he had declared in 1940, "is mainly concerned with distribution," not total production. That delimitation continued to color his thought. Although he asserted in 1944 that wartime full employment was "too costly to be a practical objective for peacetime," he did not deprecate the obvious value of increased total production. In 1959 he conceded that "social security is pretty meaningless unless we have full employment or near full employment." But even though "full employment is a first essential," he wrote in 1946, "it is my philosophy that we will not make people secure until we start making *some* people secure." "Full employment," he emphasized repeatedly, "does not make social security unnecessary."[8]

People became sick and disabled, and some children lived without support, he reminded audiences and readers, no matter how plentiful were the opportunities for employment. Even unemployment continued in the most prosperous times, owing to frictional, seasonal, and technological causes. Workers also grew old. When, in the 1950's, gerontologists, psychiatrists, and others increasingly emphasized the values of employment to the aged, Witte agreed; but he warned them not to underrate the continued necessity of social security. He suspected that much of the popularity among the well-to-do of noneconomic approaches to problems of aging stemmed from concern over rising public costs of aged support. More concretely, he cited statistics that the average retirement age already was not 65 but 69, and that the great majority of the dependent aged were women. Employment was, he agreed, economically best for the aged and indeed necessary in view of the lengthening span of life. But he doubted that more than 50 per cent, the peak figure even in World War II, could continue to work.[9] Full employment for all and employment for the aged specifically were important goals, but they were largely irrelevant to social security. There would continue to be unproductive elements in the population; social security was for their special benefit. It would best serve them if its central goal continued to be maintenance of a minimum income during specific contingencies, rather than maximum opportunity for employment which many could never share.

Closely akin to the heresies of the economic planners were suggestions for more centralized social security administration. They, too, raised many questions, doubts, and dissents in Witte's mind. On the surface he tried as always to be pragmatic and conciliatory. More profoundly, however, his social security thinking increasingly took the form of fixed doctrines and appeals to fundamental principles.

World War II created no scarcity of suggestions for altering welfare institutions. In its annual reports in 1942 and 1943 the Social Security Board recommended making its system more uniform and comprehensive by abandoning the federal-state approach to unemployment insurance in favor of a straight national system, and called for hospital and medical benefits and other extensions and changes. In March, 1943, Roosevelt transmitted to Congress without specific endorsement a wide-ranging report of the National Resources Planning Board on *Social Security, Work, and Relief Policies,* a report which called for an even more radically centralized approach, with integration of all programs into one system. In June, 1943, Senator Wagner and other congressmen introduced a measure embodying parts of the Resource Planning Board program, but with significant alterations and a decidedly different cast. In 1944, the Health Program Conference, a private *ad hoc* committee of twenty-nine physicians, welfare administrators, and economists (including Witte), made recommendations for health insurance.[10]

For Witte, the Resources Planning Board report was especially full of old ghosts. Most members of the committee who prepared it were persons of relief and social work orientation, such as Corrington Gill from the Works Progress Administration, and Fred Hoehler, executive director of the American Public Welfare Association. The director of research was one who had disagreed with Witte in 1934–1935, Eveline Burns. The committee chairman was William Haber of the University of Michigan, an economist friendly to but not always in agreement with Witte. Witte declared that the report represented only the views of Washington planners and relief and social security administrators. In words ironically reminiscent of Epstein's complaints eight years earlier, Witte charged that students "who held views at variance with Washington officialdom were completely ignored."[11]

The Burns-Haber report, as the Planning Board report was usually called, strongly emphasized work relief and general public assistance, and discussed social insurance as only one of a variety of measures for social welfare and full utilization of resources. It recommended extending social insurance to the disabled and broadening old-age insurance. But to Witte's disgust it did not recommend health insurance. Nor did he like its concept of social insurance: that "insurance" referred to benefits received, not to any "mathematical or actuarial relationship" between an individual's contributions and his benefits. Witte sharply criticized its failure to estimate the costs of its programs, and declared that the authors mistakenly assumed that "our resources are so ample that we can have any sort of social program we want." Because the report called for a centralized, integrated approach to social welfare problems, its champions sometimes hailed it as an "American Beveridge Plan" for an English proposal by a world-renowned social security expert whom Witte personally knew and emulated, Sir William Beveridge. Witte, however, shrewdly worked to disassociate it from the popular Beveridge Plan, pointing out that Beveridge had confined his discussion to social insurance and specific social services, had counted the costs, and had emphasized health insurance.[12]

Witte rejected the Burns-Haber report, but gave qualified support to the Wagner Bill. "I am not," he declared, "going to adopt a dog-in-the-manger attitude which the people who are behind the present proposals adopted when the original social security act was before Congress." He had deep reservations about Wagner's bill, although unlike the Burns-Haber report it had little of the relief orientation so foreign to Witte's background and thought. Instead it recommended extending social insurance to ill health as well as to physical disability, along with broadening of old-age insurance coverage. It firmly supported the contributory principle by proposing increases in payroll taxes to 6 per cent from each party, the employer and the worker. But on another issue its tenor was similar to the Burns-Haber report: centralization of administration. The bill proposed national administration of its health insurance program and, like the Burns-Haber report, federalization of unemployment insurance.[13] It was chiefly on the issue of centralization and federalization that Witte had reservations.

"I have always taken the position that whether the national or state government should undertake a task must be decided not on a theoretical basis but on a pragmatic one," declared Witte to Michael Davis, chairman of the *ad hoc* Health Program Conference, in 1943. Under either arrangement, he declared, the basic problem was the same: to develop "a popular actual administration on the local contact level." Unfortunately, federal-state co-operation involving state administration had frequently been inefficient and had invited low-caliber administrators. But national administration had too often proved to be "administration by multitudinous instructions by telegrams and telephone calls from Washington," the worst form of administration Witte could imagine. "Neither system offers a guarantee of superior administration," he concluded. For health insurance he would make his decision on his other criterion and ask, "Which system will have the best chances of enactment?" On the basis of political expediency he decided to cast his vote in the Health Program Conference for federal action with state administration.[14] Witte was impressed (and dismayed) that in the popular mind "Washington is getting the reputation that Wall Street had a generation ago." While he conceded that the resentment often stemmed from "anti-social" motives, as a product of Wisconsin progressivism he saw in it also a legitimate "desire of all Americans to control their own affairs." He was willing to make concessions to that desire.[15]

In the end the Health Program Conference called for "national action," but also for decentralized administration through "local and intermediate levels" of government. Witte's Wisconsin colleague Elizabeth Brandeis protested that the report seemed to suggest organization by regions rather than by states, "some of whose officials are related to the public through the old fashioned democratic method of elections!" Witte, however, defended the agitation for national action as a way of stimulating state legislation, and declared that he saw no prospect of immediate national action in any event. Labor was supporting the Wagner bill, but politically labor was "in the doghouse." Employers not only objected to tax increases, but, Witte charged, "the Washington administrative group" had completely alienated them by trying to destroy experience rating in unemployment insurance, and by "treating social security as a matter of concern to labor only." The American Medical Association was attacking, and most of all the American people were reacting strongly against further domestic reform.[16]

So pessimistic was Witte's assessment, and so strong were his warnings to consider political realities, that several persons in the Health Program Conferences misinterpreted him as being completely defeatist about health legislation. Witte's true position however, was what it had been in 1938 at an earlier National Health Conference—that the only way to meet organized opposition was for health insurance advocates to agree on a program and then close ranks in a solid phalanx. He believed that in 1938 and 1939 the advocates had not heeded him and had underestimated the opposition. So he warned once again that the only way to counteract the American Medical Association's attacks on "socialized medicine" and "Washington bureaucrats" was to meet the association "on its own ground." Therefore, he "suggested that it was about time to open up on the A.M.A. and take the attack away from it." In its final report, however, the Health Program Conference confined its efforts largely to outlining the principles of a health insurance program.[17]

Witte expressed a similar desire for pragmatism and political expediency on the issue of the federalization of unemployment insurance. The chief argument for federalization was the old one of improving standards of administration and benefits. Witte declared in 1941 that he had "always felt that on a purely theoretical basis a federal system of unemployment compensation is likely to be the most satisfactory—assuming especially that I could write the terms." That, he argued, "is what all of us always assume," but he believed from his 1934–1935 experience that in all probability Congress would legislate "standards that suit Mississippi" rather than "standards that suit New York." Although he believed that national administration was weak at the crucial local level, he suggested pointedly that perhaps national administration was the better alternative if federal-state co-operation meant having state administrators do the local work with Washington officials sitting in judgment on them. Despite his theoretical assent, Witte declared that federalization was not really a "fundamental" issue. He always took a dim view of such proposals.[18]

In part Witte was merely trying to steer a middle and characteristically conciliatory course on an issue that sharply divided his circle of friends. By the early 1940's, Altmeyer and Cohen had become advocates of federalization—reluctantly, Cohen asserted, after the Social Security Board had tried repeatedly "to get the state administrators to take a constructive attitude" towards improving the federal-state system. On the other side, the Raushenbushes of Wisconsin were leaders of the state administration camp.[19]

For his middle course Witte produced his usual practical arguments. He constantly pointed to the hostility of Congress to the extension of federal power. During the war, when Congress might have acceded on grounds of need for central control in the emergency, he argued that such proposals merely caused troubles with state administrators—troubles that interfered with the war effort. The wartime proposals insulted the state administrators by implying that "Washington people . . . were the only Americans who really want to win this war." He argued further that the emphasis on federalizing unemployment insurance deflected support from more fundamental reforms, such as adding health insurance.[20]

Yet the unemployment insurance battles also revealed that Witte's hostility to centralization went far deeper than conciliation, pragmatism, and political expediency. Opposition to centralization was ingrained in his fundamental assumptions and principles. Although the "belief of the people back home that Washington is going to deprive them of any effective voice in their government . . . is overdrawn," Witte told Cohen in 1943, he confessed that at times he shared their fears. When Cohen argued that centralized operation of social insurance was not the equivalent of centralized governmental regulation, Witte indicated that he still conceived social insurance to be "a form of labor legislation," and hence of regulation. When Cohen argued the value of a nationwide pooling of risk, Witte asserted that a small rural fire insurance company typically returned much more of the premium to the policyholder than did a huge corporation such as the Prudential Insurance Company. "I know that I am out of touch with the thinking of the highbrow planners," he declared, but "as an old time Progressive, I have the La Follette-Brandeis fear of bigness."[21]

Most fundamentally, Witte cited the fact that the Constitution of the United States had established a federal system of government. The issue, he asserted, should not become one of states' rights versus a unitary form of government. The task was rather to create "a co-operative type of government" in which the state political institutions were "part and parcel of the Government of the United States." He feared not that the state governments would pass away, he advised Miss Brandeis in 1942, but that they would become impotent "rotten boroughs." Despite the many *de facto* constitutional changes during his lifetime, Witte continued until the end to approach social security questions in terms of a truly federal governmental framework. He suggested, therefore, that a unified, integrated, comprehensive system of social insurance (such as Beveridge suggested in 1942 and Witte himself had once considered in 1934) did not suit the United States, however ideal it might be. Social insurance in America, he admitted, had "grown like Topsy," disconnected and uncoordinated. But that fact did not disturb him. Until the close of his life he continued to hope for additional progress through further piecemeal growth.[22]

Witte was "inclined to be conservative," he declared in 1958, for he believed that if Americans built upon principles and insitutions already established, steady improvement of social security would occur. The improvements would come "not quite as rapidly as I would like, but quite certainly."[23] Relative to many of the economic, administrative, and constitutional doctrines against which he warned, his approach was indeed conservative.

It was, however, conservativism at its most constructive—not static but progressive, without a trace of reaction.

Whenever he considered provisions for financing and qualifying to be sound, Witte was friendly to liberalizing social security benefits, whether of the social insurance, quasi-relief, or general social service programs. In 1938, at the peak of his battle in the Social Security Advisory Council for the *status quo* in structure and principle, he not only advocated dependents' benefits even at the cost of compromise, but also suggested other generous changes. Partly from a conservative desire to forestall Townsendism, he suggested exempting a certain amount of the income of an old-age assistance recipient when applying the needs test, and forbidding states to confiscate the recipient's property during his lifetime. He also suggested a requirement that states maintain a given average level of pensions in order to qualify for federal aid. In line with his belief that federal grants-in-aid were not so much to provide a lever of federal control as to redistribute wealth among the states, he proposed aiding poorer states by increasing the percentage of assistance for the first $15 of the state pension. He also favored raising the inconsistently low levels of aid to dependent children, and throughout his life deplored the inadequacy of general public assistance allowances. Social security benefits, he believed, should maintain minimum income at levels that reflected not merely increasing costs, but increasing standards of living.[24]

While he always resisted transforming the contributory insurance programs into gratuities, Witte constantly worked also for their extension and liberalization. After the 1939 amendments, he advocated easing qualifications for receiving old-age and survivors' insurance benefits, increases of benefits to keep pace with rising living costs and with old-age assistance levels, addition of disability insurance, and broadening of coverage to agricultural, domestic, and various governmental workers. In unemployment insurance also he constantly favored higher benefits, especially after it became clear in the late 1930's and early 1940's that benefits were low relative to contribution levels, and that many employers were demanding lower contributions. Witte deplored the fact that among its opponents "experience rating," which he continued to favor, took on the onus of a device for keeping costs and benefits down. He disapproved when he thought that social insurance reformers allowed demands for federalization to becloud the drive for improvements in unemployment insurance benefits.[25]

Finally, Witte was a sincere advocate of health insurance. To be sure, in 1938, as in 1935, he advised against incorporating health insurance in the major social security bill; but he supported Senator Wagner's 1939 National Health Bill, which embodied the program of the 1938 National Health Conference— federal aid for a variety of state and local preventive health programs, hospital construction, and temporary disability insurance, but not outright health insurance. In 1943 and 1944 he supported Wagner's new bill that included compulsory health insurance, largely because he believed its consideration would keep the health insurance issue alive. In his own utterances Witte attempted to turn the doctors' slogans against them. He referred to his opponents as the medical "bureaucracy," and insisted that contributory health insurance was not socialistic. Real "socialized medicine," Witte twitted the doctors, consisted of the very preventive programs and gratuitous medical assistance that the medical profession frequently supported, since society at large paid for such programs through the general treasury.[26]

When changes did come in a postwar period that was not conspicuous for bold domestic reform, they were largely along lines that Witte favored. By 1950 Congress at last allowed advances in old-age and survivors' insurance tax rates that it had been delaying since 1942, so that the rates could rise above the low level of 1 per cent each from employers and workers. In 1950 it went further in the direction of Witte's principles by providing a contribution schedule for full, self-sustained financing for the indefinite future, even at the risk of creating an old-age insurance reserve fund of $80 billion or more. To

Witte, 1950 was the year in which Congress finally confirmed the principle of contributory insurance. In 1950 also, Congress extended old-age and survivors' insurance to ten million new workers, including agricultural and domestic workers. It liberalized requirements for receiving benefits, removing some of the inequities to which Witte had objected in 1939, and raised benefits to match real 1939 levels. In 1952 it further liberalized benefits, in 1954 included self-employed persons and further increased benefits, in 1956 added disability insurance for persons over fifty years old who were permanently disabled, and in 1958 increased benefits again. Meanwhile in the late 1940's and the 1950's it had increased old-age assistance grants and put them on a sliding scale that helped poorer states. It also liberalized various other assistance and health programs, in 1950 adding aid for the permanently and totally disabled, and in 1956 aid for medical care to the indigent aged. It retained the unemployment insurance system with little change beyond increases in benefits, largely to meet inflation. At the end of Witte's life Congress had not passed health insurance, and he was not entirely satisfied with all other features and benefit levels. But in 1958, two years before his death, he observed with satisfaction that "even in a long period of a pronounced trend toward conservatism, our social security institutions have been improved."[27]

More phenomenal in the postwar period was the progress of private group efforts for individual security. In the decade from 1946 to 1956 industrial health, pension, and welfare plans proliferated from coverage of about 1,250,000 to 14,000,000 American workers. By the late 1950's both the cost to the employers and the total accumulated reserve funds of such systems had exceeded those of the old-age and survivors' insurance system, and in addition some unions were demanding supplementary unemployment benefits. Witte served as public trustee of one of the funds, that covering 30,000 members of the International Brotherhood of Electrical Workers, and with some qualification welcomed the development. He believed that industrial welfare plans provided the employer a means of meeting responsibility that he felt to faithful employees, and contributed to improvements in industrial relations. Most of all, with his view that the government could and should provide no more than minimum income security, he saw in them a sound means of supplementing social security benefits. As in the case of public security institutions, however, and indeed somewhat more relevantly, he insisted upon structural soundness, and especially upon full reserve financing and the vesting of the employee's right of benefit. Nor did he believe that private efforts were a substitute for public action. Many persons supposedly covered under the private plans would never receive benefits for lack of vesting, he pointed out, and the plans covered at best only a minority elite of workers. He insisted that there would always be need for social security, and refused to define the term broadly enough to include the private institutions.[28] Witte's brand of conservatism and appeal to established principles did not include insistence on private over public activity.

Witte was relatively satisfied with conservatively fostered progress and supplementary private effort, but he had little patience with those who aimed to reverse the pace of social security; indeed, he had even less patience for them than for Washington planners and theorists. In 1946 Lewis Meriam of the Brookings Institution published a book, *Relief and Social Security*, in which he failed to distinguish between social insurance built as much as possible upon individualism (such as Witte advocated) and proposals oriented towards broad social responsibility. Consequently, he used some ideas similar to Witte's to attack the entire principle of contributory insurance. Meriam objected to compulsory contributions in an insurance system on the ground that they compelled persons to pay for hazards to which they were not exposed, an idea implicit in Witte's support of separate, specialized systems for separate hazards. He objected that governments did not set premiums by insurance principles, a concern Witte expressed by favoring experience rating. Much as Witte insisted upon equity, Meriam objected to unneeded windfall benefits in the old-age and survivors' insurance system. Meriam's most fundamental objection, however, was that social insurance became a tool for redistributing wealth. With that objection Witte half agreed, for he insisted to the end of his life that the redistribution of wealth was no more than an incidental effect of social security, and argued that total equality of wealth was not desirable. Meriam based his objection on a different concept of social insurance: he assumed that wealth redistribution was a conscious purpose of contributory systems, and insisted that transfer of wealth from the rich to the poor violated constitutional property rights. He even opposed extensive redistribution of wealth from richer to poorer states.[29]

To such extreme application of constitutionalism and individualism Witte could not subscribe. Meriam insisted flatly that the primary purpose of social security was the traditionally accepted one of relief of need, and proposed transforming it into a system of grants-in-aid to states to give relief, strictly on the basis of established need, regardless of the cause or of contributions. To finance his program he proposed elimination of employer contributions and the substitution of a universal, flat income tax upon all business and individuals. Witte noted that Meriam would remove much of the burden of relief cost from progressive taxes. And, of course, Witte rejected out of hand the proposals to revert from contributory insurance to parsimonious relief.[30]

Meriam's proposals confronted Witte with the old paradox that, starting from different assumptions and proposing somewhat different programs, pronounced conservatives and pronounced liberals often shared a relief psychology. In 1952 Witte once more saw the specter of Baby Townsendism, but (unlike in 1940) the new specter stood on conservative assumptions and tax proposals. Paradoxically, instead of the liberal economic planners who had earlier called up Baby Townsendism, its new conjurers were none other than the United States Chamber of Commerce and Witte's erstwhile antagonist on the 1937–1938 Social Security Advisory Council, M. Albert Linton of Provident Mutual Life Insurance Company.[31]

Linton had continued active in social security discussions.

Early in 1952 he published an article in the Chamber journal, *American Economic Security*, that harked back to 1934–1935 and 1937–1938. Once more he proposed to dispense with the old-age assistance grants-in-aid and to pay at least a minimal pension to all the aged from old-age and survivors' insurance funds, regardless of need or of previous contribution. In effect his proposal was for a universal pension system financed entirely from payroll taxes, with extra benefits to some contributors depending upon their previous average wage. The gratuitous and minimal pensions would have been low, and he proposed leaving further aid on the basis of need entirely to the states. Such a system, he argued once more, would observe the sound social insurance principle that persons currently working should support the aged, would halt accumulation of the reserve fund, and would tie benefits clearly to current taxes so as to guard against demands for undue liberalization. He noted further that it would relieve the federal treasury of old-age assistance costs amounting to $800 or $900 million annually.[32]

Witte quickly predicted that the article represented "what Linton and his gang hope to put across if the 'right' President and the right Congress are elected in November." The Republican platform seemed to give some support for Linton's proposal, for it promised "a thorough study of universal pay-as-we-go pensions plans." Within two weeks after Dwight Eisenhower's election the Chamber of Commerce suggested the plan as a legislative proposal. Nevertheless, in submitting his legislative program to Congress in February, Eisenhower did not specifically endorse the Linton-Chamber plan, but called for extending coverage of "the Old Age and Survivors Insurance Law" to millions more citizens. When Senator Robert Taft of Ohio and House Speaker Joseph Martin urged delay and further study, and Congress failed promptly to extend the existing system to new groups, Witte feared that legislators were warming to the Linton-Chamber plan. After a year's delay, however, Congress chose to extend the system along established lines. To Witte, the decision was very much to Congress' and Eisenhower's

credit. Witte saw in Linton's and the Chamber's plan an attempt to shift old-age assistance costs to payroll taxes and to state
sales and property taxes. He predicted that it would have destroyed the old-age and survivors' insurance system "and, in the
end, probably would have left us nothing but old age assistance
on a needs basis financed from state funds."[33] Like the Meriam
proposal, Linton's plan came to naught. But it gave Witte a
time of concern and demonstrated how different was his from
other nominally conservative approaches.

Witte yielded to nobody, least of all to self-proclaimed conservatives, in his insistence that his methods for social security
were entirely compatible with American traditions. While he
recognized that existing security legislation was largely a product of a desperate depression situation, he emphasized that the
depression's effect had been not to revolutionize but rather to
stimulate new action based on established traditions. Ancient
codes as diverse as those of Moses and of the Peruvian Incas
had enjoined the care of the needy, he pointed out. Especially
as World War II caused him and other Americans to contemplate America's values, Witte increasingly emphasized that social security was one expression of a "Christian and civilized
society." He constantly pointed to the fact that security legislation had come to America with the earliest colonists, in the
form of the English Poor Laws. Subsequently the aspiration
of a secure existence for all had become "the dream of American democracy throughout our history." Businessmen, he declared with a trace of mischief, had been among the most secur-
ity-minded—speaking of individualism but associating and organizing to protect the security of their own interests at every
opportunity. And the government had aided business. The
welfare statism that promoted social security was not the buga-
boo that its critics claimed, he insisted, but was a defensible
tradition clearly grounded in the federal Constitution.[34]

In Witte's mind the state's promotion of the general welfare
involved no antithesis of individualism. America had to go
beyond mere relief to contributory insurance, he had declared

in 1937, partly because of its "Puritan heritage which places such a high value upon individual initiative and thrift." In later years he seldom invoked Puritanism, but he continued to insist that his belief was in social security that "leaves wide scope for individual initiative and thrift." The proper function of the government was merely "to provide an underpinning for economic security, the superstructure of which must be provided through private enterprise and individual savings." Social security "cannot become a substitute for industry, initiative, and invention," he declared, and any notion of the government's providing comforts and luxuries regardless of individual effort was "completely false" and alien to the social security movement. Social security provided not a featherbed but a net or even a hard floor under those who fell, he declaimed in a favorite metaphor. And he approved of that. "Today and in the foreseeable future," he asserted in 1958, "social security in the United States can provide only a minimum income sufficient for a standard of living compatible with prevailing concepts of needs and possibilities. . . . Providing such a necessary minimum income as a protection against the worst economic consequences of the personal hazards of life is the objective of social security, as I see it." Such a concept of social security, he insisted to the end of his life, "operates to make our democracy the more valuable and to strengthen our system of free enterprise."[35]

*   *   *   *   *

Witte made his great direct contribution to social security and to American development in 1934 and 1935. Capitalizing upon a propitious moment in history, he and his colleagues pulled together an amorphous body of social welfare ideas, formulated a new program for meeting a fundamental problem of human existence, and helped to persuade wary politicians to accept it. It was in 1934 and 1935, as he faced practical problems in a charged political atmosphere, that his specific and lasting social insurance doctrines took shape. Because of the circumstances of their inception and of his general habits of thought, his ideas were not so bold as they were commonsensical. He did not offer brilliant new conceptualizations of human problems and their solution, but he did analyze ideas carefully and apply them creatively to the realities of life. Sometimes he underrated the possibilities for political and constitutional changes in American development. But he entered the process of historical change with ideas that helped form a link of continuity between older, individualistic concepts and newer, more social approaches.

Beyond question Witte's principles of qualified individualism, equity, and institutional safeguards remained highly relevant to solving social problems long after 1935, since the overwhelming majority of Americans still looked largely to individual effort, sanctity of contract, and constitutionalism to protect their human rights. His commonsense approach aimed to create institutions that would win the lasting consensus of a responsible electorate. And although at times after 1935 he seemed to defend the *status quo*, he continued in fact to work for progress and improvement upon the principles of 1935. He did so even while fighting what he saw as heresies of the Left and the Right.

Witte had chosen a circumspect middle way. An intemperate and reactionary iron-mine operator from Minnesota, Carl J. Calvin, half misconceiving Witte's belief to be that "the *Government* should assume responsibility for the 'prevention of dependency of its citizens'," once accused him of contributing to the "insatiable appetite for public pap"; to which Witte replied that "I have so often been denounced by radicals who feel that the program I have been advocating does not go far enough" that Calvin's attack was "something of an assurance that my ideas must be somewhere near right."[36] Actually, Witte's path was more purposeful than mere blind groping between extremes. It followed the deliberate method of the institutional economist: defining a specific social problem carefully in a particularistic way, and then attempting to solve it in full recognition of all impinging economic, political, and social factors, neither abstracting it into hypothetical fiction nor losing sight of it in the shadow of any peripheral consideration. The goal he pursued was an effective, well-functioning socio-economic institution.

Witte's way was, as he himself pointed out, firmly grounded in "the older Commons-Brandeis approach." Yet he recognized that "social security stems not alone from labor legislation but also from poor relief legislation." (Significantly, he ignored the social insurance expert-propagandist root.) His great fear was that Washington officials would lose sight of the labor legislation root. He believed, he declared in 1943, that it was possible to reconcile the two points of view. Witte advocated his social security doctrines not in a spirit of unyielding insistence, but rather in a spirit of conciliation that he believed, characteristically, to be necessary "to insure further progress in social security."[37] It was the same spirit that made him effective in another area of practical problems, that of industrial mediation.

10

Labor Mediator

NINETEEN HUNDRED AND THIRTY-FIVE was the year not only of the Social Security Act, but also of the Wagner National Labor Relations Act. The Wagner Act promoted collective bargaining, not by creating collective bargaining institutions so much as by providing a legal framework within which capital, labor, and their mediators could evolve voluntary patterns. Witte feared, as he said in 1937, that unless Americans solved the labor-relations problem "we may create a situation where our very institutions are in real danger,"[1] and he turned his hand to develop the new institutions. As he did, his contribution was, on the surface, paradoxical. When he actually worked as mediator in particular labor disputes, he promoted orderly, rationalized wage and job structures and systematized relationships between disputants. When he was influencing public policy, on the other hand, he opposed the structure and rigidity that too much law might create, and advocated as broad a range as possible for flexible negotiation and voluntarism.

Characteristically, except for a bit of work for the National Industrial Recovery Administration in 1934, Witte began extensive labor-relations work at the level of state policy and action. Early in 1937 he aided the United States Department of Labor in drafting a model state labor-relations bill, and, at the request of Governor Philip La Follette, helped with a similar bill in Wisconsin.[2] Witte emphasized a mediating rather than a policing role for government. Labor departments, he warned, should not identify so closely with labor that they lost effectiveness with employers.[3] And he tried to frame state labor-relations laws around the primary purposes of avoiding and settling strikes and lockouts and of fostering industrial self-government, in contrast to the Wagner Act's approach of accepting industrial conflict as inevitable and setting up rules for containing it. Witte promoted responsibility in unions' behavior, but not in the way that some state labor acts in the late 1930's and later the 1947 national Taft-Hartley Act sought it—*i.e.*, by designating certain union practices as unfair and adding them to the Wagner Act's list of unfair employer practices. That merely created more law. The method he helped write into the 1937 Wisconsin act was to direct the state's leading employer and labor organizations respectively to form committees to foster contructive collective bargaining attitudes and policies within their own camps. Reminiscent of Commons' earlier attempts to involve representatives of interest groups in the formulation and enforcement of law, the committees were to Witte a means whereby "both industry and labor shall have an opportunity to set their own houses in order without governmental intervention."[4] After the Wisconsin bill became law, La Follette made Witte a charter member of the three-man Wisconsin Labor Relations Board it created. The Board retained the same spirit, and pursued mediation and informal procedures more than strict, legalistic enforcement.[5] From 1937 to 1939 Witte and his colleagues achieved ample successes in particular disputes, though by no means did they end the labor strife which was chronic in Wisconsin as elsewhere.

Witte tried to resign from the Wisconsin board when its initial guidelines were set, but La Follette refused his resignation. When Julius Heil, an anti-union governor, was elected late in 1938, Witte's performance and reputation were such that even he did not release Witte for some months, although under the Board unionism had grown apace. Then Heil, with the backing of conservative business and farm organizations, put forward a new "Employment Peace Bill" which borrowed the "unfair union practices" approach from an Oregon law and was otherwise sharply anti-labor. Violating his usual discretion, Witte boldly testified against the measure, denouncing it as both inequitable and likely to worsen rather than improve industrial relations. Thereupon Heil released him.[6]

The editor of the conservative *Wisconsin State Journal*, however, found Witte's departure regrettable. Witte was "liberal minded," thought the editor, but he was "not an extremist," had used "tact and good judgment," and had advocated "negotiations rather than force in labor relations." The editor had correctly perceived Witte's method. The prime prerequisites for successful labor relations, Witte believed, were not law so much as acceptance of unionism and collective bargaining by employers, and responsible behavior by unions. No law, he declared in 1939, could "create the mutual confidence upon which alone, good relations can be built." What was needed was not externally imposed "government of industry," but "government in industry," using internal, democratic, collective bargaining.[7]

*   *   *   *   *

Ironically, Witte's most extensive and significant mediation assignment was for a federal agency very much involved in "government of industry," the National War Labor Board of 1942–1945. By its very nature, the Board was hardly a vehicle for Witte to pursue his ideal of collective bargaining developed by industry and labor themselves, without government interference in negotiations or settlement terms. But it did enable him to work for rationalized wage and job structures, to promote consistency and regularity between companies and their workers, and so to help institutionalize collective bargaining.

Witte had little opportunity to influence the Board's broad labor policy guidelines, except indirectly through serving in 1941 on a seven-man Twentieth Century Fund committee that made recommendations for wartime labor policy. As finally constituted, however, the Board represented a mixture of voluntar-

ism and compulsion that he could well accept. As defense production got underway, Witte warned against introducing too
much government control over labor relations, the position
that the Twentieth Century Fund report also took. Yet, as
usual, he did not follow his ideas to their radical conclusion,
and he warned both labor and employers that the public would
not tolerate many stoppages of defense production. By May,
1942, with the nation actually at war, he declared that when
labor and management refused to co-operate in wartime, "something more than voluntary mediation is called for."[8] The evolution of Witte's thought paralleled that of public policy. Early
in 1941 Roosevelt created the National Defense Mediation Board,
appointing as its chairman William H. Davis, an attorney and
mediator with whom Witte had worked as early as 1934 and
who had recently headed the committee of the Twentieth Century Fund. The Mediation Board represented the voluntary
approach, but C.I.O. unions boycotted it and by late 1941 its
method was breaking down. Congress proposed the compulsory
approach, in the form of bills to outlaw strikes in defense industries. To avoid such an extremity, Roosevelt called a Labor-
Management Conference in January, 1942, again under Davis'
leadership, and got representatives of both camps to pledge that
there would be no strikes or lockouts during wartime. The
Conference recommended that Roosevelt establish a board to
adjudicate disputes, and on January 12 Roosevelt issued an executive order creating the National War Labor Board with a tripartite system of equal representation (four each) from labor,
management, and the public. In June, 1943, Congress accorded
the Board legal recognition.[9]

Reflecting its mixed origins, the Board interspersed quasi-
compulsion and voluntarism. Although it normally accepted
only cases in which all conventional avenues for conciliation
had been exhausted, it could not compel obedience, the courts
eventually ruling that there was no legal penalty for noncom-
pliance with its decisions. But it could turn such cases over to
the President. The element of compulsion was strong enough

that it had to take that step in only 300 of 21,000 cases. On the side of voluntarism, the Board had the pressure of public opinion against stoppages, the no-strike/no-lockout pledges, and most importantly, its tripartite organization. The presence of labor and management representatives on the Board enabled it to settle many cases "in the hall," and to establish liaison with the disputing parties to secure compliance. The representatives could easily have boycotted and perhaps destroyed the Board. Yet they did not, and invariably they supported the Board's final decision once it was made. And so while the Board used elements of compulsion, it kept them in the background, and its structure and operation approximated that of voluntary collective bargaining. Witte was quick to defend it against the charge that it practiced compulsory arbitration.[10]

From the very beginning of mobilization for World War II Witte handled labor cases for the National Defense Advisory Council, the National Defense Mediation Board, and War Manpower Commission. In 1942 Roosevelt appointed him to a wartime National Railway Labor Panel. Meanwhile he began to take cases for the National War Labor Board itself and chaired a council advising its Chicago branch. In January, 1943, the Board set up a new Regional War Labor Board in Detroit, and appointed Witte as its first chairman, a post he filled for the next thirteen months.

Witte's experience in Detroit did little to convince him of the wisdom of governmental meddling in labor disputes except as an emergency measure. The Board had established the regional boards as a decentralization move, because it had gotten bogged in a mire of undecided cases.[11] Witte found the situation in Michigan highly unstable. Wages were high, but the Detroit area was gaining population at the rate of 20,000 per month, creating maladjustments and shortages of housing and food. Much as he tried to placate all interest groups and factions in the composition of his board, he could not establish satisfactory relations with the United Auto Workers, who included 80 per cent of all union members in Michigan. He got on well with the union's president, Rolland J. Thomas, and found it quite possible to work with its communist-leaning secretary-treasurer, George Addes. But a right-wing faction under vice-president Walter Reuther was attempting to wrest control from the Addes group, and constantly criticized the union for co-operating with the government on wages and even on the no-strike pledge. With labor so restive, Witte's board was faced with as many as fifteen to twenty wildcat strikes per week. "The largest single center of war production in the United States," Witte found, was "quite a hot spot in industrial relations."[12]

Frank Rising, an industrialist on Witte's board, later recalled that

> *In the terrible winter of forty-three*
> *Our Board was convened for the whole world to see...*
> *With snarling and shouting the rest all pitched in*
> *And made Dr. Witte's life hotter than sin....*

Witte indeed felt that he was "sitting on the top of a volcano." His chief complaints were not, however, against the restless workers. Them he defended, pointing out that the auto workers' union was unstable primarily because it was genuinely democratic, that because of shortages workers felt poor despite high wages, and that the most publicized strikes really had the character of much-needed vacations.[13] His complaints were against government policies. He chafed under a presidential wage order of April, 1943, which, because Detroit wages were already very high, allowed very little flexibility for wage adjustments. He disliked the Labor Disputes Act which Congress passed in June of 1943. Apparently under the assumption that union members did not really want to strike but their leaders misguided them, Congress required that unions give thirty days' notice before striking and compelled the National Labor Relations Board to conduct a strike vote. The elections invariably authorized leaders to proceed, and Witte, like most other Board officials, believed the procedure merely increased the number of strikes and strike threats. Washington authorities, Witte observed, sometimes forgot that the primary goal was to win the war, not to stabilize wages.[14]

For his problems Witte characteristically put forward no grand solutions, attempting rather to solve each one pragmatically with "every bit of energy and ingenuity I have." As Rising put it:

> *Those were the times, boys, those were the times!*
> *When the unions came in for their nickels and dimes;*
> *When Leo yelled yes! And Lovett screamed no!*
> *And Witte and staff had a tough row to hoe. . . .*
> *Oh, let us recall as in wassail we join,*
> *The wage rates we set by the toss of a coin. . . .*
> *We've said it before and we'll say it again:*
> *(If you worked for the Board you will utter amen)*
> *That no one lived through it who could be quite sure*
> *That his favorite theories were totally pure.*

Witte had few theories. When a journalist once mentioned that the "short and rotund" chairman was wearing a Phi Beta Kappa key, Witte assured the newsman that he was not "just another one of those smart college professors expounding his theories again."[15] If Witte had any theory it was an implicit one, that the most productive settlements resulted when negotiations were fluid, with the fewest possible constrictions imposed on procedures or terms from the outside. Observing that belief as far as he could, he kept his volcano from blowing up, and later he noted with satisfaction that the government had never needed to seize a plant in Michigan despite its prime importance to defense production. When Witte left Detroit his Disputes Director, Ronald Haughton, observed wryly that at least he was not leaving town on a rail.[16]

In February, 1944, President Roosevelt called Witte to Washington to become one of a new group of "alternate" members of the national Board, whose regular members had long since laid down major policy guidelines. They continued to handle troublesome cases such as Montgomery Ward President Sewell Avery's highly publicized refusals to accept the Board's directives, and the United Mine Workers' equally notorious challenge from the union side. It was they who made important recommendations late in the war regarding wages and reconversion policy. The alternates, by contrast, were a "junior varsity." Much of their work was mundane—reviewing appeals, holding compliance hearings, and deciding mine-run cases—and although Witte considered his job important he found it tedious.[17] Gradually, however, he got involved in work of some import. In 1944 he performed much of the research on coal mine cases, which were potentially very troublesome and among other issues involved the emerging practice of portal-to-portal pay.[18] With his Detroit background he acted as the Board's expert on the automotive industry, and in the winter of 1944–1945 made the major recommendations for a settlement between General Motors and United Auto Workers. The issues included such large questions as a guaranteed weekly wage during postwar reconversion, and whether wages should conform to local levels as the company wished or be uniform company-wide as the union advocated. (On the former issue, Witte recommended further study; on the latter, he advised that uniform company rates would upset national stabilization policy.)[19] In 1945 he supervised a series of Western Union Company cases. He found the firm's wage practices "a mess," with inexplicable wage variations and scarcely any proper job classifications, and helped the company develop consistent wage structures.[20]

Out of the mundane, Witte was quietly fostering patterns and structure for collective bargaining. No cases better illustrated this than those arising from the meatpacking industry. In mid-1944 Witte took charge of all meatpacking cases. Although he worked chiefly with the Big Four packers—Swift, Armour, Cudahy, and Wilson—a historical trend among small packers to "follow the leaders" made his influence nearly as broad as the industry. In the spring of 1945 he got the Board to set up a Meat Packing Commission, with labor economist Clark Kerr as chairman but under Witte's own general direction, which helped the packers and unions to work together towards simplifying the industry's ridiculously complex job and wage categories. Witte, with the Board's backing, introduced the portal-to-portal principle in the industry, so that workers were paid for the considerable time they spent sharpening tools and changing clothes. He strongly encouraged a pattern the industry had already established, a guaranteed work week, and got the Board to extend it from thirty-two to thirty-six hours.[21] His influence with the industry did not end with the war. In January and February, 1946, when the meatpackers were among the first to be hit with postwar strikes, he served as chairman of a new fact-finding board. Again in 1951, during the Korean conflict, he headed a Meat Packing Panel for the Economic Security Agency. Throughout, Witte and his colleagues often made pace-setting decisions on very immediate considerations. But frequently they seemed also to be working quite deliberately to promote more orderly, rational procedures. That effort was Witte's greatest contribution as a War Labor Board member, and his most lasting contribution to collective bargaining.

Witte hoped that his position with the Board would enable him also to influence events in the postwar reconversion period, for he detected that the Truman administration was adrift in its labor policies. But he found that the Board's prestige declined rapidly in 1945, as first the Germans and then the Japanese surrendered and public opinion grew hostile to wartime labor controls. Many key members of the Board and its staff resigned in the latter half of the year. Those who remained lost practically all leverage on the Truman administration.[22] With his usual loyalty, Witte stayed with the Board until its demise on December 31, but he had virtually no chance to influence reconversion policy. Early in 1946 he returned to the University of Wisconsin.

*   *   *   *   *

Despite his wish that the government guide labor relations during reconversion, fundamentally Witte opposed compulsion and excessive legalism in collective bargaining as much as ever.

Unlike much of the public, he accepted postwar labor struggles calmly—much more calmly than his social security hassles—and dismissed the wave of strikes during late 1945 and 1946 as "unavoidable." Instead of calling for new laws, he preached return to first principles. His language was rather vague, didactic, and commonplace among collective bargaining advocates; it was nevertheless quite basic. Strikes, he pointed out, could be the "safety valve" for industrial harmony, even for democracy itself. Industrial peace was a goal that had to be compromised with other goals such as productivity in labor-management relations. Freedom was another such goal, but Witte declared over and over that a more constructive slogan than the oft-repeated cry of "free collective bargaining" was "genuine collective bargaining." "Genuine collective bargaining means more than the right to strike and the right to oppose the unions," he preached. Labor had to accept the system of free enterprise, quit using the language of class struggle, and take care not to offend the public. Management had to stop idolizing the pre-union "good old days," and let unions cease fighting for their very existence. Only by common commitment to make bargaining work, he prophesied, could the parties avert government control of their relations and, in the end, of the economy.[23]

Given his philosophy of collective bargaining, Witte could only oppose the cooling-off periods and fact-finding commissions, legal restrictions on unions, and even compulsory arbitration proposed in Congress in 1945 and 1946. He thought the Taft-Hartley Act of 1947 "a bad mistake" which, instead of equalizing labor relations as it was supposed to do, created a new imbalance against labor. Its anti-closed-shop provisions, restriction of unions' political activity, requirements of noncommunist affidavits and financial reporting, and assertions that such traditional union practices as the "secondary boycott" against handling nonunion made goods were unfair union practices left labor worse off, he argued, than if Congress had merely repealed the Wagner Act. The new law, though fostered by conservatives, injected much more government into labor relations by prescribing collective bargaining procedures, requiring new reports, and giving vast new powers to the National Labor Relations Board. Most fundamentally, it was a "law geared to industrial conflict rather than to harmonious labor-management relations," for it gave new weapons to belligerent employers and only created problems for those who wished to live peaceably with unions.[24]

Over the years Witte had evolved a more or less coherent set of rules he thought government should observe. It should be impartial, avoid compulsory arbitration except in the gravest of emergencies, and not prohibit strikes, revive the labor injunction, or in any other way hinder unions from functioning effectively. Neither should it specify exactly how negotiations should proceed, nor declare certain issues such as the right to discharge an employee off limits for collective bargaining. Positively, government could promote research and education on matters of collective bargaining and be a clearinghouse of information. It should obligate both employers and workers by law to bargain in good faith. It should provide an impartial mediation service, and, where bona fide bargaining broke down, help define and arbitrate unresolved issues. Though any arbitration in the process of forming the contract should be voluntary, the law should compel arbitration and prohibit strikes to settle disputes over interpreting the contract once it was signed.[25] There would inevitably be strikes in the process of forming contracts, and when they produced genuine national emergencies Witte was willing to allow government to intervene "with all the powers at its command." But he warned that intervention would be ineffective if practiced too frequently.[26]

Witte espoused his principles, but not as a great crusade against the Taft-Hartley Act. He favored the Act's repeal, yet defended its enforcement.[27] Pragmatism was a stronger element of his reformism than was moral indignation, and he knew better than to insist on legislative change when political trends were running against him as in the late 1940's and the 1950's. Even more, however, he perceived the problem to be not so much a question of legal and institutional structures as of right attitudes and wills.

In 1948 President Harry S. Truman confronted Witte with

a concrete labor-relations problem. Because of troubles between private contractors and unions in the nation's atomic energy installations at Oak Ridge, Tennessee, Truman created a President's Commission on Labor Relations in Atomic Energy Installations. To it he appointed Witte and New York attorney Aaron Horvitz, with William Davis once more as chairman.

Earlier a committee consisting of former War Labor Board Chairman George W. Taylor, former Wisconsin law dean Lloyd Garrison, and Undersecretary of Labor David Morse had taken the structural approach, and recommended that to establish uniformity the government should dictate many of the terms of labor at the installations. Both contractors and unions had opposed that course, the A.F. of L. especially objecting to having its terms made uniform with those of the C.I.O. Negotiations had broken down to the point where they threatened to stop vital defense work. There was abroad, in the Joint Congressional Committee on Atomic Energy and elsewhere, an assumption that compulsory arbitration might be necessary. Davis, Witte, and Horvitz moved quickly to reverse the drift away from collective bargaining. Instead of special legislation or procedures to guarantee absolutely that there should be no strike, they proceeded on a principle that Davis had enunciated in War Labor Board days: if the governmental machinery could somehow be kept "behind a bush," the parties might actually bargain their differences.[28]

The three men could not of course keep government entirely off the scene, but they used it with more voluntarism and flexibility than even the War Labor Board had managed. Their strategy was to refuse to set up rigid, predictable avenues of appeal, on grounds that the parties, when it appeared to be to their advantage, would quickly take recourse to these rather than bargain in good faith. Recommending that the Atomic Energy Commission keep interference with terms of employment at a minimum, they insisted that management and unions accept moral responsibility for keeping the plants operating. Both parties were to give semivoluntary pledges not to change conditions of employment without prior agreement, and, before any strike or lockout, to give a special Atomic Energy Labor Relations Panel time to make recommendations. The panel would not intervene automatically; it would have absolute flexibility both as to whether it would intervene, and if so whether and what to recommend. Its one limitation was that it could not arbitrate with compulsion. If its conciliatory efforts failed, it, like the War Labor Board, could only refer the case to the President. Contractors and unions, despite strong reservations, agreed to accept the plan if Davis, Witte, and Horwitz comprised the new panel.[29] In June, 1949, Truman appointed them, and Witte served until Dwight Eisenhower took over the presidential office and accepted his routine resignation early in 1953.

The Davis Panel was not quite the "standby" agency which would "never have to go into action," as Witte had initially hoped. But in its three and a half years of life it intervened officially in only fifty-nine cases, although it offered unofficial counsel in many others. It found itself making recommendations at an increasing rate, but it gave first emphasis to mediation, as Witte had long advocated. At the end of its existence it could boast that despite some work stoppages none had occurred in facilities considered vital to national defense.[30] Congress did not find it necessary to pass no-strike legislation. The Davis Panel vindicated the policy of maximum voluntarism and flexible structure even in the most sensitive of industrial relations.

While he worked to avoid excessive legal structure, Witte continued in the postwar period to help institutionalize collective bargaining and develop its forms. He often served as a mediator or arbitrator, taking cases through either public agencies such as the Federal Mediation and Conciliation Service or private groups such as the American Arbitration Association. With his writing and advice on private health and welfare plans he helped collective bargaining expand rapidly in the area of fringe benefits. In the 1950's, as economic advisor to both the United Auto Workers and the American Motors Corporation, he aided the movement for a guaranteed annual wage that resulted in company-financed unemployment benefits supplementing those from states. He was one of the seven original members of a United Auto Workers watchdog, the Public Review Board. At Wisconsin he helped to form one of the many industrial relations centers that were springing up on university campuses, and served as chairman of the faculty committee overseeing it. Nationally, in 1946 and 1947 he participated in organizing an Industrial Relations Research Association and became its first president, despite (as he said) a "high and holy" promise to Mrs. Witte not to take on the extra work.[31] The group wanted a man "nationally known and universally respected, someone about whom there is no element of controversy."[32] They found Witte sufficiently prominent, suitably lacking in color, and unable to say no.

Mediation work suited well Witte's approach of eschewing theory and deciding matters on immediate considerations. There were no objective standards, he believed, for the mediator or arbitrator to apply. Disputants in labor conflicts cared nothing for economic theory, and they used statistical arguments only for argument's sake. So he advocated such rules as New York State Board of Mediation Chairman Arthur Meyer's advice to work within the parties' "area of expectation," or George W. Taylor's principle simply of finding "what it takes to settle a strike." In a field heavily studded with lawyers, Witte warned against a legalistic style, reminding his colleagues that the parties had "to continue to live with each other, no matter who wins the arbitration case." Although he was among the most successful practitioners, Witte had few firmly conceptualized ideas to offer industrial mediators and arbitrators beyond such rules of thumb. To him their practice was "an art" that required "an understanding of human nature," "an 'uncanny' ability to grasp the real situation amid pretenses and arguments," and "imagination and ingenuity for finding acceptable bases of settlement." "Problems of human relations," he firmly believed, "cannot be solved by formulas."[33]

At one level Witte helped develop rationality and structure in collective bargaining. Yet he did not seek the absolute guarantees and assurances in law that he sought for social welfare. In social welfare the goal was security, and he believed that the institutions to achieve that goal had to be compulsory and quite rigid. In labor relations the goal was co-operation between groups and between classes, and for that goal he thought voluntarism and flexibility more important than clear structure and legal sanction. Practical and pragmatic as he was, the concepts he worked to institutionalize in one field did not have necessarily to resemble closely those in another.

11

Professor Witte

WITTE'S DECISION TO JOIN THE University of Wisconsin faculty in 1933, at the age of forty-six, proved to be a decision for life. Thereafter he left the Madison campus for his intermittent government service, and for academic assignments of up to one semester at the University of Washington, at Harvard, and elsewhere; but he always returned, despite frequent offers of positions carrying great prestige and high salaries. Of all offers, a proposal in 1946 that he become Commissioner of Labor Statistics tempted him most. "If I were younger," he declared, "I would jump at the opportunity." But after his War Labor Board service in Washington both he and Mrs. Witte yearned for Madison. Also, at fifty-nine, Witte thought that he had "reached an age where I must do the research and writing I have planned if I am ever to do so."[1] Such considerations, plus the broader ideal of an academic career in the institution and the tradition of John R. Commons, kept him tied firmly to the university. But although his academic life remained the base for his larger career, it contained elements of tragedy. And the tragedy fed on the same ingredients that made his reformism cautious.

The ideal of writing books intrigued Witte not only in 1946; it also attracted him to the university in 1933, and stayed with him to the end of his life. Yet by 1933 he had already published the single major work of his lifetime, *The Government in Labor Disputes*. The subsequent success of that book was ambiguous.

It was a substantial work which demonstrated Witte's capacity for extensive research and mastery of detail, with a writing style that was logical and lucid, though hardly vivacious. No less a commentator than Felix Frankfurter, who knew the subject thoroughly and of course had worked with Witte on the Norris-La Guardia bill, had nothing but praise for Witte's book. Other reviewers generally concurred, although Frankfurter's junior colleague at the Harvard Law School, James Landis, noted that "the style of the writer [was] somewhat flat." Despite the book's favorable reviews, however, the Norris-La Guardia Act, coming almost simultaneously, corrected many of the problems Witte had discussed and killed most of the interest in the subject. Within a dozen years the volume's sales had dropped to near zero, and the publisher let it pass out of print.[2]

Witte always hoped to publish other books, but circumstances and shifts in his interests seemed always to intervene. In 1933 he contemplated a work on American labor legislation, a logical sequel to his 1932 volume. But the call to Washington in 1934 shifted his interest to social security. Thereupon he began to think of a book to popularize the new economic security system. While he did not wish, "like a 'Moses', to set forth the law from the mountain top," he hoped "to make converts for the social security program, particularly among business men." But before he got to writing that book, the public demonstrated that in general it had already accepted social security. So in the late 1930's he shifted his plans to a history of social security and a social security textbook. But then came his expanding work of industrial mediation, including his World War II assignments in Detroit and Washington, and he again delayed the writing of his books. After the war he thought of a volume on "Government and Business," the subject of one of his university courses, then dropped it in favor of his projected works on social security.[3] But just as he had never finished his bachelor's or his master's thesis as a student, as a professor he let a busy schedule of teaching, lecturing, mediating, sabbaticals, and several extended trips abroad displace his writing.

Witte had a weakness for consenting to immediate tasks, and

persons and institutions with work to be done exploited his willing nature. Perhaps none interfered with his writing more than
the department of economics at his own university. It was a
department constantly torn by factionalism, so that once after
reading a professor's contemptuous satire of state legislators Witte
responded sardonically that an intelligent legislator might de-
scribe universities just as humorously and just as critically. In
1936 the department selected him as its chairman, and he served
until 1941. While he was away for his wartime work the dissen-
sions worsened, and at war's end his colleagues insisted that he
was the one man behind whom they could unite. Confessing
privately that it was "probably a foolish thing to do," he yielded
to their importunities, and served from 1946 to 1953. Of his
twenty years as full-time professor, he held the departmental
chairmanship for twelve.[4]

Yet even the chairmanship and like duties did not fully account for his inability to produce books. Actually he wrote
voluminously, but in shorter stretches. After the mid-1930's, except for the war years, he normally produced six or eight articles
per year, besides numerous lectures, book chapters, pamphlets,
and booklets. A few of his writings found their way into a half-
dozen languages from French to Japanese and Indonesian. In
1936 he composed a lengthy manuscript on the workings of the
Committee on Economic Security and on the committee's program in Congress, later published posthumously as *The Development of the Social Security Act*. In 1951 the University of Puerto
Rico published a series of addresses he had given there as a book
entitled *Five Lectures on Social Security*.[5]

Witte's writing revealed his habit of thinking particularistical-
ly. He could treat limited, immediate problems and subjects
incisively and lucidly, but he did not conceptualize in a grand
manner. Even his *The Government in Labor Disputes* and *The
Development of the Social Security Act*, though each possessed
an internal consistency, were organized by compiling information paragraph by paragraph and section by section, rather than
building on a framework of large central theses. Witte did not

write books partly because his mind was not attuned to the large topics and the broad questions that writing full-length works entailed. Had Witte published nothing, of course, he would still have made his contribution to reform. But he wanted to produce books, so much so that there was an almost tragic cast to his failure to do so. For it was not merely the press of work and circumstances that prevented him; it was also the particularism that lay at the center of his reformism.

Equally poignant in his academic career was Witte's sense of alienation from fellow economists. Scarcely had he returned to the university in 1933 when he published a spirited review in *The New Republic* of a book in which seven Harvard professors of the classical, laissez-faire school of economics criticized New Deal recovery measures. Witte ridiculed the seven for their certainty that they "*are* economists, not politicians," and their assurance that they "know their science well enough to know that there *are* economic laws." Under the title "Seven Economists Dancing on the Point of a Needle," he dismissed their deductive method of reasoning with a quotation from the German economic historian Werner Sombart that such economics was "closer to medieval scholasticism than almost any other intellectual activity in the modern world." Nobody could expect government policy makers to pay much heed to such rarefied economics.[6]

Concern for questions of public policy over theory, indeed a contempt for theory as irrelevant to public policy, was the key to Witte's alienation. "Theorizing when there is fighting to do does not appeal to me," he once declared of social security. As time passed and proponents of the broad economic growth theories of John Maynard Keynes replaced classicists in many chairs of economics, Witte remained unsympathetic. With professional realism he encouraged young economists to study Keynes's ideas so long as they were in vogue, but he professed not to understand them when he read them.[7] Unquestionably he underestimated the impact that economic theories such as those of Keynes would have on public policy in the long run.

It was by his preoccupation with questions of public policy

that Witte, in his academic career, best reflected the tradition of Commons. As a teacher he offered courses and seminars on Wisconsin's economic problems, the legislative process, and general problems of state government; on labor problems, labor legislation, government and labor, and collective bargaining; a regular course on social security; broad seminars on general governmental economic problems and the role of the government in the economy; and, because no other faculty member was available to teach it in 1933, a "Government and Business" course which he liked so well that he continued it until he retired in 1957. The range of Witte's subject matter was so broad that students often could elect to take their credits for his courses in political science, law, or social work; but it also had cohesion, for all of it dealt with aspects of public policy.[8] Witte had neither Commons' erudite grasp of great ideas in the history of economic thought, nor his mentor's ability to move beyond the practical problem, through sustained, tenacious thought, to overarching ideas. Consequently he never tried to develop his institutionalism into an extensive, profoundly conceptualized system, as Commons had tried in his later writings. But with his direct concern for public policy he, along with other colleagues, especially labor economist Selig Perlman, kept the institutionalist tradition alive at Wisconsin.

Witte's feeling of alienation from his profession approached its peak in the late 1940's. Twice, in 1945 and 1949, he was nominated for vice-president of the American Economics Association, and then not elected. The rejections gave color to his complaint that identifying himself as an institutionalist seemed to many in his profession "equivalent to admitting that I am not an economist at all." In the early 1950's Witte began to fight back, most vigorously in a 1953 address to a Central New York Economic Conference, which he published in *The Southern Economic Journal* in 1954. Emphasizing that institutionalists focused on questions of public economic policy, Witte declared that Commons' scholarship had truly represented "political economy," the older term for the field, rather than "economics." He admitted that institutionalists had never fully developed "a complete, self-contained, independent theory of the price mechanism or the functioning of the economic system." Rather than a "connected body of thought," institutionalism was "a method of approaching economic problems." It sought not so much to explain all economic phenomena as to find solutions to "particular problems of immediate significance."[9]

In seeking practical solutions, Witte continued, institutionalists did not confine themselves to what the more orthodox classed as economic data, but freely included "social, psychological, historical, legal, political, administrative, and even technical" considerations. Instead of thinking in terms of "timeless and placeless" economic laws, they assumed that institutions were "manmade and changeable," and therefore probed "the institutional background of the time, place, and situation." To the charge that such an approach made those of his persuasion descriptive, not analytical, Witte replied that it made them "generally inductive rather than deductive." They had "a great regard for statistics and field studies," and they were usually pragmatists, studying the facts not for their own sake but to make "a better world to live in." In that pursuit institutionalists did use reason and develop theories even though they had no all-inclusive economic models. Of their number, for instance, Wesley Mitchell had developed an understanding of the business cycle, Thorstein Veblen of noneconomic motives in economic behavior, Commons of industrial relations, and Perlman of organized labor. And whether they were institutionalists or not, Witte insisted, economists in government and other practical assignments used the institutional approach rather than classroom theory.[10]

Witte closed his defense with a plea that his minority views be given a larger place in the teaching of economics and generally in the profession.[11] Shortly after his vigorous defense appeared in print, a committee of the American Economics Association accorded him the profession's highest honor. It nominated him for president of the association for the year 1956, an action that was by custom tantamount to election. Although Witte thought he had detected a renewed interest in institutional economics even before 1953, he professed complete surprise at his selection, declaring that he "had no more thought of being president of the AEA than I might of flying under my own power." In fact, he mused, "I have often doubted whether I am an economist at all—very certainly I am something of a late-comer as I spent half my active life in public positions." But he accepted the position, as an honor to himself, the Wisconsin department, and the tradition of institutional economics.[12]

In December, 1956, seizing the opportunity that his presidential address to the association provided, Witte once again defended his kind of economics. The founders of the American Economics Association in 1886 had had as one of their original purposes "the historical and statistical study of actual conditions," he pointed out, and as individuals economists had always addressed themselves to questions of public policy. Academically, however, they had too often left the study of government to political scientists, treating government as an outside interference in economic life. Thus they failed to explore government's positive economic roles as rule maker, umpire, definer of property rights, financier, and producer, purchaser, and purveyor of goods and services. Too often economists wanted to limit themselves to the so-called strictly economic questions that they could treat exactly, mathematically, "scientifically." Economists had to be scientific, Witte argued, if the word meant completely honest and impartial. But when they resorted to language that not even he as a colleague in the profession could understand—much less practical-minded business, labor, and government officials—they only made themselves ineffectual. As his own criterion for fruitful economic research, Witte suggested that the economist should choose a problem in which he was genuinely interested, but also one that reflected the belief that men could better their circumstances and improve their institutions. After another plea for tolerance among the economists, Witte closed with words from Theodore Roosevelt. "It is not the critic who counts . . . ," he averred. "The credit belongs to the man who is actually in the arena; . . . who knows the great enthusiasms, the great devotions, and spends himself in a worthy cause."[13]

Witte's two major expositions of institutionalism were calls to economists to come back to the world of everyday realities, not the grand attempts Commons had made to provide fresh, overarching postulates about economic behavior. In his antitheoretical approach he ignored any distinction between academic and practical functions, and the possibility that the freedom of the classroom might best be used to pursue that truth which comes only by abstraction. He too easily assumed that the human mind could readily grasp raw facts and data and find practical meaning in them, with little systematic effort to delineate the patterns in the reality that the data reflected. Witte could grasp and find meaning in much larger doses of raw data than could most men. But even he acted on an assumption—*i.e.*, that the policies and reforms he advocated would lead to betterment and progress—without really examining and proving that assumption. Fortunately, in his usual style he did not follow his premises to their ultimate conclusion. He admitted that his call to draw facts from all fields was "a well-nigh impossible prescription . . . in this complex age," and he was careful to concede that there was room for theoreticians within the profession.[14] With those qualifications, his utterances added up to an appeal for a better balance in a profession growing increasingly esoteric.

At the close of Witte's presidential address the economists greeted his remarks with a standing ovation—reputedly a tribute with few precedents in the history of the association.[15] The honor was for a man and an address that were full of common sense, however, not for any bold foray among uncharted ideas; it had about it the ring of veneration, rather than of men enlisting for battle. For institutionalism as a definable school of economic thought was fast passing from the scene. Witte would retire in 1957, Perlman in 1959, and even the Wisconsin department would virtually abandon the faith. Thus Witte's uneasiness in his profession was more than alienation; it was prescience coupled with a note of genuine tragedy.

Unable to produce his hoped-for books, an honored devotee of a diminishing school of thought, Witte did not make his reputation as an academician. Neither did he make it from any personal flair. With no unfriendliness, John Newhouse of the *Wisconsin State Journal* saw him a few months after his presidential address as "a little man," not handsome, bald, "of the type that you could easily lose in a crowd." He was not quick with a quip; neither did he win renown by being a prophet in the critical, dissenting style. He was ready with platitudes describing the American government as "the best on earth" or the Constitution as "the finest document ever conceived by man"—although (very crucially) he did not, by such utterances, endorse individualism and laissez faire, as did most of his contemporaries.[16] Without monumental scholarship, personal mystique, or intellectual acerbity, Witte nevertheless made his reputation. In the course of his life the son of Ebenezer won appreciation from presidents and other high American officials, and, on occasion, even from foreigners.

And from students. However ambiguous his successes within the economics profession, Witte drew praise from those eager to learn. In the classroom he was not brilliant with oratory and originality, but he delivered vast amounts of high-quality factual information through his lectures and through the up-to-date mimeographed materials for which he became famous. One student, Lloyd Ulman, later a professor at Berkeley, found his instruction so full of substance that fifteen years later he professed still to feel an ache in his wrist from taking notes. Beyond facts, Witte, like Commons before him, transmitted his outlook. Of his teaching William Knowles declared, after he had become Director of the Industrial Relations Study Center at Puerto Rico's Inter-American University, "The Witte point of view . . . usually compromised the liberal goal by what was politically feasible." It "took the heat and emotion out of the issue, relied heavily upon statistical facts, concentrated on the immediate problem and avoided ideological issues." To Knowles, study under Witte provided a valuable lesson "on how to approach any socio-economic problem." Witte drew praise from students also for his personal commitment to public service as an ideal and his own personification of that ideal, praise that came too spontaneously and frequently to have been mere rhetoric. In a moment of discouragement in 1937 one student remembered one of Witte's lectures, and wrote of her "need of one of your inspiring talks on the good to be done in this world, and the opportunities to do it." Always deeply conscientious, Witte insisted on grading papers and otherwise giving students personal attention, even when he was very busy and might have delegated the tasks to assistants. Students especially appreciated his liberality with his ample research files and his time—and occasionally even his money, for despite the modesty of his financial resources he sometimes made personal loans to needy young scholars. Had he collected more honoraria he would have had more money, but in keeping with the Wisconsin Idea of the university in service to the state, he refused to accept payment for his frequent lectures to audiences in Wisconsin. It was for his generosity of spirit, more than for his academic ideas, that Witte elicited extraordinary praise.[17]

The warmth which Witte evoked expanded far beyond the University of Wisconsin. In the spring of 1957 came Witte's final semester of teaching, and former students, colleagues, and friends arranged a two-day "Government and Labor" symposium at Wisconsin to express their feelings. The speakers reflected the range of Witte's accomplishments. They included American Motors vice-president Edward Cushman; Milwaukee labor leader Jacob Friedrich; labor mediator William H. Davis; Wilbur Cohen, who had gone to Washington in 1934 as Witte's protégé and would eventually become Secretary of Health, Education, and Welfare; United States Senator Wayne Morse, who had once been a student in Witte's classes; and former Secretary of Labor Frances Perkins. Their remarks ranged from Cushman's giving Witte a key to Detroit for his wartime mediation work there, to Miss Perkins' reminiscences of the man "of strength, a miracle of intelligence, imagination, and flexibility," who in 1934 "drove a team of wild horses" to produce the social security program in six short months. Former President Harry S. Truman, recalling Witte's labor mediation in atomic energy installations, sent congratulations. Ronald Haughton, Director of the Institute of Industrial Relations at Wayne State University, and formerly one of Witte's favorite students, presented gifts totaling $2,800 from many well-wishers. Three hundred attended a testimonial banquet, and many others were among the 260 who wrote their sentiments and had them bound into a volume for Witte and his family to cherish.[18] Other honors—the presidency of the economics association and the Doctor of Laws degree that Marquette University conferred on Witte the following June— were professional. The symposium was intensely personal as well: Witte had been a success in his public life, and personally he was a man with many friends, and no enemies.

Witte had been an active lecturer and teacher too long to recede to his study upon retirement. At once he accepted a post as Distinguished Visiting Professor at Michigan State University for the academic year 1957–1958. At the year's end Loyola University conferred upon him a second honorary Doctor of Laws degree, a fitting recognition for a man who had worked in the field of legislation quite as much as in economics. Immediately thereafter he, with Mrs. Witte, made his fourth extended trip abroad, and then returned to Madison. Though emeritus, he resumed part-time teaching at the university, and continued it until his final sickness and death. Witte had always taken satisfaction in the fact that except for one illness in 1919 he rarely missed a day of work because of sickness, and few for any other reason. But he was aging, and his cardiovascular system was deteriorating. On January 11, 1959, a week after his seventy-second birthday, came his first severe warning—a heart attack. He recovered partially, and remained as active as he dared for another year, trying especially to get to his writing. But he had to submit to hospital confinement on several occasions. In February, 1960, a mild cerebral hemorrhage disabled him further. Again he tried to return to active life, and on April

13 he was in Sheboygan, Wisconsin, lecturing, as usual. There he again became ill. Soon after he got home he suffered a new, paralyzing cerebral attack. On May 20, after five weeks in a semicoma, he died.[19]

*   *   *   *   *

Thus passed a man who, without fanfare, had done more than his share of society's work. As a reformer Edwin E. Witte was a link between ideas and their realization, a practitioner who took what he found to be workable in abstract ideas and implemented it into laws and institutions. A social engineer, he directed his inventiveness towards working out the technical details of new legal and institutional structures. His genius lay there, rather than in conceiving radical new designs for the social order. As he designed institutions, he used blueprints that were compatible with what he understood to be prevailing American political and economic concepts. His education under Commons and his practical experience in government convinced him to take a reform course that was, in a progressive way, conservative. With his concern for the particular problem, for practicality, and for preserving American traditions, his role was commonsensical, circumspect, and cautious. Yet it was a crucial role, essential to the reform process. For without implementation and translation into working laws and institutions, reform ideas have no impact.

NOTES

CHAPTER 1

[1] Genealogical and other family documents in possession of Mrs. Florence Witte, Madison, Wis.; *Souvenir of the Centennial, Ebenezer Moravian Church,* (June 11–14, 1953); interview with Mrs. Herbert Kant, Dec. 17, 1963, Watertown, Wis.

[2] John R. Weinlick, "The Moravian Church: An Historical Sketch," in *Five Hundredth Anniversary Service of the Moravian Church Or Unitas Fratrum, 1457–1957* (The Moravian Church in America, March 3, 1957). Interviews with Mrs. Florence Witte, Nov. 15, 1963, Madison, Wis.; with Mrs. William Gehrke, Dec. 17, 1963, Watertown, Wis.; with Mrs. Clara Witte, Jan. 31, 1964, Madison, Wis.; with Henry Rabbach, Feb. 5, 1964, Watertown, Wis.; and with David Saposs, Sept. 8, 1964, Madison, Wis. (Saposs interview taped, with tape in the possession of the State Historical Society of Wisconsin, Madison, Wis.)

[3] Interviews with Mrs. Clara Witte and with Rabbach (cited note 2); and with Gerhard Trachte, Feb. 5, 1964, Watertown, Wis. Witte Diaries, in the Papers of Edwin E. Witte, State Historical Society of Wisconsin, Madison, Wis., IV, Dec. 24, 1909–Jan. 2, 1910, Feb. 19, 1910, and *passim.* Interviews with Herman Else, Feb. 5, 1964, Watertown, Wis.; with Mrs. Kant (cited note 1); with George Fischer, Dec. 6, 1963, Watertown, Wis.; and with Mrs. Florence Witte (cited note 2); *Souvenir of the Centennial, Ebenezer Moravian Church* (June 11–14, 1953); "Nachruf," *Watertown Weltbürger,* May 2, 1903; Town of Watertown Record Book, 1871–1906, pp. 105, 108, 182, 496. The quotation was from Rabbach.

[4] "New Schools to be Organized for Jefferson County," *The Watertown Gazette,* Nov. 8, 1901; interview with Trachte (cited note 3); "Population of Wisconsin by Minor Civil Divisions," *Census Bulletin No. 91* (Washington, July 9, 1891), 2, 8; John Henry Ott, ed., *Jefferson County, Wisconsin, and Its People, a Record of Settlement, Organization, Progress and Achievement* (Chicago, 1917), I, 72, 74–75, 153; Ralph Blumenfeld, *Home Town: Story of a Dream That Came True* (London, New York, 1944), 10, 7; *Watertown Gazette,* 1885–1905, *passim,* especially the Feb. 13, 1903, issue which was devoted to Watertown's progress, and "Watertown," Dec. 30, 1904.

[5] Interviews with Trachte (cited note 3); with Mrs. Gehrke (cited note 2); with Arthur Radtke, Dec. 17, 1963, Watertown Wis.; and with Fischer (cited note 3); Gilbert Greene to Witte, Apr. 18, n. y. (from internal evidence, 1946), box 10, Witte papers. "High Schools Debate," *The Watertown Gazette,* May 5, 1905; "High School Commencement Week a Busy One," *The Watertown Gazette,* June 30, 1905.

[6] Interviews with Fischer (cited note 3) and with Mrs. Kant (cited note 1).

[7] Witte Diaries, I, Oct. 6, 1905, and III, Oct. 7, 1909; interview with Douglas Anderson, July 16, 1963, Madison, Wis. (taped, with tape in the possession of the State Historical Society of Wisconsin, Madison, Wis.), tape 1.

[8] Witte Diaries, I, Sept. 26, Oct. 14, 15, Nov. 5, 8, 1905; II, Oct. 7, 15, 1906; and *passim.*

[9] Myron Utgard to author, Dec. 15, 1963. Witte Diaries, III, Nov. 13, 1909; V, Aug. 21–28, 1910; IV, Jan. 6, 1910; I, Oct. 9, 1905; and *passim.* Interviews with Mrs. Kant (cited note 1) and with Fischer (cited note 3).

[10] Witte Diaries, IV, June 4–Aug. 6, 1910; membership records, First Methodist Church, Madison, Wis. Witte to George Wehrwein, Oct. 14, 1938, box 4; Witte to Wilbur Cohen, Aug. 2, 1941, box 6; Witte to Kirtley Mather, Apr. 28, 1941, box 6; all in the Witte Papers.

[11] See, for instance, Witte, "Why Social Security—Does It Meet Our Problem?", address of June 18, 1940, box 258, Witte Papers; and Witte, "Public Policy on Economic Security," *Business Topics,* 5 (May, 1958), 7.

[12] Witte, "Opportunities for the Professionally Trained," remarks of Oct. 8, 1948, box 256, Witte Papers.

[13] For general description of the University of Wisconsin during the presidency of Charles R. Van Hise see Merle Curti and Vernon Carstensen, *The University of Wisconsin: A History, 1848–1925* (Madison, 1949), II, 3–122, and *passim;* and Maurice M. Vance, *Charles Richard Van Hise: Scientist Progressive* (Madison, 1960), 91–136.

[14] Interviews with Mrs. Gehrke (cited note 2) and with Trachte (cited note 3). Witte Diaries, I, Oct. 12, 22, Nov. 14, 1905; IV, Dec. 27, 1909, Jan. 1, Apr. 24, June 4–Aug. 6, 1910; V, Sept. 11, 1910; and *passim.* Witte to Carol Oetzel, Feb. 20, 1947, box 11, Witte Papers.

[15] Interviews with Saposs (cited note 2), tape 2; and with Anderson (cited note 7), tape 1. Myron Utgard to author, Dec. 15, 1963; Witte Diaries, *passim.*

[16] Interview with Saposs (cited note 2), tape 2; Witte to Clarence Blair, Jan. 13, 1930, correspondence files, Wisconsin Legislative Reference Bureau, Madison, Wis.; Curti and Carstensen, *The University of Wisconsin,* II, 500–02.

[17] Interview with Saposs (cited note 2), tape 2; Witte Diaries, V, Oct. 4, 1910.

[18] Witte Diaries, V, Oct. 10–21, 1910; VI, Oct. 27, 1910–June, 1911.

[19] Witte Diaries, IV, Apr. 25, 1910; V, Aug. 25, 28–Sept. 2, 5, 6, 1910; VI, Oct. 27–Nov. 20, 1910. Interview with Rabbach (cited note 2); records of Town of Watertown voting, *Wisconsin Blue Book*[s], 1888–1905. The evidence is contradictory as to the political views of Witte's father, but most probably he was a conservative Democrat.

[20] Witte Diaries, III, Nov. 8, Dec. 13, 1909; IV, Jan. 10, Apr. 5, June 4–Aug. 6, 1910; VI, Oct. 27–Nov. 20, 1910.

[21] "Hesperia Wins Joint Debate," *Daily Cardinal* (University of Wisconsin), Dec. 19, 1908; Witte Diaries, III, Dec. 10, 1909; interview with Anderson (cited note 7); *The 1910 Badger* (University of Wisconsin yearbook), XXIV, 101.

[22] Witte Diaries, III, Oct. 8, 1909; Myron Utgard to author, Dec. 15, 1963.

[23] Interview with Anderson (cited note 7); "Literary Societies," *Daily Cardinal* (University of Wisconsin), Mar. 24, 1906; Witte Diaries, VII; Witte to Mrs. Lucile McCarthy, Oct. 28, 1924, correspondence files, Wisconsin Legislative Reference Bureau, Madison, Wis.; Witte, "Institutional Economics as Seen by an Institutional Economist," *Southern Economic Journal,* 21 (Oct., 1954), 131; "Preparing for Joint Debate," *Daily Cardinal* (University of Wisconsin), Dec. 8, 1905; Witte Diaries, II, Oct. 22, Nov. 9, 1906.

[24] Interview with Saposs (cited note 2); "Hesperia Wins Joint Debate," *Daily Cardinal* (University of Wisconsin), Dec. 19, 1908. Witte Diaries, IV, Apr. 24, 1910; VI, Nov. 21–23, 1910. "Degrees Are Given to 577 Students," *Wisconsin State Journal* (Madison), June 23, 1909; "Commencement Oration, June 23, 1909: The Security for Industrial Peace" (Ms. in Witte's handwriting), box 255, Witte Papers; Witte, "The Role of the Courts in Labor Disputes" (unpublished Ph. D. dissertation, University of Wisconsin, 1927); Witte, *The Government in Labor Disputes* (New York and London, 1932). The Danbury hatters' court case was *Loewe v. Lawlor*, 208 U. S. 274, 28 Sup. Ct., 301 (1908).

[25] "What Socialism Aims at," *Jefferson County Union* (Ft. Atkinson, Wis.), July 30, 1909. Witte Diaries, III, Nov. 19, 1909; IV, Apr. 28–June 4, 1910.

[26] Witte Diaries, IV, June 4–Aug. 6, 1910; V, Oct. 13, 1910; III, Nov. 19, Dec. 21, 1910; II, Oct. 21, 1906; VI, n. d.

[27] Witte Diaries, III, Oct. 15, 1909; IV, Feb. 17, 21, Apr. 27, 28–June 4, June 4–Aug. 6, 1910; V, Oct. 13, 1910; and *passim*.

[28] Myron Utgard to author, Dec. 15, 1963; transcripts of Edwin Witte's grades, University of Wisconsin files; *The 1910 Badger* (cited note 21); unsigned letter to H. E. Hoagland, Aug. 3, 1916, in the John R. Commons Papers, State Historical Society of Wisconsin, Madison, Wis. Witte Diaries, III, Oct. 15, Nov. 2, Dec. 21, 1909; IV, Feb. 6, 17, 1910; V, Sept. 28, 1910; and *passim*.

[29] Witte Diaries, IV, Feb. 6, 1910, and *passim*; Witte to Wm. Leiserson, Jan. 12, 1910, Witte file, in the William Leiserson Papers, State Historical Society of Wisconsin, Madison, Wis.

[30] Witte Diaries, IV, June 4–Aug. 6, Apr. 21, Feb. 6, 1910; VI, n. d.; Witte, "Institutional Economics as Seen by an Institutional Economist" (cited note 23), 131.

CHAPTER 2

[1] For insight into Commons' personality, see especially his autobiography, *Myself* (New York, 1934; Madison, 1963). For exposure to his intellect see especially his *Institutional Economics* (New York, 1934). Witte, "John R. Commons as a Teacher, Economist, and Public Servant," remarks of Oct. 10, 1950, box 257, Witte Papers.

[2] Witte to Kenneth Parsons, May 14, 1945, box 9, Witte Papers.

[3] For a summary of Ely's doctrines see Theron F. Schlabach, "An Aristocrat on Trial: The Case of Richard T. Ely," *Wisconsin Magazine of History*, 47 (Winter, 1963–1964), 148–51. For a Commons statement resembling Ely's thought, see Commons, *The Christian Minister and Sociology* (Publications of the Christian Social Union No. 4; undated, but copy in Wisconsin State Historical Library bears in pencil the plausible date 1892). For the best concise statement of Commons' theory of institutional economics, see Commons, "Institutional Economics," *American Economic Review*, 21 (Dec. 1931), 647–58; for the full treatise see Commons, *Institutional Economics*. For commentary on Commons' ideas see Kenneth Parsons, "John R. Commons' Point of View," *Journal of Land and Public Utility Economics*, 18 (Aug., 1942), 245–56, reprinted in Commons, *The Economics of Collective Action* (New York, 1950), 341–75.

[4] Commons, "Institutional Economics," 648; Commons, *Institutional Economics*, 586, 115; Commons, *Legal Foundations of Capitalism* (New York, 1939), vii.

[5] Parsons, "John R. Commons' Point of View," 374–75, 343–44.

[6] Commons, "Institutional Economics," 652; Commons, *Institutional Economics*, 330–33.

[7] Commons, *Myself*, 74, 93; Commons, *Legal Foundations of Capitalism*, 6; Commons, "Institutional Economics," 648, 650.

[8] Commons, quoted in Lafayette G. Harter, *John R. Commons: His Assault on Laissez Faire* (Corvallis, Ore., 1962), 165; Commons, "Karl Marx and Samuel Gompers," *Political Science Quarterly*, 41 (June, 1926), 284.

[9] Commons, *Legal Foundations of Capitalism*, 6; Commons, "Marx Today: Capitalism and Socialism," *Atlantic Monthly*, 136 (Nov., 1925), 684–685; Commons, *Industrial Goodwill* (New York, 1919), 37–43.

[10] Standard Oil Co. of New Jersey *v.* United States, 221 U. S. 1 (1911); Commons, *Institutional Economics*, 343–44, 330–33, 683; Commons, *Industrial Goodwill*, 30–31.

[11] Commons, *The Christian Minister and Sociology* (cited note 3); Commons, *Institutional Economics*, 741–42.

[12] Commons, "Marx Today," 3–14; Commons, *Institutional Economics*, 742.

[13] Loewe *v.* Lawlor, 208 U. S. 274 (1908); Commons, *Institutional Economics*, 522–23, 394.

[14] Commons, *Industrial Goodwill*, 1–19, 30–31.

[15] Commons, "Marx Today" (cited note 9), 6.

[16] Witte to Walter Hempstead, Feb. 5, 1932, correspondence files, Wisconsin Legislative Reference Bureau, Madison, Wis.

[17] Commons, *The Industrial Commission of Wisconsin: Its Organization and Methods* (Industrial Commission of Wisconsin, n. d.; copy in Wisconsin Legislative Reference Bureau Library bears the plausible date 1913), 4–22. The original Wisconsin workmen's compensation law was Chapter 50, Laws of Wisconsin, 1911, now embodied in Wisconsin Statutes, Sec. 102; the "safe place" law was Chapter 485, Laws of Wisconsin, 1911, now Wisconsin Statutes, Sec. 101.06. See also Arthur Altmeyer, *The Industrial Commission of Wisconsin: A Case Study in Labor Law Administration* (Madison, 1932), especially 123–125, 171; and Commons and John B. Andrews, *Principles of Labor Legislation* (New York, 1916), especially 443–453.

[18] Witte, "Work Done in Political Economy," document, May 4, 1915, in the Richard T. Ely Papers, State Historical Society of Wisconsin, Madison, Wis.; *Liability Insurance Rates* (Bulletin of the Industrial Commission of Wisconsin, Vol. 1, No. 6), 289–99; Altmeyer, *The Industrial Commission of Wisconsin*, 294.

[19] Interview with David J. Saposs, Sept. 8, 1964, at the State Historical Society of Wisconsin, Madison, Wis. (taped, with tapes in the possession of the Society).

[20] *Antitrust Legislation* (63d Cong., 3d Sess.), H. R. Report No. 627, Pt. 3; for evidence that Witte wrote the report see Witte to Alpheus Mason, Mar. 3, 1933, box 1, Witte Papers.

[21] Remarks of John M. Nelson, *Congressional Record*, 51 (63d Cong., 3d Sess.), Pt. 9, p. 9166; *Antitrust Legislation* (cited note 20).

[22] Witte, "Preliminary Report upon Studies on Trade Union Law," United States Commission on Industrial Relations files, Record Group 174, National Archives, Washington, D. C. (hereinafter cited as CIR files).

[23] Commons to Witte, Nov. 11, 1913, in the John R. Commons Papers, State Historical Society of Wisconsin, Madison, Wis.

[24] For a list of Witte's reports, see Witte entry in the checklist of investigators' reports, CIR files. Witte's main report was "Injunctions in Labor Disputes," Feb. 27, 1915, CIR files (a second copy, lacking Appendix A, is in the possession of the State Historical Society of Wisconsin, Madison, Wis.). Witte, "A Partial Draft of the Labor Disputes Act," Feb. 3, 1914; Witte, "Speech," Feb. 3, 1914; Witte, "Injunctions in Labor Disputes," Feb. 27, 1915; all in CIR files.

[25] Harter, *John R. Commons*, 156, 138, 147.

[26] *Industrial Relations: Final Report and Testimony Submitted to Congress by the Commission on Industrial Relations* (64th Cong., 1st Sess.) Senate Doc. No. 415, Vol. I, pp. 17–269, especially pp. 90–92, 214.

[27] Commons and Andrews, *Principles of Labor Legislation*, 91–124; for evidence that Witte wrote this section see Witte to Nathan Katz, Dec. 26, 1926, and Witte to John Landesco, Dec. 12, 1927, box 1, Witte Papers. Commons, David J. Saposs, Helen Sumner, E. B. Mittleman, H. E. Hoagland, John B. Andrews, and Selig Perlman, *History of Labour in the United States* (New York, 1918), I, xi; II, 504, n. 92.

[28] "U. W. Economist Chosen to Investigate Labor Hours," *Milwaukee Journal*, June 1, 1916; Industrial Commission of Wisconsin, *Report on Allied Functions for the Two Years Ending June 30, 1917*, 44–47.

[29] Unsigned letter to H. E. Hoagland, Dec. 12, 1913, Commons Papers.

[30] Interviews with Mrs. Florence Witte, Apr. 15, 1964, and June 8, 1965, Madison, Wis.; Witte to Wm. Leiserson, Oct. 10, 1915, Witte file, in the William Leiserson Papers, State Historical Society of Wisconsin, Madison, Wis.

[31] Interviews with Mrs. Hazel Rasmussen Kuehn, Oct. 30, 1963, Monona Village, Wis.; with John Dorney, May 16, 1965, Clintonville, Wis.; and with Mrs. Florence Witte (cited note 30).

[32] Witte to Mrs. Witte, Aug. 4, 19, 1931, documents in the possession of Mrs. Witte, Madison, Wis.

[33] Interviews with Mrs. Florence Witte (cited note 30); Mrs. Margaret Witte Weeks to author, June 27, 1966; interview with Mrs. John Witte, July 3, 1966, Ft. Atkinson, Wis.

[34] Witte to Mrs. Witte, July 25, June 24, July 12, 1931, documents in the possession of Mrs. Florence Witte, Madison, Wis. Witte to John Witte, July 5, n. y. (from internal evidence, 1935), on microfilm; Witte to Wilbur Cohen, Oct. 14, 1938, box 4; Witte to Robert Salzstein, Oct. 5, 1939, box 5; Witte to Ronald Haughton, May 4, 1946, box 10; all in the Witte Papers. Also interviews with Mrs. Florence Witte (cited note 30).

[35] Witte to Richard Ely, June 26, Aug. 24, 1916, box 293, Witte Papers; Commons to Ely, Oct. 5, 1916, and Ely to Commons, Oct. 11, 1916, box 105, Ely Papers.

[36] Witte to Commons, Oct. 12, 1916; Witte to Ely, Dec. 28, 1916; box 293, Witte Papers. "Few Changes in State Politics," *Wisconsin State Journal* (Madison), Dec. 31, 1916.

[37] Witte to Commons, July 4, 1944, box 9, Witte Papers.

CHAPTER 3

[1] Arthur J. Altmeyer, *The Industrial Commission of Wisconsin: A Case Study in Labor Law Administration* (Madison, 1932), 105–09, 126.

[2] Minutes of the Industrial Commission of Wisconsin (unpublished documents in the offices of the Industrial Commission, Madison, Wis.), II (March 30, 1922), 386; "State of Wisconsin Before the Industrial Commission of Wisconsin," being a "Petition of Wisconsin Federation of Labor, Milwaukee Council of Social Agencies, and Wisconsin Consumers League for a hearing and determination as to the hours of labor of women," typewritten Ms., June 29, 1917, file C1384.2, correspondence of the Industrial Commission of Wisconsin, at the offices of the Industrial Commission, Madison, Wis. (hereinafter cited as IC correspondence); Altmeyer, *The Industrial Commission of Wisconsin*, 192–95. Material in file 1384.3; "In the Matter of the Petition of Russell Brothers for Rescinding, Can-

celling and Vacating General Order No. 6095 of the Industrial Commission," Jan.
31, 1922, file C387; Witte, "Recent British Reports Upon Desirable Limitation
of Hours of Labor," April 4, 1917; IC correspondence. Industrial Commission
of Wisconsin, *Report on Allied Functions*, 1917, p. 33.

[3] Industrial Commission of Wisconsin, *Report*[s] *on Allied Functions;* 1918, pp.
36–39; 1919, p. 37; 1922, pp. 31–33.

[4] G. H. Cook to Tracy Copp, Dec. 15, 1917, file C1384.5; "Before the Industrial
Commission of Wisconsin," Jan. 26, 1918, file C1384.6; Witte to Henry Ohl, Feb. 6,
1918, file C1384.6; J. J. Handley to Geo. Hambrecht, Feb. 2, 1918, file C1384.6;
Tracy Copp to Witte, Dec. 14, 1917, file C1384.5; Tracy Copp to G. H. Cook,
Dec. 14, 1917, file C1384.5; IC correspondence. The Industrial Commission of
Wisconsin, *Report on Allied Functions,* 1918, p. 36. "Women Unlikely to Aid on
Street Cars," *The Milwaukee Free Press,* May 19, 1918, Pt. 1, p. 5.

[5] Industrial Commission Minutes, I (Mar. 13, 1918), 106.

[6] The Industrial Commission of Wisconsin, *Report on Allied Functions,* 1920,
pp. 57–65; Witte to Ekern, July 19, 1924, correspondence of the Wisconsin Legislative Reference Library, Wisconsin Legislative Reference Bureau, Madison, Wis.
(hereafter cited as LRL correspondence); The Industrial Commission of Wisconsin,
Report[s] *on Allied Functions,* 1926, pp. 40–41, and 1928, p. 44. The new "oppressive" wage law was Chapter 176, Laws of Wisconsin, 1925.

[7] Witte, "The Growing Role of Employment Security," *Employment Security
Review,* 25 (June, 1958), 24–27; Witte to R. D. Scoon, Feb. 16, 1938, box 4,
Witte Papers. John B. Densmore to Geo. Hambrecht, Feb. 20, 1918, file C597;
material in files C597 and C597.5; IC correspondence.

[8] Witte to Wm. Leiserson, Dec. 22, 1921, Witte file, in the William Leiserson
Papers, State Historical Society of Wisconsin, Madison, Wis.

[9] Witte to R. D. Scoon, Feb. 16, 1938, box 4, Witte Papers; Witte, "What's
Ahead in Employment Security," address of Oct. 9, 1940, box 258, Witte Papers.

[10] Isaac M. Rubinow, "Health Insurance: The Spread of the Movement," *The
Survey,* 36 (July 15, 1916), 407; Altmeyer, *The Industrial Commission of Wisconsin,*
26; Isaac M. Rubinow, *Social Insurance, with Special Reference to American Conditions* (New York, 1913), 181–82; *Liability Insurance Rates,* Bulletins of the
Industrial Commission of Wisconsin, Vol. 1, No. 6 (Dec. 20, 1912), 280–92.

[11] Witte, "Treble Compensation for Injured Children," *The American Labor
Legislation Review,* 13 (June, 1923), 123–29; Altmeyer, *The Industrial Commission
of Wisconsin,* 26–30, 63–64, 59; Witte, John Callahan, E. L. Philip, "State of Wisconsin, Plan of Cooperation," June 20, 1920, IC correspondence; Witte to Karl
Ashburn, Aug. 6, 1938, box 4, Witte Papers.

[12] Witte, "The Theory of Workmen's Compensation," *The American Labor Legislation Review,* 20 (Dec., 1930), 411–18.

[13] *Ibid.*

[14] John H. Leek, *Legislative Reference Work: A Comparative Study* (Philadelphia, 1925), 46ff.

[15] "Reply to Open Letter from C. P. Cary," unidentified clipping consisting of a
letter from Howard Ohm to Cary, box 108, Witte Papers; M. G. Toepel, "The
Legislative Reference Library: Serving Wisconsin," *Wisconsin Law Review,* 1951
(Jan., 1951), 114–24; Edward A. Fitzpatrick, *McCarthy of Wisconsin* (Morningside
Heights, N. Y., 1944), 41–42, 48–52; Leek, *Legislative Reference Work,* 58–59; Horace
Plunkett, "McCarthy of Wisconsin: The Career of an Irishman Abroad as it
Appears and Appeals to an Irishman at Home," pamphlet reprinted from *The
Nineteenth Century,* June, 1915; Harold J. Laski, "The Elite in a Democratic
Society," *Harper's Magazine,* 167 (Sept., 1933), 456–64.

[16] "The Reference Library," *The Evening Sentinel* (Milwaukee, Wis.), Feb. 25, 1922.

[17] Interview with Reuben G. Knutson, Dec. 19, 1963, Madison, Wis.

[18] Witte, "Essentials in Legislative Reference Work," Ms. attached to a letter to the American Legislators Association of Oct. 27, 1933, indicating that the Ms. was a copy of Witte's address to that association, box 254, Witte Papers.

[19] Minutes of the Wisconsin Free Library Commission, Feb. 20, 1922, at the offices of the Commission, Madison, Wis.; "Witte Accepts Post as Head of Library," *Wisconsin State Journal* (Madison), Mar. 2, 1922, p. 1.

[20] Fitzpatrick, *McCarthy of Wisconsin*, 244, 226–233; "Dr. Charles McCarthy Dead," *Wisconsin State Journal* (Madison), Mar. 27, 1921. Fitzpatrick attempted to explain the reasons for McCarthy's senatorial bid, but his penchant for always ascribing the best motives to McCarthy's ventures made his explanation unreliable.

[21] Fitzpatrick, *McCarthy of Wisconsin*, 90–97, 114; Charles McCarthy, *The Wisconsin Bill Factory* (pamphlet, n. d., no explanation, copy in University of Wisconsin Library); John R. Commons, *Myself* (New York, 1934; republished, Madison, 1963), 107–09; Witte to Lucile McCarthy, Oct. 28, 1924, LRL correspondence.

[22] Fitzpatrick, *McCarthy of Wisconsin*, Ch. 8, *passim*, and Ch. 7, *passim*; Fred Holmes, quoted in Irma Hochstein, "Work of Charles McCarthy in Fields of Minimum Wage, Child Labor and Apprenticeship Legislation in Wisconsin," 1929, Ms. in library of the Wisconsin Legislative Reference Bureau, Madison, Wis., p. 12.

[23] "Report[s] of the Legislative Reference Library," 1925–1926, 1928–1929, 1930–1931, 1932–1933, box 108, Witte Papers.

[24] Leek, *Legislative Reference Work*, 37.

[25] Witte to Olen A. Peters, Feb. 6, 1930, LRL correspondence.

[26] Charles McCarthy, *The Wisconsin Idea* (New York, 1912), 197.

[27] Interview with Mrs. Hazel Rasmussen Kuehn, Oct. 30, 1963, Monona Village, Wis.; Witte to Eugene Smith, Feb. 25, 1930, LRL correspondence; Witte, "Governmental Agencies for the Improvement of Statute Law in Wisconsin," *Phi Beta Kappa Quarterly*, 8 (May, 1926), 51; interview with John C. Schuman, Dec. 17, 1963, Watertown, Wis.; Witte, "Essentials in Legislative Reference Work" (cited note 18).

[28] Fitzpatrick, *McCarthy of Wisconsin*, 85; Witte, "A Law Making Laboratory," *State Government*, 3 (April, 1930), 7.

[29] Witte, "Essentials of Legislative Reference Work" (cited note 18); Witte, "A Legislative Reference Librarian's Conception of His Job," address of Oct., 1931, box 259, Witte Papers; Witte, "A Law-Making Laboratory," 6.

[30] Witte, "Essentials in Legislative Reference Work" (cited note 18); Witte, "A Law-Making Laboratory," 6, 7.

[31] Witte to Kaiser, Nov. 30, 1932, LRL correspondence.

[32] Witte, "Essentials in Legislative Reference work" (cited note 18); Witte, "Technical Services for State Legislators," *The Annals of the American Academy of Political and Social Science*, 195 (Jan., 1938), 142–43; *Aids to Legislation* (pamphlet recording a discussion among Witte, Henry Toll, and DeWitt Billman over NBC radio, May 9, 1933; Chicago: University of Chicago press, Government Series III, Lecture No. 19), 8.

[33] Witte, "The Research Work of Legislative Reference Bureaus," address of Dec. 27, 1933, box 257; Witte to J. Finley Christ, Mar. 12, 1932, box 1; Witte Papers. Interview with Mrs. Kuehn (cited note 27); Fitzpatrick, *McCarthy of Wisconsin*, 45–47; Witte, "Governmental Agencies for the Improvement of Statute Law in Wisconsin" (cited note 27), 48–49; Miss Augusta Best to State Reference Library [*sic*], Mar. 27, 1932 (filed with 1931 correspondence), LRL correspondence; "Report[s] of the Legislative Reference Library," 1930–1931, 1932–1933, box 108, Witte Papers.

[34] Witte, "The Research Work of Legislative Reference Bureaus."

[35] Correspondence and indexed materials in the library of the Wisconsin Legislative Reference Bureau, Madison, Wis., *passim.*

[36] Witte, "The Research Work of Legislative Reference Bureaus." For examples of speeches or speech outlines that Witte wrote for conservatives, see Witte to Evan Davies, June 6, 1930, with attached Ms. ostensibly by Davies, "A Constructive Program for Agriculture"; and Witte to Herman Boldt, Apr. 8, 1931, and Ms., "Statement of Senator Boldt on the Necessity for a Legislative Holiday at This Time from Further Regulation and Taxation"; LRL correspondence. For examples of speeches and speech outlines for progressives, see "Plutocracy's Attack on Government," Ms. marked in Witte's handwriting "April 1932 for Col. John J. Haman"; and Witte to Philip La Follette, Dec. 31, 1932; LRL correspondence.

[37] Witte to V. S. Keppel, Sept. 21, 1928; Witte to Geo. Schneider, Sept. 29, 1928; Hubert Peavey to Witte, Jan. 11, 1932; Witte to Peavey, Jan. 13, 1932; Witte to Philip La Follette, Feb. 27, 1932; Witte to H. V. Schwalbach, May 23, 1930; LRL corespondence.

[38] LRL correspondence, 1922–1933, *passim*; Witte, "Essentials in Legislative Reference Work" (cited note 18).

[39] Witte, "Unemployment Insurance," address of Mar. 2, 1928, box 257; Witte, "What the Labor Movement Means to the Community," address, box 255; Witte Papers.

[40] Witte to Howard Kaltenborn, Dec. 18, 1940, box 6, Witte Papers; Witte to Nelson, Nov. 26, 1924, LRL correspondence.

[41] Interview with Mrs. Kuehn (cited note 27). LRL correspondence, 1922–1933, *passim.* See, for example, Witte to A. C. Reis, Apr. 29, 1929; and Witte to Philip La Follette, Dec. 20, 1930, with attached paper, "Agriculture—Possibilities for Legislation"; LRL correspondence.

[42] Witte to *Wisconsin State Journal* editor A. M. Brayton, June 20, 1932; Witte to Oscar Morris, Sept. 30, 1933; LRL correspondence.

[43] Interview with Schuman (cited note 27); Witte, "Essentials in Legislative Reference Work" (cited note 18); Witte to Wm. Leiserson, Feb. 7, 1913, Witte file, Leiserson Papers.

[44] " 'Bill Factory' Under Attack," *Milwaukee Journal*, Mar. 19, 1927; J. C. Ralston, "Heavy Job Left for Legislature," *Milwaukee Journal*, July 10, 1927; "Pay Trips Home," *Wisconsin State Journal* (Madison), June 11, 1929.

[45] State of Wisconsin, Joint Resolutions Nos. 90-S and 136-A, 1929, enrolled June 19, 1929; see *Index to the Journals of the Fifty-Ninth Session of the Wisconsin Legislature*, 1929, p. 224.

[46] "Pay Trips Home," *Wisconsin State Journal* (Madison), June 11, 1929.

[47] State of Wisconsin, Joint Resolution No. 177-A, 1933.

[48] "Letters and Resolutions Commending Service Rendered by the Wisconsin Legislative Reference Bureau," a collection of clippings in the library of the bureau, *passim;* LRL correspondence, 1922–1933, *passim;* J. D. Millar to Witte, Dec. 27, 1929, LRL correspondence.

[49] Witte, "Essentials in Legislative Reference Work" (cited Note 21). Geo. Yantis to Witte, Dec. 9, 1932; Witte to Yantis, Dec. 19, 1932; Witte to Jos. Harris, Dec. 24, 1932; LRL correspondence. Henry Toll to Witte, Sept. 14, 1933, with attached notes, box 1, Witte Papers. Witte to Rodney Mott, June 12, 1933; Witte to A. R. Hatton, Dec. 19, 1930; Witte to Henry Toll, Oct. 12, 1931; Witte to Harriet Long, Feb. 20, 1931, LRL correspondence.

[50] John H. Leek, "The Legislative Reference Bureau in Recent Years," *American Political Science Review*, 20 (Nov. 1926), 826; "Report of the Legislative Reference Library," 1930–1931, box 108, Witte Papers; Witte, "Essentials in Legislative Reference Work" (cited note 18).

[51] Witte, "Essentials in Legislative Reference Work" (cited note 18); Witte, form letter to each legislative committee chairman of the Wisconsin legislature, Jan. 28, 1933, LRL correspondence; interview with John Schuman (cited note 27); Witte to A. R. Hutton, Dec. 19, 1930, LRL correspondence. "Report of the Legislative Reference Library," 1930–1931, box 108; Witte to Felix Frankfurter, June 6, 1928, box 1; Witte Papers. "Some Brief Comments on the Organization and Operation of the Legislative Reference Library," Ms. attached to M. G. Toepel to Members of the Free Library Commission, n.d., which indicates that Ms. was product of request of the commission made on Dec. 2, 1958, in files of the Free Library Commission, Madison, Wis.; interview with Mrs. Kuehn (cited note 27). E. G. Smith to Witte, Feb. 3, n. y. (filed with 1931 correspondence); Legislative Interim Committee on a Retirement System for State Employes, to All State Officers and Employes, Dec. 3, 1930; LRL correspondence.

[52] Wisconsin Legislature, *Report of the Interim Committee on Administration and Taxation* (Madison, Dec., 1926), especially pp. 50–61, 28–53.

[53] LRL correspondence, 1926–1933, *passim*. Witte, "Taxation Problems in Wisconsin," address, Oct. 28, 1926, box 259; Witte to Otto Mueller, Nov. 24, 1934, box 63; Witte Papers. Witte to J. W. Carow, Feb. 12, 1932, LRL correspondence; "Important Legislation of the 1933 Session," Ms., no author given but written very much in Witte's style, in library of the Wisconsin Legislative Reference Bureau; "Mr. Witte's Speech for Sen. Wagner—before a Communist Group—Wash. Auditorium in Oct., 1934," Ms. in box 3, Committee on Economic Security files, Record Group 47, National Archives, Washington, D. C.

[54] University of Wisconsin "Instructional Reports," 1933–1953, University of Wisconsin Archives, Madison, Wis. Wisconsin State Recovery Administration material, box 64; Wisconsin State Planning Board material, box 64; Witte to Andrew P. Een, Jan. 9, 1936, box 2; Wisconsin Citizens Committee on Public Welfare material, box 63; Wisconsin Labor Relations Board material, box 63; President's Committee on Administrative Management material, box 43; Witte Papers. Witte, "The Preparation of Proposed Legislative Measures by Administrative Departments," in The President's Committee on Administrative Management, *Report of the Committee With Studies of Administrative Management in the Federal Government* (Washington, 1937), 357–78.

[55] Witte to John Cashman, Sept. 23, 1933, LRL correspondence; Witte, "Essentials in Legislative Reference Work" (cited note 18).

[56] Witte, "Essentials in Legislative Reference Work" (cited note 18).

CHAPTER 4

[1] Witte, "The Doctrine That Labor Is a Commodity," *Annals of the American Academy of Political and Social Science,* 69 (Jan., 1917), 139.

[2] "The Security for Industrial Peace," Ms. in Witte's handwriting marked "Commencement Oration, June 23, 1909"; "Labor's Count Against the Doctrine of Malicous [*sic*] Conspiracy," Ms. marked in Witte's handwriting, "Address in University Speech Contest, 1909," and "Senior Open Oration, 1909"; box 255, Witte Papers.

[3] Witte, *The Government in Labor Disputes* (New York and London, 1932), 265–68.

[4] Witte, *The Government in Labor Disputes,* 268–69; Witte, "The Doctrine That Labor Is a Commodity," 133; Witte, "The Clayton Bill and Organized Labor," *The Survey,* 32 (July 4, 1914), 360.

[5] Witte to Alpheus T. Mason, Mar. 3, 1933, box 1, Witte Papers.

[6] Witte, "The Clayton Bill and Organized Labor," 360–61; Witte, "The Doctrine That Labor Is a Commodity" (cited note 1), 134–36.

[7] Witte, "A Partial Draft of the Labor Disputes Act; Presented to the Industrial Relations Commission Feb. 3, 1914"; Witte, "Preliminary Report Upon Studies on Trade Union Law," Sept. 1, 1914; files of the Commission on Industrial Relations, Record Group 174, National Archives, Washington, D. C. (hereinafter cited as CIR files). Witte, "Summary of the Report on Injunctions in Labor Disputes," Feb., 1915, bound with "Injunctions in Labor Disputes," an unpublished report to the United States Industrial Relations Commission, Feb. 27, 1915, Mss. in State Historical Society of Wisconsin Library, Madison, Wis., and in CIR files; Witte, "Injunctions in Labor Disputes" (cited immediately above); 72–75; Witte, *The Government in Labor Disputes*, 316.

[8] Witte, *The Government in Labor Disputes*, 316; Witte, "Injunctions in Labor Disputes," 72–75; Witte, "Summary of the Report on Injunctions in Labor Disputes."

[9] John R. Commons and John B. Andrews, *Principles of Labor Legislation* (New York, 1916), 116. Witte wrote pages 91–125 of the Commons and Andrews book anonymously.

[10] Witte, "Summary of the Report on Injunctions in Labor Disputes."

[11] Witte to C. E. Swayzee, May 12, 1928, box 1, Witte Papers.

[12] J. Finley Christ, "The Federal Courts and Organized Labor, I," *Journal of Business*, 3 (Apr., 1930), 205, n. 1.

[13] Witte, "Preliminary Report Upon Studies on Trade Union Law" (cited note 7).

[14] Witte to Nelson, Nov. 26, 1924, Wisconsin Legislative Reference Library correspondence, Wisconsin Legislative Reference Bureau, Madison, Wis. Witte to Greene, Jan. 13, 1930; Witte to Shearer, Oct. 21, 1929; box 1, Witte Papers.

[15] Witte, "Results of Injunctions in Labor Disputes," *American Labor Legislation Review*, 12 (Dec., 1922), 201.

[16] This paragraph is synthesized from four of Witte's leading articles on the injunction question: "Results of Injunctions in Labor Disputes," 197–201; "Value of Injunctions in Labor Disputes," *Journal of Political Economy*, 32 (June, 1924), 335–56; "The Labor Injunction—A Red Flag," *American Labor Legislation Review*, 18 (Sept., 1928), 315–17; "Social Consequences of Injunctions in Labor Disputes," *Illinois Law Review*, 24 (Mar., 1930), 772–85.

[17] Witte, "Injunctions and Acts of Violence in Labor Disputes: Introductory Outline," Oct. 31, 1914, Appendix C of "Injunctions in Labor Disputes" (cited note 7).

[18] Witte, "Value of Injunctions in Labor Disputes," 355–56.

[19] Witte, "Results of Injunctions in Labor Disputes," 201.

[20] This paragraph is synthesized from the four articles cited in note 16.

[21] Witte, "The Role of the Courts in Labor Disputes" (unpublished University of Wisconsin Ph.D dissertation, 1927), quotation from p. 3.

[22] *Ibid.*, 40–57.

[23] *Ibid.*, 116, 3–5.

[24] Witte, *The Government in Labor Disputes*, 221–24; Gertrude Schmidt, "History of Labor Legislation in Wisconsin" (unpublished University of Wisconsin Ph.D. dissertation, 1933), 288–95.

[25] Witte, " 'Yellow Dog' Contracts," *Wisconsin Law Review*, 6 (Dec., 1930), 31.

[26] Witte, *The Government in Labor Disputes*, 270; Witte to Matthew Woll, Jan. 12, 1926, box 1, Witte Papers.

[27] Schmidt, "History of Labor Legislation in Wisconsin," 299, 286–88.

[28] Witte to Woll, Jan. 12, 1926, box 1, Witte Papers.

[29] S. 1482, 70th Congress, 1st Session; Andrew Furuseth to Geo. W. Norris, June 7, 1928, copy in box 1, Witte Papers.

[30] Blaine to Witte, Feb. 13, 1928; Witte to Blaine, March 6, 1928; box 1, Witte Papers. *Limiting Scope of Injunctions in Labor Disputes: Hearing Before a Subcommittee of the Committee on the Judiciary, United States Senate, Seventieth Congress, First Session on S. 1482, A Bill to Amend the Judicial Code and To Define and Limit the Jurisdiction of Courts Sitting in Equity, and for Other Purposes,* Feb. 3–Mar. 22, 1928 (Washngton, 1928), 1; Geo. W. Norris, *Fighting Liberal: The Autobiography of George W. Norris* (New York, 1945), 312; Norris to Witte, Apr. 1, 1928, box 1, Witte Papers.

[31] Penned notes on a "Tentative Draft" of the Norris subcommittee bill, May 1–3, 1928, box 1, Witte Papers; Norris, *Fighting Liberal*, 312–13; notes penned in margin of page 313 of Witte's copy of Norris' book, in the possession of Mrs. Florence Witte, Madison, Wis.

[32] Frankfurter to Witte, April 24, 1928, and attached Mss., "Revision of An Act Concerning Labor Organizations," dated Apr. 9, 1923, and "Revision of An Act Concerning the Granting and Enforcement of Injunctions," dated April 9, 1923, box 1, Witte Papers.

[33] Schmidt, "History of Labor Legislation in Wisconsin" (cited note 24), 290.

[34] "Tentative Draft," May 1–3, 1928; Witte to Sayre, May 26, 1928; Witte correspondence of May, 1928, *passim*; box 1, Witte Papers.

[35] Witte to Sayre, May 26, 1928; Witte to Wm. Green, July 14, 1928; Frankfurter to Witte, Apr. 24, May 29, 1928; Witte to Blaine, Nov. 3, 1928; copy, Richberg to Norris, May 18, 1928; copy, Oliphant to Frankfurter, May 21, 1928; box 1, Witte Papers. "Text of the Substitute Anti-Injunction Bill," *Law and Labor,* 10 (Dec., 1928), 267–68.

[36] Frankfurter to Witte, May 29, 1928, box 1, Witte Papers.

[37] "Restrictions of the Use of Injunctions in Labor Disputes," Ms. marked in Witte's handwriting, "Prepared by Me for the Subcommittee of the Committee on the Judiciary which reported the Norris-LaGuardia Anti-Injunction Bill, 1928," box 1, Witte Papers.

[38] *Ibid.;* "Text of the Substitute Anti-Injunction Bill" (cited note 35); Witte to Wm. Green, July 14, 1928, box 1, Witte Papers.

[39] "Text of Substitute Anti-Injunction Bill"; Witte, "Restrictions of the Use of Injunctions in Labor Disputes."

[40] Witte, "Restrictions of the Use of Injunctions in Labor Disputes."

[41] Hyman Weintraub, *Andrew Furuseth, Emancipator of the Seamen* (Berkeley and Los Angeles, 1959), 114, 130, 186; Felix Frankfurter and Nathan Greene, *The Labor Injunction* (New York, 1930), 207; *Limiting the Scope of Injunctions* (cited note 30), 18, 24; copy, Furuseth to Norris, June 7, 1928, box 1, Witte Papers; Norris, *Fighting Liberal*, 312.

[42] Frankfurter to Witte, June 15, 1928; copy Oliphant to Frankfurter, June 16, 1928; Witte to Oliphant, June 28, 1928; box 1, Witte Papers.

[43] *Report of the Proceedings of the Forty-Seventh Annual Convention of the American Federation of Labor Held at Los Angeles, California, October 3 to 14, Inclusive, 1927* (Washington, 1927), 291, 308. *Report of the Proceedings of the Forty-Eighth Annual Convention of the American Federation of Labor, Held at New Orleans, Louisiana, November 19 to 28, Inclusive, 1928* (Washington, 1928), 251–53. Witte, "The Federal Anti-Injunction Act," *Minnesota Law Review,* 16 (May, 1932), 639.

[44] *Report of Proceedings of the Forty-Ninth Annual Convention of the American Federation of Labor, Held at Toronto, Ontario, Canada, October 7th to 18th, Inclusive, 1929* (Washington, 1929), 194–98, 318–19, 352; John P. Frey, *The Labor*

Injunction: An Exposition of Government by Judicial Conscience and Its Menace (Cincinnati, [1923?]); Witte, "Results of Injunctions in Labor Disputes" (cited note 15), 198; Schmidt, "History of Labor Legislation in Wisconsin" (cited note 24), 280–90.

[45] Copies, Frankfurter to Norris, Jan. 28, 1930, and attached Ms., "Observations on Amendments Proposed by the American Federation of Labor to the Injunction Bill Drafted by the Sub-Committee of the Senate Committee on the Judiciary"; Witte to Norris, Dec. 6, 1929; Witte to Richberg, March 13, 1930; Witte to Frankfurter, Jan. 21, 1930; "Observations on Injunction Bill Endorsed by A. F. of L.", Ms. attached to Frankfurter to Witte, Jan. 14, 1930; box 1, Witte Papers.

[46] Subcommittee bill as printed in Senate Report No. 1060 (71st Congress, 2nd Session), Part 1, pp. 1–4; *Report of Proceedings of the Fiftieth Annual Convention of the American Federation of Labor, Held at Boston, Massachusetts, October 6th to 17th, Inclusive, 1930* (Washington, 1930), 355–57, 364, 371; *Report of Proceedings of the Fifty-First Annual Convention of the American Federation of Labor, Held at Vancouver, B. C., Canada, October 5th to 15th, Inclusive, 1931* (Washington, 1931), 465.

[47] Witte, "The Federal Anti-Injunction Act," 639–40; see especially the publication of the League for Industrial Rights, *Law and Labor*, Vols. 10–13 (1928–31).

[48] Senate Report No. 1060 (71st Congress, 2nd Session), Part 1, pp. 6–10.

[49] Witte, "Labor and Anti-Labor Bills in the Legislature: Record to August 10, 1929," Ms. in library of the Wisconsin Legislative Reference Bureau; Witte to Irma Hochstein, and to James Landis, Oct. 16, 1931, and to J. J. Handley, May 17, 1930, Wisconsin Legislative Reference Library correspondence, Wisconsin Legislative Reference Bureau, Madison, Wis.; Schmidt, "History of Labor Legislation in Wisconsin" (cited note 24), 290–93, 303–07; Gordon Haferbecker, *Wisconsin Labor Laws* (Madison, 1958), 161. The "Wisconsin Labor Code" was Chapter 376, Laws of Wisconsin, 1931; later Wisconsin Statutes, Sec. 103.51-103.62.

[50] Witte, "The Federal Anti-Injunction Act" (cited note 43), 639–43; Senate Report No. 163 (72nd Congress, 1st Session), Parts 1 and 2.

[51] Witte, *The Government in Labor Disputes* (New York, 1932). The quotation is taken from page 290. Witte gave his recommendations in Ch. XIII, "Future Policies."

[52] Witte to Sumner Slichter, Feb. 8, 1934, box 1, Witte Papers; *To Create a National Labor Board: Hearings Before the Committee on Education and Labor, United States Senate, Seventy-Third Congress, Second Session, on S. 2926, A Bill to Equalize the Bargaining Power of Employers and Employees, to Encourage the Amicable Settlement of Disputes Between Employers and Employees, to Create a National Labor Board, and For Other Purposes*, Part I, pp. 240–44; Witte, "The Labor Injunction Bill—A Red Flag" (cited note 16), 317; Witte, "Socio-Economic Reasons Why the Injunctions Sought by the Interborough Rapid Transit Company Against the American Federation of Labor Should Not Be Allowed," Dec., 1927, box 255, Witte Papers.

[53] National Labor Relations Board, *Legislative History of the National Labor Relations Act* (Washington, 1949), II, 3271.

CHAPTER 5

[1] Franklin D. Roosevelt, *Review of Legislative Accomplishments of the Administration and Congress* (Message to Congress, June 8, 1934), United States House of Representatives Document No. 397 (73d Congress, 2d Session), 2, 4.

[2] *Ibid.*, 2–4.

[3] Industrial Relations Counselors, Inc., *An Historical Basis for Unemployment Insurance* (Minneapolis, 1934), 3–8; Isaac M. Rubinow, *The Quest for Security* (New York, 1934), 595–97, 599–601; Witte, book review in *Harvard Law Review*, 55 (June, 1942), 1414; Abraham Epstein, *The Challenge of the Aged* (New York, 1928), 352.

[4] Rubinow, *The Quest for Security*, 599–601; Massachusetts Commission on Old Age Pensions, Annuities and Insurance, *Report of the Commission on Old Age Pensions, Annuities and Insurance* (Boston, 1910); Lloyd F. Pierce, "The Activities of the American Association for Labor Legislation on Behalf of Social Security and Protective Labor Legislation" (unpublished University of Wisconsin Ph.D. dissertation, 1953), 150–67; Isaac Rubinow, "First American Conference on Social Insurance," *The Survey*, 30 (July 5, 1913), 478–80; Isaac Rubinow, *Social Insurance, With Special Reference to American Conditions* (New York, 1913).

[5] Abraham Epstein, *Insecurity, A Challenge to America: A study of Social Insurance in the United States and Abroad* (New York, 1933), 18.

[6] Walter Linn, "Social Insurance: Constructive Destruction," *Annals of the American Academy of Political and Social Science*, 170 (Nov., 1933), 7–9, 16; Noel Sargent, "Do We Need Compulsory Unemployment Insurance? No," *Annals of the American Academy of Political and Social Science*, 170 (Nov., 1933), 32, 38.

[7] Frederick L. Hoffman, "American Problems in Social Insurance," *Proceedings of the National Conference of Charities and Corrections* (1914), 346–55; Henry R. Seager, *Social Insurance: A Program of Social Reform* (New York, 1910), 120–24, 140–44; Louis D. Brandeis, "Our New Peonage: Discretionary Pensions," *The Independent*, 73 (July 25, 1912), 187–91; Samuel Gompers, "Not Even Compulsory Benevolence Will Do: Infringement of Personal Liberty," in *Compulsory Health Insurance* (Annual Meeting Addresses of the National Civic Federation, Jan. 22, 1917), 6–7.

[8] Domenico Gagliardo, *American Social Insurance* (New York, 1955 ed.), 131; Epstein, *Insecurity*, 148, 517; Barbara N. Armstrong, *Insuring the Essentials: Minimum Wage Plus Social Insurance—a Living Wage Program* (New York, 1932), 531; Bryce M. Stewart, "American Voluntary Attempts at Unemployment Benefits," *Annals of the American Academy of Political and Social Science*, 170 (Nov., 1933), 53–64.

[9] Narayan Viswanathan, "The Role of the American Public Welfare Association in the Formulation and Development of Public Welfare Policies in the United States, 1930–1960" (unpublished Columbia University Ph.D. dissertation, 1961), 33–35, 46, 49–51; Robert M. Kelso, "The Transition from Charities and Correction to Public Welfare," *Annals of the American Academy of Political and Social Science*, 105 (Jan., 1923), 21–25; Rubinow, *The Quest for Security*, 342; Rubinow, "Needed: A Social Insurance Revival," *The Survey*, 56 (May 15, 1926), 233.

[10] Walter Gifford, "Pensions, Charity, and Old Age," *Atlantic Monthly*, 145 (Feb., 1930), 259–65; Sargent, "Do We Need Compulsory Health Insurance? No," 31.

[11] Viswanathan, "The Role of the American Public Welfare Association," 70–115.

[12] The books referred to are Rubinow, *Social Insurance;* Abraham Epstein, *Facing Old Age* (New York, 1922), *Challenge of the Aged*, and *Insecurity;* Paul Douglas, *Standards of Unemployment Insurance* (Chicago, 1932); and Barbara Armstrong, *Insuring the Essentials*.

[13] Rubinow, *Social Insurance*, 8–9; Rubinow, "Labor Insurance," *Journal of Political Economy*, 12 (June, 1904), 362.

[14] Epstein, *Insecurity*, 319, 38–39; Rubinow, *Social Insurance*, 490–91.

[15] Isaac Rubinow, "Conflict of Public and Private Interests in the Field of Social Insurance," *Annals of the American Academy of Political and Social Science*, 154 (Mar., 1931), 108–16; Epstein, *Insecurity* (1936 ed.), 558–60, 245, 303.

[16] Epstein, *Insecurity* (1936 ed.), 245, 303.

[17] Samuel Gompers, quoted by Rubinow in *The Quest for Security*, 541.

[18] Witte Diaries, IX, entry of June 30, 1931, Witte Papers.

[19] John R. Commons, *Myself* (New York, 1934), 143.

[20] Pierce, "Activities of the AALL" (cited note 4), 5–10.

[21] For a detailed account, see *ibid.*, 91–93, 254–94; for another extensive and more interpretive account, see David H. Clark, "An Analytical View of the History of Health Insurance, 1910–1959" (unpublished University of Wisconsin Ph.D. dissertation, 1963), Ch. 3. For a contemporary and a later account by a participant, see Isaac Rubinow, "Health Insurance: the Spread of the Movement," *The Survey*, 36 (July 15, 1916), 407–09; and Rubinow, *The Quest for Security*, 207–17. For a critic's contemporary views, see Frederick L. Hoffman, *Facts and Fallacies of Compulsory Health Insurance* (Newark, 1920).

[22] Clark, "History of Health Insurance," 41–48, 54; Pierce, "Activities of the AALL" (cited note 4), 270–75, 287–91, quoting Hoffman on 270–71; Gompers, "Not Even Compulsory Benevolence Will Do" (cited note 7), 5–10.

[23] Ada J. Davis, "The Evolution of the Institution of Mothers' Pensions in the United States," *American Journal of Sociology*, 35 (Jan., 1930), 573–78; Viswanathan, "The Role of the American Public Welfare Association" (cited note 9), 42; Rubinow, "Conflict of Private and Public Interest in the Field of Social Insurance" (cited note 15), 112; Epstein, *Insecurity*, 621–35; Grace Abbott, "What About Mothers' Pensions Now?" *The Survey*, 70 (March, 1934), 80–81.

[24] William E. Odom, "Do We Need State Old Age Pensions? No," *Annals of the American Academy of Political and Social Science*, 170 (Nov., 1933), 103–06; Charles Denby, Jr., "Do We Need State Old Age Pensions? Yes," *Annals of the American Academy of Political and Social Science*, 170 (Nov., 1933), 93–102.

[25] Pierce, "Activities of the AALL" (cited note 4), 387–92.

[26] Epstein, *Insecurity*, 547; Abraham Epstein, "The American State Old Age Pension System in Operation," *Annals of The American Academy of Political and Social Science*, 170 (Nov., 1933), 110–11; Rubinow, *Social Insurance*, 368, 371; Armstrong, *Insuring the Essentials*, 412, 6, 436; John B. Andrews, quoted in Pierce, "Activities of the AALL" (cited note 4), 392.

[27] Witte to Wilbur Cohen, Jan. 20, 1941, box 6, Witte Papers; Witte to Paul R. Alfonsi, June 6, 1933, Wisconsin Legislative Reference Library Correspondence, Wisconsin Legislative Reference Bureau, Madison, Wis. (hereinafter cited as LRL correspondence).

[28] Witte to Arthur Balzer, June 23, 1933; Witte to Paul Alfonsi, June 6, 1933; copy, Paul Raushenbush to John B. Andrews, Dec. 19, 1930; Witte to Raushenbush, Dec. 24, 1930; LRL correspondence.

[29] Pierce, "Activities of the AALL" (cited note 4), 389–90; Epstein, "The American State Old Age Pension System in Operation," 107–11; Epstein, *Insecurity*, 533–37.

[30] Witte Diaries, IX, *passim*, Witte Papers.

[31] Rubinow, "Labor Insurance" (cited note 13), 374–75.

[32] Commons, *Myself*, 143; John R. Commons, "Unemployment: Compensation and Prevention," *The Survey*, 47 (Oct. 1, 1921), 5–9; Commons, "Unemployment Insurance Is Coming," *La Follette's Magazine*, 14 (Dec., 1922), 190–91.

[33] John R. Commons, "Unemployment Compensation," *American Labor Legislation Review*, 20 (Sept., 1930), 249–50; John R. Commons, "The Groves Unemployment Reserves Law," *American Labor Legislation Review*, 22 (March, 1932), 8–10. Interviews with Harold Groves, Oct. 30, 1964; with Paul Raushenbush, Nov. 2, 1964; both in Madison, Wis. Edwin Witte, "Development of Unemployment Compensa-

tion," *Yale Law Journal*, 55 (Dec., 1945), 25–26. See also Paul Raushenbush, "The Wisconsin Unemployment Reserves Law," *Quarterly Bulletin of the New York State Conference on Social Work*, April, 1933; and The Industrial Commission of Wisconsin, "History and Status of Wisconsin's Unemployment Compensation Act," reprinted from the commission's *Biennial Report, 1932–1934* (Madison, 1934), 52–60.

[34] "Governors' Interstate Commission Urges Unemployment Reserves," *American Labor Legislation Review*, 22 (March, 1932), 19–23; Isaac Rubinow, "The Ohio Idea: Unemployment Insurance," *Annals of the American Academy of Political and Social Science*, 170 (Nov., 1933), 76–87; Douglas, *Standards of Unemployment Insurance;* John B. Andrews to Witte, Aug. 1, 1933, box 1, Witte Papers.

[35] Andrews to Witte, Aug. 1, 1933, box 1, Witte Papers; Pierce, "Activities of the AALL" (cited note 4), 296–306, 335–54; John B. Andrews, "Social Insurance in America," *Current History*, 33 (Feb., 1931), 719; "An American Plan for Unemployment Reserve Funds," *American Labor Legislation Review*, 20 (Dec., 1930), 349–56; John B. Andrews, "Prospects for Unemployment Compensation Laws," *Annals of the American Academy of Political and Social Science*, 170 (Nov., 1933), 90–91; Rubinow, *The Quest for Security*, 446.

[36] Pierce, "Activities of the AALL" (cited note 4), 354–55; Abraham Epstein, "Enemies of Unemployment Insurance," *New Republic*, 76 (Sept. 6, 1933), 94–96; Elizabeth Brandeis, "Employment Reserves vs. Insurance," *New Republic*, 76 (Sept. 27, 1933), 178; Paul Raushenbush, "The Wisconsin Idea: Unemployment Reserves," *Annals of the American Academy of Political and Social Science*, 170 (Nov., 1933), 69.

[37] Isaac Rubinow, "Job Insurance—The Ohio Plan," *American Labor Legislation Review*, 23 (Sept., 1933), 131–32; Raushenbush, "The Wisconsin Idea: Unemployment Reserves," 65; Paul Raushenbush, "Wisconsin's Unemployment Compensation Act," *American Labor Legislation Review*, 22 (March, 1932), 17; Harold Groves and Elizabeth Brandeis, "Economic Bases of the Wisconsin Unemployment Reserves Act," *American Economic Review*, 24 (March, 1934, 40; Elizabeth Brandeis, "An Official Challenge to Fatalism in Industry," *The American Labor Legislation Review*, 23 (June, 1933), 137–41; Epstein, *Insecurity*, 222.

[38] Notes in Witte's handwriting, "Addresses on Unemployment Insurance at the Convention of the Wisconsin Manufacturer's [*sic*] Association at Milwaukee, December 15, 1921," box 250; Witte to R. P. Cronin, June 17, 1940, box 6; "Factors Affecting the Economic Development of the United States," summary of a May 3, 1956 address by Witte, box 259; Witte Papers. John Andrews to Witte, Nov. 7, 28, Dec. 8, 1930; Witte to Andrews, Nov. 18, Dec. 1 (telegram), 11, 1930; LRL correspondence. Witte to John R. Commons, July 2, 1921; Witte to Joseph Chamberlain, Oct. 24, 1932; Witte to Mollie Carroll, Oct. 27, 1932; Witte to Epstein, June 29, 1933; box 1, Witte Papers.

[39] Witte to William Green, Oct. 24, 1932; Witte to Joseph Chamberlain, Oct. 24, 1932; box 1, Witte Papers. Edwin Witte, "The Theory of Workmen's Compensation," *American Labor Legislation Review*, 20 (Dec., 1930), 411–18. Witte to Abraham Epstein, July 13, 1933, LRL correspondence.

[40] Witte to John Andrews, Nov. 18, 1930, LRL correspondence. Witte to Merrill Murray, Dec. 16, 1932; Witte to Andrews, Aug. 1, 1933; Witte to Abraham Epstein, June 29, 1933; box 1, Witte Papers.

[41] Viswanathan, "The Role of the American Public Welfare Association" (cited note 9), 42–43; Rubinow, *Social Insurance*, 410–12; Epstein *Insecurity*, 532–33; Malcolm S. Torgerson, "An Analysis of the Development of Old-Age Assistance in the United States" (unpublished University of Nebraska Ph.D. dissertation, 1953), 40; Witte, *The Development of the Social Security Act* (Madison, 1963), 5; Gagliardo, *American Social Insurance* (1955 ed.), 133. David J. Lewis to Roosevelt, Jan. 20,

1934; M. H. McIntyre to Perkins, Jan. 22, 1934; unsigned draft of reply for Lewis, Jan. 29, 1934; box 11, Record Group 174, National Archives.

[42] Edwin Witte, "An Historical Account of Unemployment Insurance in the Social Security Act," *Law and Contemporary Problems*, 3 (Jan., 1936), 158–59; Rubinow, *The Quest for Security*, 381–87; Robert F. Wagner, "Federal Encouragement to State Unemployment Reserve Legislation," *American Labor Legislation Review*, 22 (March, 1932), 45, 46; Robert F. Wagner, "A Federal-State Program for Unemployment Reserves," *American Labor Legislation Review*, 23 (Dec., 1933), 167–69. William Green to Witte, Sept. 20, 30, Oct. 17, 1932; Witte to Green, Sept. 28, Oct. 11, 19, 1932; "Draft as prepared by Professor Sayre"; box 1, Witte Papers. *Report of the Proceedings of the Fifty-Second Annual Convention of the American Federation of Labor*, Nov. 21–Dec. 2, 1932 (Washington, 1932), 41–44, 360. "Chronological History of Administration's Unemployment Insurance Program," box 48, Committee on Economic Security files, Record Group 47, National Archives, Washington, D.C.

[43] "Chronological History" (Ms. cited in note 42); "Unemployment Insurance Urged by Governor of New York," *American Labor Legislation Review*, 20 (Sept., 1930), 254–55; "Roosevelt on Unemployment Insurance," *American Labor Legislation Review*, 21 (June, 1931), 219–20; Witte Diaries, IX, entry of Aug. 21, 1931, Witte Papers; interview with Paul Raushenbush, Nov. 2, 1964, Madison, Wis.; Frances Perkins, "Unemployment Insurance: An American Plan to Protect Workers and Avoid the Dole," *Survey Graphic*, 20 (Nov., 1931), 117–19, 173; Frances Perkins, "Job Insurance," *American Labor Legislation Review*, 23 (June, 1933), 117–20.

[44] Interview with Paul Raushenbush, Nov. 2, 1964, Madison, Wis.; confidential source; Witte to Elizabeth Brandeis, May 7, 1942, box 35, Witte Papers; Witte, "Historical Background of Employment Security," *Proceedings of the Institute Cosponsored by Minnesota Department of Employment Security, University of Minnesota Center for Continuation Study, and Minnesota Chapter, International Association of Personnel in Employment Security*, Oct. 22–23, 1957, p. 6; *Economic Security Act: Hearings Before the Committee on Ways and Means, House of Representatives, Seventy-Fourth Congress, First Session on H. R. 4120* (Washington, 1935), 576; Witte to Abraham Eptstein, Feb. 9, 1934, box 1, Witte Papers; Witte, "An Historical Account of Unemployment Insurance," 159–60; Paul Douglas, "Toward Unemployment Insurance," *The World Tomorrow*, 17 (March 20, 1934), 161–62; Rubinow, *The Quest for Security*, 448–49. R. L. Doughton to Roosevelt, March 16, 1934; note on Department of Labor paper n.d.; Perkins to Roosevelt, March 21, 1934; draft of Roosevelt to Doughton, March 23, 1934; Official file 121-A, Franklin D. Roosevelt Library, Hyde Park, New York. Witte, *Development of the Social Security Act*, 5.

[45] "Unemployment Insurance Urged by Governor of New York," 254–55; Witte, *Development of the Social Security Act*, 4–5; Paul Douglas, *Social Security In the United States* (New York, 1936), 26. David J. Lewis to Roosevelt, Jan. 20, 1934; Roosevelt to Lewis, Jan. 29, 1934; copies in box 11, Secretary Perkins files, Record Group 174, National Archives.

[46] Witte to Ray Westerfield, July 20, 1934, box 33; Witte to John B. Andrews, June 19, 1934, box 2; Witte Papers.

[47] "Plan for Study of Economic Security, Ms. marked "Prepared for Presentation to the President, June, 1934, by Dr. A. J. Altmeyer, assisted by Meredith B. Givens and Bryce Stewart," box 5, Committee on Economic Security files, Record Group 47, National Archives; Witte, *Development of the Social Security Act*, 12–13; Perkins to author, Oct. 26, 1964; "Factors Affecting the Economic Development of the United States" (cited note 38).

[48] Witte to John B. Andrews, Aug. 1, 1934, box 54, Committee on Economic Security files, Record Group 47, National Archives.

CHAPTER 6

[1] Witte to William Rice, Nov. 19, 1934, box 15, Committee on Economic Security files, Record Group 47, National Archives. (Hereinafter cited as CES files).

[2] Louis Stark, "Roosevelt Bars Plans Now for Broad Social Program; Seeks Job Insurance Only," *New York Times,* Nov. 15, 1934; Louis Stark, "Experts Push Plan for 'Real' Job Bill With Federal Aid," *New York Times,* Nov. 16, 1934.

[3] Witte to Frankfurter, Nov. 19, 1934, box 56, CES files.

[4] Kellogg to Witte, Dec. 12, 1934; attached clipping, "Dr. Defoe Tells New York Audience Story of Birth of Dionne Quintuplets," marked "N. Y. World-Telegram –Dec. 11, 1934"; box 16, CES files.

[5] Interview with Murray W. Latimer, Aug, 8, 10, 1964, Washington, D. C.; notes in Witte's handwriting, "The Twentieth Anniversary of the Social Security Act," outline of a talk, Dec. 5, 1955, box 259, Witte Papers; "Plan for Study of Economic Security," Ms. marked "Prepared for Presentation to the President, June 1934, by Dr. A. J. Altmeyer, assisted by Meredith B. Givens and Bryce Stewart," box 5, CES files.

[6] Edwin E. Witte, *The Development of the Social Security Act: A Memorandum on the History of the Committee on Economic Security and Legislative History of the Social Security Act* (Madison, 1963), 28–35, 19, 23–25; Witte to George Robinson, Dec. 6, 1948, box 35, Witte Papers; Frances Perkins to author, Oct. 26, 1964; Witte, "The Twentieth Anniversary of the Social Security Act."

[7] Statement of the Republican National Committee, quoted in "Republican Declaration of Policy," *New York Times,* June 7, 1934; "The President's Planned Society," *Chicago Daily Tribune,* June 11, 1934; "The Republicans Take the Field," *Chicago Daily Tribune,* June 9, 1934; "A Disappointing Message," *New York Herald Tribune,* June 9, 1934; "The President's Message," *Birmingham Age-Herald,* June 9, 1934; "The President's Vision," *New York Times,* June 9, 1934; "Now Social Insurance," *Journal of Commerce and Commercial* (New York), June 9, 1934.

[8] "Information Primer: The Committee on Economic Security," box 1, CES files; Witte, *Development of the Social Security Act,* 48–53, 41–45; Witte, "Memorandum on the Views Relating to the Work of the Committee on Economic Security Expressed by Various Individuals Consulted on a Trip to New England and New York on August 19–21, 1934," Witte folder, CES files; memorandum, Altmeyer to members of the Committee on Economic Security, Aug. 13, 1934, and "List Which Does Not Take into Account Geographical Representation," box 154, Secretary Perkins files, Record Group 174, National Archives (hereinafter cited as Perkins files).

[9] Witte to Edgar Sydenstricker, Oct. 6, 1934, box 16, CES files; Witte, "The Twentieth Anniversary of the Social Security Act" (cited note 5).

[10] The summary of the security committee organization's formal structure has been derived from many sources, especially the primary documents extant from the committee; see especially the "Plan for Study of Economic Security" (cited note 4), and Witte, *Development of the Social Security Act,* 19, 23–24, 55.

[11] Frances Perkins to author, Oct. 26, 1964; "Memorandum from the Secretary [certainly Perkins] to Mr. Altmeyer," July 20, 1934, box 154, Perkins files; memorandum, C. E. Wyzanski, Jr., to Altmeyer, June 30, 1934, box 56, CES files; interview with Wilbur Cohen, July 28, 1964, Washington, D. C.

[12] Frances Perkins to author, Oct. 26, 1964. Interviews with Wilbur Cohen, July 28, 1964, Washington, D. C.; with Murray Latimer, Aug. 8, 10, 1964, Washington, D. C.; and with Arthur Altmeyer, June 17, 1966, Madison, Wis.

[13] Witte, "What Should We Expect from Social Security," address of April 17, 1942, box 258, Witte Papers.

[14] Witte, *Development of the Social Security Act,* 4–5; Witte, "Suggestions of Hon. John J. Raskob Regarding the Handling of Reserve Funds," memorandum of Oct. 19, 1934, Witte folder, "Report of the Industrial Relations Committee, Business Advisory and Planning Council, September 19, 1934," box 17, CES files; message of President Franklin D. Roosevelt to Congress, *Review of Legislative Accomplishments of the Administration and Congress,* United States House of Representatives Document No. 297 (73rd Congress, 3rd Session); Arthur Altmeyer, *The Formative Years of Social Security* (Madison, 1966), 11.

[15] Witte, "What Should We Expect from Social Security" (cited note 13). Witte to Paul Kellogg, Nov. 23, 1934, box 15; document labeled "Mr. Witte's speech for Sen. Wagner—before a communist group—Wash. Auditorium in Oct. 1934," box 3; CES files.

[16] Witte, "Preliminary Outline of the Work of the Staff of the Committee on Economic Security," marked in Witte's handwriting, "Presented to the Technical Board at Its Meeting, August 10, 1934," box 5, CES files; Alvin Hansen, "The Investment of Unemployment Reserves and Business Stability," in Hansen *et al., A Program for Unemployment Insurance and Relief in the United States* (Minneapolis, 1934); "Preliminary Outline of the Work of the Staff of the Committee on Economic Security: Submitted to the Technical Board, August 10, 1934, and Informally Agreed Upon as Basis for Beginning Work," box 5, CES files; interview with Murray Latimer, Aug. 8, 10, 1964, Washington, D. C.; Frances Perkins to J. N. Peyton, Aug. 20, 1934, box 154, Perkins files.

[17] Witte, "What Should We Expect from Social Security."

[18] "Preliminary Outline[s]."

[19] Witte, "Possible General Approaches to the Problem of Economic Security: First Tentative Outline, August 16, 1934," Witte folder; Witte, "Views of Miss Edith Abbott of the University of Chicago on a Feasible Program for Economic Security: Conference with Miss Abbott in Washington, August 25, 1934," and attached letter, Witte to Altmeyer, Aug. 25, 1934, box 54; CES files.

[20] Witte, *Development of the Social Security Act, 77;* memorandum, Thos. Eliot to Frances Perkins, Dec. 31, 1934, box 11, Perkins files.

[21] Witte to Wilbur Cohen, Sept. 7, 1940, box 6, Witte Papers; Witte, *Development of the Social Security Act,* 13–14.

[22] "Mr. Witte's speech for Sen. Wagner" (cited note 15).

[23] "President Roosevelt's Remarks to the National Conference on Economic Security, November 14, 1934," box 1, CES files; "Minutes of the Meetings of the Technical Board," Sept. 27, 1934, box 65, Witte Papers; "Preliminary Report of the Technical Board to the Committee on Economic Security," one draft marked "For Cabinet Committee Oct. 1, 1934 E.W.," box 1, CES files.

[24] Roosevelt, *Review of Legislative Accomplishments* (cited note 14); "Some Suggested Lines of Inquiry Regarding Social Insurance," marked "Prepared Prior to the Organization of the Committee on Economic Security by Meredith B. Givens and A. J. Altmeyer," box 5, CES files; "Roosevelt Cabinet Group to Gather National Data for Wide Social Program," *New York Times,* June 30, 1934.

[25] Document marked "Green Bay Address—Written for the President by Edwin E. Witte," Aug. 3, 1934, box 16, CES files; "Text of President's Speech," *New York Times,* Aug. 10, 1934.

[26] "Possibilities of a Unified System of Insurance Against Loss of Earnings," marked "Outline Sept. 1934, by Witte," box 5, CES files; Technical Board Minutes, Sept. 27, 1934; "Minutes of the Meetings of the Committee on Economic Security," Oct. 1, 1934, box 65, Witte Papers; Witte, *Development of the Social Security Act,* 20.

[27] Frances Perkins, *The Roosevelt I Knew* (New York, 1946), 188; interview with

Arthur Altmeyer, June 17, 1966, Madison, Wis.; Frances Perkins to author, Oct. 26, 1964.

[28] Witte to Charlotte Abbott, July 19, 1939; Witte to Edith Abbott, Oct. 18, 1939; box 5, Witte Papers. Witte to Grace Abbott, Aug. 17, 1934, box 16, CES files; Technical Board Minutes, Nov. 30, 1934; Witte, *Development of the Social Security Act*, 162–71; CES Minutes, Dec. 4, 1934; *Report to the President of the Committee on Economic Security* (Washington, 1935), 35–38.

[29] Interview with Murray Latimer, Aug. 8, 10, 1964, Washington, D. C.; Technical Board Minutes (cited note 23), Sept. 27, 1934; Witte to Don Lescohier, Oct. 6, 1934, box 15, CES files.

[30] Witte, "Committee on Economic Security; Report on Progress of Work," Sept. 25, 1934, box 1, CES files; Abraham Holtzman, *The Townsend Movement: A Political Study* (New York, 1963), 35–40; "The Biggest Mass Meeting Ever Held in All the World," and "Suggestions As to the Holding of Mass Meeting on Oct. 28, 1934," mimeographed documents by F. E. Townsend and R. E. Clement, from internal evidence for use of Townsend organizers, box 24, CES files. Witte, "Old Age Pension Organizations: Warning Against Organizations Which Collect Money for Old Age Pension Propaganda," Sept. 6, 1934; K. P. Aldrich to Witte, Sept. 18, 25, 1934; Witte to Aldrich, Sept. 20, 1934; Witte to James Farley, Sept. 7, 1934; box 43, CES files. Witte to Alice Sturtzen, Nov. 15, 1935, box 1, Witte Papers. Witte to Abraham Epstein, Sept. 28, 1934, box 56; document marked "went to Miss Perkins for Press Release E. E. W.," Oct. 25, 1934, box 3; CES files.

[31] Witte, *Development of the Social Security Act*, 17–18.

[32] Document marked in Witte's handwriting, "Material Prepared for Speech of President at the National Conference on Economic Security, Nov. 14, 1935 [*sic*]. Delivered to Miss Perkins, Nov. 11, 1935 [*sic*]. By E. E. Witte," box 3, CES files; drafts of Roosevelt's Nov. 14, 1934, speech, with corrections in Roosevelt's handwriting, file #7046, Presidential Speech Files, Franklin D. Roosevelt Library, Hyde Park, N. Y.

[33] Arthur Krock, "In Washington," *New York Times*, Nov. 20, 1934. Witte, *Development of the Social Security Act*, 45–47; Stark, "Roosevelt Bars Plans Now for Broad Social Program" (cited note 2), 1; Stark, "Experts Push for 'Real' Job Bill" (cited note 2), 1–2; Witte to Josephine Goldmark and many others, Nov. 17, 1934, box 15, CES files.

[34] Interview with Murray Latimer, Oct. 8, 10, 1964, Washington, D. C.; Witte, *Development of the Social Security Act*, 46; interview with Arthur Altmeyer, June 17, 1966, Madison, Wis.; Technical Board Minutes (cited note 23), Nov. 12, 1934; Louis Stark, "See Billion a Year for Job Insurance," *New York Times*, Nov. 17, 1934.

[35] "Recovery Gaining, President Assures Mayors of Country," *New York Times*, Nov. 23, 1934.

[36] "Preliminary Recommendations on Old Age Security, Presented to the President's Committee on Economic Security, by Its Executive Director and His Staff, November 27, 1934," box 5, CES files; CES Minutes (cited note 26), Nov. 27, 1934.

[37] Roosevelt, *Review of Legislative Accomplishments* (cited note 14); Witte, "Memorandum on the Views Relating to the Work of the Committee on Economic Security" (cited note 8); Abraham Epstein to Witte, Sept. 25, 1934, box 56, CES files; Isaac Rubinow, *The Quest for Security* (New York, 1934), 217; Witte to Edgar Sydenstricker, Oct. 23, 1934, box 56, CES files; Witte, *Development of the Social Security Act*, 174–75.

[38] Witte, *Development of the Social Security Act*, 174–79. Witte to Abraham Epstein, Sept. 28, 1934, box 56; copy of letter, apparently to Mrs. Eleanor Roosevelt, prepared by Witte for Miss Perkins' signature, Oct. 12, 1934, box 59; Witte to

Altmeyer, Oct. 6, 1934, box 2; Witte to Sydenstricker, Oct. 6, 23, 1934, box 16; Witte, "The Health Insurance Study of the Committee on Economic Security," Dec. 18, 1934, box 5; CES files. *Report to the President of the Committee on Economic Security,* 38–43; Kellogg to Witte, Dec. 31, 1934, box 16, CES files.

[39] Witte, "The Health Insurance Study of the Committee on Economic Security"; Witte, *Development of the Social Security Act,* 178–80; Cushing-Roosevelt correspondence in file #1523, President's Personal Files, Franklin D. Roosevelt Library, Hyde Park, N. Y. Cushing to Witte, Nov. 26, 1934, box 2; Cushing to Sydenstricker, Nov. 17, 1934, box 16; Bierring to Witte, Cushing to Witte, Feb. 4, 1935, box 2; CES files. Cushing to Roosevelt, Feb. 1, 1935, file #1523 (noted above).

[40] Witte, *Development of the Social Security Act,* 182, 187–88; *Report to the President of the Committee on Economic Security,* 6, 41–43. Sydenstricker to Witte, Feb. 21, 1935; Witte to Sydenstricker, Feb. 23, 1935; box 16, CES files.

[41] Roosevelt, *Review of Legislative Accomplishments* (cited note 14); interview with Murray Latimer, Aug. 8, 1964, Washington, D. C.; "Chronological History of Administration's Unemployment Insurance Program," box 48, CES files; confidential source; Altmeyer, *Formative Years of Social Security,* 11.

[42] Interview with Arthur Altmeyer, June 17, 1966, Madison, Wis.; interview with Murray Latimer, Aug. 8, 10, 1966, Washington, D. C.; Witte to Felix Frankfurter, July 27 and Aug. 9, 1934, box 56, CES files.

[43] Confidential source; Eliot, "Discussion of Constitutionality of Possible Federal-State Plans for Unemployment Insurance and Old-Age Pensions," Aug., 1934, box 18, CES files; Witte, "Memorandum on the Views Relating to the Work of the Committee on Economic Security" (cited note 8). Frankfurter to Witte, Aug. 4, 1934, box 56; memorandum, Eliot to Witte, Oct. 8, 1934, box 18; "Report of Industrial Relations Committee, Business Advisory and Planning Council, September 19, 1934," box 17; CES files.

[44] Memorandum, Eliot to Witte, Oct. 8, 1934, box 18, CES files; Witte, *Development of the Social Security Act,* 33 n., 65, 112; Witte, "Memorandum on the Views Relating to the Work of the Committee on Economic Security" (cited note 8).

[45] Memorandum, Eliot to Witte, Sept. 12, 1934, box 18, CES files; interview with Murray Latimer, Aug. 8, 10, 1964, Washington, D. C.; Technical Board Minutes (cited note 23), Sept. 26, 27, 1934. Mrs. Armstrong, "Outline of Old Age Security Program Proposed by Staff," Nov. 9, 1934; Mrs. Armstrong, "Memorandum on Section 5: Old Age Retirement," n. d.; box 23, CES files. *Economic Security Act: Hearings Before the Committee on Ways and Means, House of Representatives, Seventy-Fourth Congress, First Session, On H. R. 4120* (Washington, 1935), 227; "Preliminary Recommendations on Old Age Security, Presented to the President's Committee on Economic Security, by Its Executive Director and His Staff, November 27, 1934," box 5, CES files; *Report to the President of the Committee on Economic Security.*

[46] Witte, *Development of the Social Security Act,* 111–12; *Economic Security Act,* 1092–93; memorandum, Eliot to Witte, Oct. 8, 1934, box 18, CES files; interview with Arthur Altmeyer, June 17, 1966, Madison, Wis.

[47] "The Technical Board on Economic Security: Report of Committee on Unemployment Insurance," Sept. 26, 1934; "Preliminary Report of the Technical Board to the Committee on Economic Security," one draft marked "For Cabinet Committee Oct. 1, 1934 E W"; box 1, CES files. Witte, *Development of the Social Security Act,* 117; *Economic Security Act,* 400. Two drafts of "Report of the Technical Board on the Major Alternative Plans for the Administration of Unemployment Insurance," one marked "Prepared by Edwin E. Witte for Consideration of the Executive Com-

mittee of the Technical Board, November 8, 1934," in box 1, CES files; the other, a somewhat revised version, in box 71, Witte Papers, and printed in *Economic Security Act*, 874–76.

⁴⁸ Two drafts of "Report of the Technical Board on the Major Alternative Plans for the Administration of Unemployment Insurance."

⁴⁹ *Ibid.;* Technical Board Minutes (cited note 23), Oct. 25, 1934; Bryce Stewart, "Arguments in Support of the Subsidy Plan," Dec. 4, 1934, box 24, CES files.

⁵⁰ Technical Board Minutes (cited note 23), Nov. 8, 1934; Witte, *Development of the Social Security Act*, 117–18; CES Minutes (cited note 26), Nov. 9, 1934; Perkins, *The Roosevelt I Knew*, 291; drafts of Roosevelt's Nov. 14, 1934, Economic Security Conference speech (cited note 32).

⁵¹ "Minutes of Meeting on [*sic*] Unemployment Insurance Experts, Conference on Economic Security, Morning of November 15, 1934," and memorandum, Stewart to Witte, Nov. 21, 1934, box 1; memorandum Witte to Stewart, Nov. 12, 1934, box 16; CES files.

⁵² Witte, *Development of the Social Security Act*, 121–22; Stark, "Experts Push Plan for 'Real' Job Bill" (cited note 2), 1. According to Murray Latimer (interview, Aug. 8, 10, 1964, Washington, D. C.), Stark had many contacts for receiving information on the inside workings of the Committee on Economic Security. His misunderstanding of the subsidy issue here suggests, however, that his direct contact was someone outside of the committee organization, and the emphasis on general revenue contributions suggests that the source was Epstein. Epstein's influence was even more clear in a later Stark attack, on Jan. 20, 1935 (see note 71, below). For Epstein's views see especially his "Social Security—Fact or Fiction," *American Mercury*, 33 (Oct., 1934), 129–38; his two contributions to the *New Republic* series on "Security for Americans," 81 (Nov. 21, 1934, and Jan. 2, 1935), 37–39, 212–15. For his congressional testimony, see Ch. 7.

⁵³ Witte to Frankfurter, Nov. 19, 1934, box 56; Stewart to Witte, Nov. 22, 1934, box 16; Frankfurter to Witte, Nov. 27, n. y., box 56; CES files.

⁵⁴ For a fuller account of the segregated reserves versus pooling issue, see Ch. 5.

⁵⁵ Witte, "The Government and Unemployment," *American Labor Legislation Review*, 25 (March, 1935), 5–12.

⁵⁶ "Report of Industrial Relations Committee" (cited note 43); drafts of Roosevelt's Nov. 14, 1934. Economic Security Conference speech (cited note 32); Witte, *Development of the Social Security Act*, 75, 111, 28, 127; "States Free to Choose Type of Unemployment Compensation Legislation," document marked "By E. E. Witte, Dec. 11, 1934, for Miss Perkins," box 3, CES files; Witte to Harry Millis, Oct. 26, 1938, box 4, Witte Papers; *Economic Security Act* (cited note 45), 372–73; CES Minutes (cited note 26), Nov. 9, 1934; *Report to the President of the Committee on Economic Security*, 15–18; Witte, "The Government and Unemployment" 11.

⁵⁷ Witte to Mary Dawson, Nov. 28, 1934, box 16, CES files; Frances Perkins to author, Oct. 26, 1964; Witte, *Development of the Social Security Act*, 117, 56; Eliot, "Subsidy Plan," Nov. 8, 1934, box 18, CES files; Stewart, "Arguments in Support of the Subsidy Plan" (cited note 49); "Advantages of Federal Subsidy Plan," by "B. N. A." (Barbara Nachtrieb Armstrong), Nov. 9, 1934, box 17, CES files; "Minutes of Meeting on [*sic*] Unemployment Experts" (cited note 51); "Report of the Advisory Council to the Committee on Economic Security," printed in *Economic Security Act* (cited note 45), 885–86; *Report to the President of the Committee on Economic Security*, 11; Advisory Council Minutes, Nov. 15, 16, 1934, box 65, Witte Papers.

⁵⁸ Advisory Council Minutes, Nov. 15, 16, Dec. 7, 1934; Witte, *Development of the*

Social Security Act, 122, 58–61; Stewart, "Arguments in Support of the Subsidy Plan" (cited note 49); Stark, "Job Insurance by States, With a Federal Subsidy, Roosevelt Council's Plan," *New York Times*, Dec. 15, 1934.

[59] Interview with Murray Latimer, Aug. 8, 10, 1964, Washington, D. C.; "Plan for Study of Economic Security" (cited note 5).

[60] Bryce Stewart *et al.*, "Committee on Economic Security, Staff Report on Unemployment Insurance," Dec. 24, 1934, box 71, Witte Papers; Perkins, *The Roosevelt I Knew*, 291–92; Witte, *Development of the Social Security Act*, 124–28.

[61] "Report of the Advisory Council to the Committee on Economic Security" (cited note 57), 882–93; Advisory Council Minutes, Nov. 15, 16, 1934. "Supplementary Statement, Advisory Council on Economic Security," Box 14; Kellogg to Witte, Feb. 21, 1935, box 16; CES files. *Economic Security Act* (cited note 45), 871–93. Kellogg to Louis Howe, Jan. 31, Feb. 12, 1935, Official file #1086, Franklin D. Roosevelt Library, Hyde Park, N. Y.

[62] Tugwell to Roosevelt, Dec. 17, 1934, Official File #121-A; memorandum, "F. D. R." to "L. H.," Feb. 4, 1935, and Howe to Kellogg, Feb. 7, 1935, Official File #1086; Franklin D. Roosevelt Library, Hyde Park, N. Y.

[63] Technical Board Minutes (cited note 23), Nov. 12, 16, 22, Dec. 12, 1934; Witte to Arthur Altmeyer, Dec. 18, 1934, box 54, CES files.

[64] Technical Board Minutes (cited note 23), Nov. 12, 16, 22, Dec. 12, 1934. "Report of the Staff on old Age Security to the Technical Board Executive Committee," Nov. 16, 1934, box 1; Witte to Altmeyer, Dec. 18, 1934, box 54; CES files. Witte, "Old Age Security in the Social Security Act," *Journal of Political Economy*, 45 (Feb., 1937), 29; "Old Age Security Staff Report to Mr. Witte," n. d., box 5, CES files; "Preliminary Recommendations on Old Age Security" (cited note 36), Witte to M. Albert Linton, Dec. 28, 1934, box 57, CES files.

[65] "Preliminary Recommendations on Old Age Security" (cited note 36); Altmeyer, *Formative Years of Social Security*, 26; Technical Board Minutes (cited note 23), Nov. 22, Dec. 12, 1934; "Committee on Economic Security, Agenda of Meeting, Wednesday, December 19, 1934," box 1, CES files; CES Minutes (cited note 26), Dec. 19, 1934; Witte, *Development of the Social Security Act*, 149, 73–74; Witte to Geo. Robinson, Dec. 6, 1948, box 35, Witte Papers; memorandum, Haas to Morgenthau, Jan. 5, 1935, "Henry Morgenthau, Jr., Diary," III, Franklin D. Roosevelt Library, Hyde Park, N. Y.; CES Minutes (cited note 26), Nov. 27, Dec. 4, 7, 18, 19, 28, 1934; document (from internal evidence a transcript of a telephone conversation between Morgenthau and Harry Hopkins), Jan. 7, 1935, "Henry Morgenthau Jr., Diary," III (cited above); CES Minutes (cited note 26), Jan. 7, 1935.

[66] Witte, *Development of the Social Security Act*, 74, 147–51; Witte to Geo. Robinson, Dec. 6, 1948, box 35, Witte Papers; Altmeyer, *Formative Years of Social Security*, 29.

[67] See Ch. 8, *infra*.

[68] Witte to Geo. Robinson, Dec. 6, 1948, box 35, Witte Papers; Witte, *Development of the Social Security Act*, 68–74.

[69] *Report to the President of the Committee on Economic Security*.

[70] Witte to David Saposs, Aug. 27, 1934, box 15, CES files.

[71] Stark, "Wagner Social Security Plan Attacked by Experts as 'Hazy'," *New York Times*, Jan. 20, 1935.

[72] Grace Abbott to Witte, Jan. 19, n. y. (from internal evidence, 1935), box 16; Kellogg to Witte, Feb. 21, 1935, box 16; Witte to Saposs, Aug. 27, 1934, box 15; Witte to Wm. Rice, Jr., Nov. 19, 1934, box 15; Witte to Frankfurter, Nov. 19, 1934, box 56; CES files.

[73] Witte, "Social Welfare Legislation in the Nineteen Thirties," synopsis of address of Feb. 16, 1956, box 259, Witte Papers.

CHAPTER 7

[1] Witte card no. 4, Faculty Information Cards, University of Wisconsin Archives, Madison, Wis.; *The Development of the Social Security Act: A Memorandum on the History of the Committee on Economic Security and Drafting and Legislative History of the Social Security Act* (Madison, 1963), 100. Witte to Jack T. Salter, Mar. 11, 1963, box 8; paper by Wilbur Cohen, "Legislative History of the Social Security Act," box 65; Witte Papers.

[2] See Witte's testimony in *Economic Security Act: Hearings Before the Committee on Ways and Means, House of Representatives, Seventy-Fourth Congress, First Session, on H. R. 4120,* Jan. 21–Feb. 12, 1935 (Washington, 1935) (hereinafter cited as House Hearings), 1–172; and in *Economic Security Act: Hearings Before the Committee on Finance, United States Senate, Seventy-Fourth Congress, First Session, on S. 1130,* Jan. 22 to Feb. 20, 1935 (Washington, 1935) (hereinafter cited as Senate Hearings), 31–99, 187–249.

[3] House Hearings, 3, 122–23, 9, 63, 173, 125 and *passim;* interview with Murray W. Latimer, Aug. 8, 10, 1964, Washington, D. C.

[4] House Hearings, 5–9, 141, 169, and *passim.* Witte's House testimony was his best over-all statement, but he made the same points in Senate testimony and numerous articles and addresses.

[5] "An Important Milestone," *Richmond Times-Dispatch,* Jan. 19, 1935; "The Program for Social Security," *New York Herald Tribune,* Jan. 18, 1935. Roosevelt's words, alluded to by almost all editors, and quoted in full in "The Social Security Plan," *Detroit Free Press,* Jan. 19, 1935, were: "It is overwhelmingly important to avoid any danger of permanently discrediting the sound and necessary policy of Federal legislation for economic security by attempting to apply it on too ambitious a scale before actual experience has provided guidance for the permanently safe direction of such benefits." "The Social Insurance Program," *Journal of Commerce and Commercial* (New York), Jan. 18, 1935; "The President's Program," *New York Times,* Jan. 18, 1935; "Daily Price Index of Stocks," *Journal of Commerce and Commercial* (New York), Jan. 21, 1935; "A Line O' Type or Two," *Chicago Daily Tribune,* Jan. 19, 1935.

[6] "Security for All and Forever," *Boston Evening Transcript,* Jan. 17, 1935; "The Social Security Plan," *Detroit Free Press,* Jan. 19, 1935; "President Insists on Actuarial Insurance," *San Francisco Chronicle,* Jan. 18, 1935; "A Smooth Article," *Chicago Daily Tribune,* Jan. 22, 1935; "Social Security Plans," *St. Louis Globe Democrat,* Jan. 19, 1935; "The President's Program," *New York Times,* Jan. 18, 1935.

[7] House Hearings, 957; Witte to Wm. T. Evjue, Aug. 24, 1938, box 4, Witte Papers; unsent letter, Cohen to Ervin I. Aaron, Mar. 13, 1935, box 43, Committee on Economic Security files, Record Group 47, National Archives, Washington, D. C. (hereinafter cited as CES files); interview with Cohen, July 28, 1964, Washington, D. C.; Witte, "Why the Townsend Old-Age Revolving Pension Plan is Impossible," in House Hearings, 894–96; House Hearings, 110.

[8] Witte to Raymond Moley, May 10, 1935, box 15; Witte to Mary Gilson, April 11, 1935, box 15; Witte, "Balance of Power," n. d. (from internal evidence probably early Apr., 1935), Witte folder; CES files. Witte, "The Social Security Act and the Business Men," synopsis of address of Apr. 18, 1935, box 257, Witte Papers; Witte, "Old Age Security," June 18, 1935, Witte folder, CES files.

⁹ Witte, "The Lundeen (Workers' Unemployment and Social Insurance Bill) [sic]: An Analysis of its Provisions and of the Arguments Advanced by its Supporters," April, 1935, box 9, CES files; Witte, *Development of the Social Security Act*, 80; for a well-measured defense of the Lundeen Bill see Mary Van Kleeck, "Security for Americans IV; The Workers' Bill for Unemployment and Social Insurance," *New Republic*, 81 (Dec. 12, 1934), 121–24.

¹⁰ Rubinow favored national administration of unemployment insurance, or at least endorsement of pooling. See Rubinow, "Security for Americans II: The Ohio Plan of Unemployment Insurance," *New Republic*, 81 (Nov. 28, 1934), 64–66. But he did not testify against the administration bill.

¹¹ House Hearings, 552–83, 1086–91; Senate Hearings, 458–78, 491–516, 892–96, 1138–40. "Endorsements of the Wagner-Lewis Bill in the 73rd Congress. In testimony Before a Sub-Committee of the Committee on Ways and Means of the House of Representatives, March 21 to March 30, 1934," Witte folder; Witte to Frank Graham, March 23, 1935, box 15; CES files.

¹² See especially Epstein's *Insecurity—A Challenge to America* (New York, 1933).

¹³ Witte to E. Wight Bakke, Oct. 24, 1942, box 8, Witte Papers; Frances Perkins to author, Oct. 26, 1964; confidential source; Senate Hearings, 467–68; House Hearings, 571, 552, 561–63, 553–54; Witte, *Development of the Social Security Act*, 82–84; Witte to Epstein, Feb. 5, 1935, box 56, CES files.

¹⁴ Epstein, "Social Security—Fiction or Fact?" *American Mercury*, 33 (Oct., 1934), 129–38; see chapter 6 for Stark's attacks; Epstein, "Security for Americans," *New Republic*, 81 (Nov. 21, 1934), 38.

¹⁵ House Hearings, 554, 561; Witte to Epstein, Feb. 5, 1935, box 56, CES files; Senate Hearings, 464, 466.

¹⁶ Senate Hearings, 474. Robert Elbert, Morris Leeds, Walter Teagle, and Gerard Swope, "Business Advisory Council for the Department of Commerce: Report of Committee on Social Legislation," Apr. 10, 1935, box 11; memorandum, Witte to Joseph Harris, Apr. 26, 1935, box 16, CES files. Witte to Wilbur Cohen, July 16, 1936, box 3, Witte Papers.

¹⁷ Senate Hearings, 1138–40; House Hearings, 1086–90, 1092–96.

¹⁸ House Hearings, 3, 5, 137–38; Witte, "Features of the Economic Security Program," *The Annals of the American Academy of Political and Social Science*, 178 (March, 1935), 88–89, 92; Witte, "Major Issues in Unemployment Compensation," *The Social Service Review*, 9 (March, 1935), 1–23.

¹⁹ Witte, "Major Issues in Unemployment Compensation," 1–23; Witte, "Wisconsin's Interest in the National Security Program," address of Apr. 20, 1935, box 257, Witte Papers. House Hearings, 5.

²⁰ Arthur Altmeyer, *The Formative Years of Social Security* (Madison, 1966), 85, 134–35.

²¹ Witte, *Development of the Social Security Act*, 88; House Hearings, 384–97, 902–06, 141; Senate Hearings, 141–86, 761–68; Kellogg, "Fifteen Weeks and Insecurity," *The Survey*, 71 (Feb., 1935), 38–39; Witte, "Major Issues in Unemployment Compensation," 13, 16.

²² Witte to Kellogg, Jan. 31, 1935; Witte to Frank Graham, Feb. 1, 1935, box 16, CES files. Witte to John Winant, Oct. 7, 1935, box 33, Witte Papers. Senate Hearings, 470.

²³ Witte to Kellogg, Feb. 25, 1935, box 16, CES files. House Hearings, 902. " 'Security Next' " and "The Security Program," *The Survey*, 71 (Feb. and April, 1935), 48 and 110. Witte, "Balance of Power," n. d. (internal evidence suggests early Apr., 1935), Witte folder, CES files; Witte, " 'Federalization' of Unemployment Compensation?" *American Labor Legislation Review*, 32 (Mar., 1942), 41.

[24] Witte memoranda of interviews with John Raskob, Oct. 18, 1934; with Ralph Flanders, Morris Leeds, and William Julian, Oct. 24, 1934; and with Gerard Swope, Oct. 29, 1934; Witte folder, CES files. Gerard Swope to Frances Perkins, box 16, CES files. Soule, quoted in Louis Stark, "Economists Warn Against Inflation," *New York Times,* Dec. 28, 1934; Witte to Irma Hochstein, Jan. 28, 1935, box 15, CES files.

[25] "The Retailers' Program for Social Security," *New York Times,* Jan. 16, 1935; House Hearings, 761–72, 989–1008; Senate Hearings, 702–11, 553–89; interview with Murray Latimer, Aug. 8, 10, 1964, Washington, D. C.

[26] Senate Hearings, 913–18, 921–30; "Chamber Denounces Plans of New Deal But Advisers of President Uphold Him," *New York Times,* May 3, 1935; "Text of Chief Resolutions of Federal Chamber of Commerce," *New York Times,* May 3, 1934; House Hearings, 1020–36.

[27] Folsom, Samuel Lewisohn, Raymond Moley, Swope, and Teagle to Miss Perkins, Dec. 15, 1934, printed in House Hearings, 873–74; Robert G. Elbert, Leeds, Teagle, and Swope, "Business Advisory Council for the Department of Commerce: Report of Committee on Social Legislation," April 10, 1935, box 11, CES files; "Retailers Favor Job Insurance and Old-Age Fund," *New York Times,* Jan. 16, 1935; "The Social Security Bill," *New York Times,* June 17, 1935; "An Uncompleted Task," *Journal of Commerce and Commercial* (New York), Aug. 12, 1935; Elbert, Folsom, Leeds, Teagle, and Swope, "Business Advisory Council: Report of Committee on Social Legislation; Regarding Old Age Security Sections of the Bill H. R. 7260," Apr. 30, 1935, box 17, CES files; "Security Bill Challenged," *New York Times,* May 4, 1935; Joseph Charles Dougherty, Jr., "The Genesis of the Social Security Act of 1935" (unpublished Georgetown University Ph.D. dissertation, 1955), 193; Linton, "The Quest for Security in Old Age: Some Practical Considerations," *Proceedings of the Academy of Political Science,* 16 (June, 1935), 389.

[28] Witte to Frank Graham, Feb. 4, 1935, box 16, CES files; "Opposes 'Haste' on Security Bill," *New York Times,* Feb. 4, 1935; "Text of Chief Resolutions of Federal Chamber of Commerce," *New York Times,* May 3, 1935; "Breaking With Roosevelt," *New York Times,* May 3, 1935; "The Social Security Bill," *New York Times,* June 17, 1935.

[29] Witte to Irma Hochstein, Jan. 28, 1935, box 15, CES files; Witte, "The Social Security Act and the Business Men," synopsis of address before Minneapolis Civic and Commerce Association, Apr. 18, 1935, box 257, Witte Papers; Dougherty, "Genesis of the Social Security Act," 206; Altmeyer, *The Formative Years of Social Security,* 38. Witte to Paul Scharrenberg, May 1, 1935, box 16; Witte to Raymond Moley, May 10, 1935, box 15; CES files.

[29] Witte, *Development of the Social Security Act,* 103, 104, 98; Dougherty, "Genesis of the Social Security Act," 208–11; Harris to Grace Abbott, May 20, 1935, box 13, CES files; Roche, in "Minutes of the Advisory Council of the Social Security Board," Dec. 9–10, 1938, morning session of Dec. 10, p. 16, container 5, Social Security Administration files, Record Group 47, National Archives.

[31] Witte, *Development of the Social Security Act,* 106, 104, 95; Witte, "Twenty Years of Social Security," address of Aug. 15, 1955, box 259, Witte Papers; Witte, "President Roosevelt, The Social Security Act, and Wisconsin," paper marked "published in the *Democratic Digest for Wisconsin,* June, 1940," box 258, Witte Papers; Witte to Grace Abbott, Feb. 21, 1935, box 16, CES files; "Gag Rule Dropped on Social Security," *New York Times,* Apr. 11, 1935; "Text of Speech of President Explaining his Program," *New York Times,* Apr. 29, 1935.

[32] Witte, *Development of the Social Security Act,* 146, 93–94, 102, 105; Witte to

Wilbur Cohen, Aug. 22, Dec. 5, 1939, box 5, Witte Papers; House Hearings, 6; Dougherty, "Genesis of the Social Security Act" (cited note 27), 212.

[33] Witte, "Old Age Security in the Social Security Act," *The Journal of Political Economy*, 45 (Feb., 1937), 4–5; Senate Hearings, 71–72, 246, 298, 301, 303; Witte to Raymond Moley, Mar. 6, 1935, box 15, CES files; "Security Measures Pressed in Senate," *New York Times,* June 15, 1935.

[34] Senate Hearings, 77; Witte to Harry Hopkins, Feb. 26, 1935, box 57; Witte to Raymond Moley, Mar. 6, 1935, box 15, CES files; "Memorandum to the President from the Secretary of Labor," May 8, 1935, marked "Prepared by Edwin E. Witte," box 11, CES files.

[35] Witte to Mary Dewson, Feb. 7, 1935, box 16; "The Case for Permitting States to Adopt the Separate Reserve Account Type of Unemployment Compensation Law and for Giving Credit to Employers Who Have Regularized Employment," no author (internal evidence suggests Witte, but not conclusively), May 21, 1935, box 11; Witte to Raymond Moley, March 6, 1935, box 15; CES files. Altmeyer, *The Formative Years of Social Security*, 34; Witte, *Development of the Social Security Act,* 130, 134, 142; House Hearings, 145.

[36] "Possible Constructive Amendments to the Social Security Act," marked "Suggested to Wisconsin Congressmen, April, 1935, E. E. Witte," box 9; Witte to Roger Hoar, Feb. 8, 1935, box 57, CES files.

[37] "The Case for Permitting States to Adopt the Separate Reserve Account Type of Unemployment Compensation Law and for Giving Credit to Employers Who Have Regularized Employment," no author (internal evidence suggests Witte, but not conclusively), May 21, 1935, box 11; "Memorandum to the President from the Secretary of Labor," May 8, 1935, marked "Prepared by Edwin E. Witte . . . ," box 11, CES files. See the account of Roosevelt's addition of passages emphasizing employment stabilization to his Jan. 17, 1935, speech, in Witte, *Development of the Social Security Act,* 128–29, 141–43.

[38] Witte, *Development of the Social Security Act,* 157. Forster to Perkins, Mar. 12, 1935, box 56; Witte to Paul Scharrenberg, June 24, 1935, box 16; "Statement Concerning the Proposed Substitute Amendment for the Clark Amendment," box 9; Witte to J. Douglas Brown, April 22, 1935, box 55; Witte to Thomas Eliot, Feb. 7, 1935, box 56; memorandum, Witte to Jos. P. Harris, Apr. 26, 1935, box 16; CES files.

[39] Witte to Philip La Follette, July 5, 1935, box 2, Witte Papers. Witte to Merrill Murray, Aug. 8, 1935, box 16; copy of radiogram, Murray to Witte, Aug. 9, 1935, box 16; Murray to Barbara Armstrong, Sept. 4, 1935, box 12; CES files.

[40] For a general summary of the specific features of and changes in the bill, see Witte, *Development of the Social Security Act,* part II.

[41] "An Uncompleted Task," *Journal of Commerce and Commercial* (New York), Aug. 12, 1935 (for evidence of this journal's essential friendliness to social insurance see "The Cost of British Social Legislation," in its issue of Aug. 10, 1935); "The Social Security Program," *Washington Post,* Aug. 11, 1935; "We Start on Social Security," *San Francisco Chronicle,* Aug. 15, 1935; "The Security Bill," *New York Times,* Aug. 11, 1935.

[42] Witte, "Are Old Age Pensions Worth Their Cost?" *American Labor Legislation Review*, 26 (March, 1936), 8–9; Witte to Paul Scharrenberg, June 24, 1935, box 16, CES files. Witte to Raymond Moley, July 5, 1935, box 33; Witte to J. Earl Baker, Nov. 29, 1935, box 2; Witte Papers.

[43] Witte to Mary Gilson, Nov. 18, 1935, box 33; Witte, "The National Social Security Act," summary of address of Nov. 19, 1935, box 257; transcript of Witte's remarks to the American Mining Congress, attached to a letter of Nov. 6, 1935, box 33; Witte to a Mr. Murphy, Dec. 12, 1935, box 2; Witte Papers. For Witte's

arguments against the Townsend plan see especially his "What's Wrong with the Townsend Plan?" in the Madison *Capital Times,* Jan. 23, 24, 26, 1936, and in other Wisconsin papers at about the same time; also his "Why I am Opposed to the Townsend Plan," which the N.E.A. newspaper service syndicated about Feb. 28, 1936. Witte to F. O. Holt, Sept. 19, 1936, box 3, Witte Papers. Witte "Old Age Security in the Social Security Act" (cited note 34), 39. Witte, "The Social Security Act and Proposed Changes," address of Sept., 1937, box 257; Witte to J. Douglas Brown, May 23, 1940, box 6; Witte to Theresa McMahon, Dec. 11, 1940, box 6; Witte Papers.

[44] Witte to James Thompson, Mar. 30, 1936, box 2, Witte Papers. Eveline Burns, *Toward Social Security: An Explanation of the Social Security Act and a Survey of the Larger Issues* (New York and London, 1936), and Paul Douglas, *Social Security in the United States: An Analysis and Appraisal of the Federal Social Security Act* (New York and London, 1936). Witte to Thompson, Oct. 22, 1935 and March 30, 1936, box 2, Witte Papers.

[45] Epstein, "Our Social Insecurity Act," *Harper's Monthly Magazine,* 172 (Dec., 1935), 55–66; Epstein, *Insecurity, A Challenge to America: A Study of Social Insurance in the United States and Abroad* (New York, rev. ed., 1936), 669–784. Witte to John B. Andrews, Feb. 12, March 11, 1936; Witte notation on Andrews to Witte, Mar. 7, 1936; box 33, Witte Papers.

[46] Witte to John B. Andrews, Mar. 11, 1936, box 33; Witte, "Consistency, Thou Art a Jewel," a paper comparing Epstein's earlier and later statements, prepared about mid-1936, box 257; Witte to Wilbur Cohen, July 16, 1936, box 3; Witte Papers. Witte, review of Epstein's *Insecurity* (1936 ed.) in *Journal of Political Economy,* 44 (Dec., 1936), 846–47.

[47] Epstein, "Our Social Insecurity Act" (cited note 45), 55. Witte, "Historical Background of Employment Security," in *Proceedings of the Institute Co-Sponsored by Minnesota Department of Employment Security, University of Minnesota Center for Continuation Study, and Minnesota Chapter, International Association of Personnel in Employment Security,* Oct. 22–23, 1957, pp. 9–10. Witte, "The Social Security Act and Proposed Changes" (cited note 43), Witte Papers. Interview with Wilbur Cohen, July 28, 1964, Washington, D. C.

[48] Witte to Wilbur Cohen, Aug. 7, 1936, box 3, Witte Papers.

[49] Witte to Douglas Anderson, Oct. 9, 1935, box 33, Witte Papers. Witte to Paul Scharrenberg, June 24, 1935, box 16, CES files. Witte to Philip La Follette, July 5, 1935, box 2, Witte Papers. Interviews with Mrs. Edwin Witte, April 15, 1964, Madison, Wis.; with Wilbur Cohen, July 28, 1964, Washington, D. C. Witte to Virginia Dean, Oct. 3, 1935, box 33, Witte Papers.

[50] Witte in "Twenty Years of Social Security," address of Aug. 15, 1955, box 259, Witte Papers. This quotation is part of material that was crossed out.

CHAPTER 8

[1] Witte to Greenman, March 16, 1937, box 34, Witte Papers.

[2] "Text of the Democratic Platform," June 26, 1936; "The Text of the Platform," June 12, 1936; both in *New York Times.*

[3] "The Text of the Platform," June 12, 1936; "Gov. Landon's Address," July 24, 1936; both in *New York Times.*

[4] "Text of Gov. Landon's Milwaukee Address on Economic Security," Sept. 27, 1936; "The Text of Governor Landon's Attack in St. Louis on the New Deal," Nov. 1, 1936; both in *New York Times.* Turner Catledge, "Industrialists Fighting

Roosevelt by Tax Warning on Pay Envelopes," *ibid.*, Oct. 24, 1936. "Text of Roosevelt Speech in New York," *Saint Paul Pioneer Press*, Nov. 1, 1936.

[5] Louis Stark, "Council of A.F.L. Condemns C.I.O. for 'Dual' Activity," Nov. 16, 1936; "Ask Major Changes in Social Security," Jan. 30, 1937; both in *New York Times.*

[6] Witte to Clarence Bond, Oct. 13, 1936, box 33, Witte Papers. Witte, "Old Age Security in the Social Security Act," *Journal of Political Economy*, 45 (Feb., 1937), 43, 17. Witte, "Financing Social Security: Reserves Versus Current Taxation," box 257; Witte to Raymond Moley, Apr. 4, 1936, box 2; Witte to J. Douglas Brown, Mar. 18, 1936, box 2; Witte Papers.

[7] Witte, "Old Age Security in the Social Security Act," 30. Witte to Altmeyer, Dec. 17, 1936, box 33; Witte to W. R. Williamson, Mar. 30, 1937, 3; Witte to Roger S. Hoar, Oct. 29, 1936, box 33; Witte Papers.

[8] "Ask Major Changes in Social Security," *New York Times*, Jan 30, 1937; *Congressional Record*, 81 (75th Congress, 1st Session), 548–50; "Senators Tackle Pension Problem," *New York Times*, Feb. 23, 1937. For more details of the events leading up to the appointment of the advisory council, see Arthur Altmeyer, *The Formative Years of Social Security* (Madison, 1966), 88–91.

[9] Mrs. McMahon to Witte, April 20, May 11, March 31, 1938, and n. d., box 34, Witte Papers. "Minutes of the Advisory Council of the Social Security Board" (hereinafter cited as AC minutes), container 5, Social Security Administration records, Record Group 47, National Archives (hereinafter cited as SS Adm. records), Nov. 6, 1937, forenoon, p. 159; Dec. 10, 1938, morning, pp. 19–20; Nov. 6, 1937, forenoon, pp. 143, 145, and afternoon, p. 120; Dec. 11, 1937, 2:00–3:30 session, pp. 12–16; and *passim.* "Mr. Iglauer's memo to SS. Advisory Council," container 4, SS Adm. records; J. Douglas Brown, The Old Age Reserve Account," *Quarterly Journal of Economics*, 51 (Aug., 1937), 716–19. "Memo by J. D. Brown, Feb., 1937," file O11. 1; J. Douglas Brown, "British Precedent and American Old Age Insurance," J. Douglas Brown folder; SS Adm. records.

[10] Witte to Hugo Zotter, Nov. 17, 1936, box 3, Witte Papers; Witte "Old Age Security in the Social Security Act," 26, 25, 31.

[11] See Ch. 6, *supra.* Linton, "The Quest for Security in Old Age," *Proceedings of the Academy of Political Science*, 16 (June, 1935), 338–39. Witte to Altmeyer, Dec. 17, 1936, box 34; Geo. B. Robinson to Witte, Feb. 7, 1945, box 35; Witte to Wilbur Cohen, Apr. 7, 1949, box 35; Witte to Cohen, Feb. 13, 1937, box 3; Witte to Thomas Konop, Mar. 6, 1937, box 3; Witte Papers. "Senators Tackle Pension Problems," *The New York Times*, Feb. 23, 1937, p. 11. Witte to W. R. Williamson, Apr. 22, 1937, box 3, Witte Papers. AC minutes, afternoon, p. 103.

[12] Linton, "The Quest for Security in Old Age," 388–89; "Sees Danger of Inflation," *New York Times*, Sept. 17, 1936; Linton, "Insuring the Future: The Burden of Old-Age Security," *Atlantic Monthly*, 162 (Oct., 1938), 544–45; Linton, "Old-Age Security for Everybody," *Atlantic Monthly*, 157 (April, 1936), 491–93. Folsom to Witte, July 21, Aug. 7, 1936, box 3, Witte Papers. AC minutes, Nov. 6, 1937, afternoon, p. 105; and Dec. 10, 1937, 2:30–4:30 session, p. 27. See the *New York Times*: "Health Plan urged by State Doctors," April 10, 1938; "No 'Real' Budget Balance," Nov. 1, 1937; "That Pseudo-Reserve Fund," Nov. 3, 1937; "Eat Your Cake Three Times," Nov. 12, 1937; "The Wrong Way Out and the Right Way Out," April 13, 1938; "Chamber Assails 'Deficit Spending'; Tax Aid Put First," April 24, 1938; "Labor Act Revision to Forbid Coercion Asked by Chamber," April 30, 1937.

[13] Linton, "The Problem of Reserves for Old Age Benefits," *American Labor Legislation Review*, 27 (March, 1937), 23–26. AC minutes, Nov. 6, 1937, afternoon, p. 101; Nov. 5, 1937, forenoon, p. 24; Dec. 10, 1937, 4:30–5:15 session, p. 11; Dec. 10,

1938, afternoon, p. 28. Linton, "Old Age Security For Everybody," 496–97; Linton, "Insuring the Future: The Burden of Old-Age Security," 547–48.

[14] "Roosevelt Scored at Chicago Rally," Aug. 5, 1938; "Republican Analysis of the Nation," Aug. 6, 1938; both in *New York Times*. Linton, "Old-Age Security for Everybody," 497; Linton, "Observations on the Old Age Security Program Embodied in the Social Security Act," box 199, Witte Papers; Linton, "Insuring the Future: The Burden of Old-Age Security," 548.

[15] Witte, "Thoughts Relating to the Old-Age Insurance Titles of the Social Security Act and Proposed Changes Therein: Revision of Statement presented by Edwin E. Witte to the Social Security Advisory Council at its meetings on February 18 and 19, 1938" (box 199, Witte Papers), 14, 16; Witte, "In Defense of the Federal Old Age Benefit Plan," *American Labor Legislation Review*, 27 (March, 1937), 31; Witte notations on a document, "Considerations as to Revision of the Federal Old-Age Insurance Program," box 199, Witte Papers.

[16] Witte, "Planned Security for an Older Population," *New York Times*, Feb. 17, 1935; Witte to W. Rulon Williamson, Feb. 4, 1938, box 34, Witte Papers.

[17] R. A. Hohaus, "Memorandum for Meeting With Social Security Advisory Council December 10, 1937," box 199, Witte Papers.

[18] Williamson to Witte, Feb. 4, 1935, box 16, CES files; Williamson, *Social Insurance Legislation* (New York, 1935; American Management Association pamphlet, Insurance Series, No. 21), 1–22. Williamson to Witte, Jan. 13, 1938; box 34; Williamson to Witte, Aug. 3, 1938, box 4; Witte Papers.

[19] Williamson to Witte, Feb. 15, 1938, box 34; Aug. 3, 19, 1938, box 4; Witte Papers.

[20] Witte to Williamson, Aug. 22, 1938; note in Witte handwriting, "The Concept of Social Insurance; Notes after a discussion of this subject by Mr. Bigge of the Social Security Board, December 11, 1937"; box 4, Witte Papers.

[21] AC minutes (cited note 9): Dec. 11, 1937, 11:30–12:30 session, pp. 1–4; and Nov. 6, 1937, forenoon, p. 147. Witte to Gerald Morgan, Nov. 7, 1938, box 34; notes in Witte's handwriting, "Views of Abe Epstein on the Amendments to the Old Age Insurance Law Presented to the Interim Committee of the Social Security Advisory Council at New York, Nov. 4, 1938," box 4; Witte Papers. AC minutes (cited note 9), Dec. 10, 1937, 12:15–1:15 session, pp. 1–27. "Health Plan Urged by State Doctors," *New York Times*, Apr. 10, 1938, p. 29; Flynn, "Fixed for Life," *Colliers*, 98 (Aug. 8, 1936), 12–13, 36–37; Witte to Philip Taft, Nov. 30, 1937, box 4, Witte Papers.

[22] "Mr. Linton's Discussion at the Saturday Morning, November 6, 1937, Session of the Advisory Council on Social Security," container 4, SS Adm. records. AC minutes (cited note 9): Feb. 10, 1938, morning, p. 62; Dec. 10, 1938, afternoon, p. 6; Dec. 9, 1938, morning, pp. 13–14; Dec. 11, 1937, 11:30–12:30 session, pp. 8–9; Nov. 6, 1937, afternoon, pp. 108–10. "Brief Summary Statement of the Deflationary Influence of the Old Age Reserve Account by Alvin H. Hansen," box 199, Witte Papers.

[23] Witte to Linton, Nov. 15, 1935, box 2, Witte Papers. AC minutes (cited note 9): Dec. 10, 1937, 2:30–4:30 session, pp. 29–36; Nov. 6, 1937, afternoon, pp. 110–24; Dec. 11, 1937, 11:30–12:30 session, p. 8. "Brief Summary Statement of the Deflationary Influence of the Old Age Reserve Account by Alvin H. Hansen," box 199, Witte Papers.

[24] Witte to Theresa McMahon, Sept. 15, 1938; Witte to Reinhard Hohaus, June 30, 1938; box 4, Witte Papers.

[25] AC minutes (cited note 9): Dec. 11, 1937, 11:30–12:30 session, pp. 12–13; Feb. 18, 1938, morning, pp. 60–63; Dec. 10, 1938, morning, pp. 32–35, and afternoon, pp. 30–31. Louis Stark, "Security Program Proposed to Cover Added 14,800,000,"

Dec. 19, 1938; "Tax Reform Urged by Manufacturers," Nov. 28, 1937; both in *New York Times*.

[26] George B. Robinson to Witte, Feb. 8, 1949, box 35, Witte Papers.

[27] Witte, "Social Security: A Wild Dream or a Practical Plan?" address of June 17, 1938, box 257, Witte Papers.

[28] Witte, "Thoughts Relating to the Old-Age Insurance Titles" (cited note 15), 2–3. Witte, "Thoughts Regarding Amendments to the Social Security Act Which Appear Feasible in the Next Session of Congress," memorandum prepared for Altmeyer, Aug., 1938, box 257; Witte to Altmeyer, Dec. 16, 1938, box 34; "Suggested Amendments to the Social Security Act—by Gerard Swope," box 199; Witte Papers.

[29] Witte, "Thoughts Relating to the Old-Age Insurance Titles" (cited note 15), 2–3. Witte to Altmeyer, April 2, 1938, box 34; Witte, "Thoughts Regarding Amendments to the Social Security Act Which Appear Feasible in the Next Session of Congress," memorandum prepared for Altmeyer, Aug., 1938, box 257; Witte to Theresa McMahon, April 26, 1938, box 34; Witte Papers.

[30] Witte to Altmeyer, Dec. 9, 1937, box 34, Witte Papers. AC minutes (cited note 9): Feb. 19, 1938, morning, pp. 25–29; April 30, 1938, morning, pp. 30–45. For copy of the Advisory Council Statement on the handling of the funds, see Advisory Council on Social Security, *Final Report*, Senate Document No. 4, 76th Congress, 1st Session (Washington, 1939; report dated Dec. 10, 1938), 29.

[31] "Considerations concerning the financing of the old-age insurance program (as amended)," a document attached to letter, Brown to Witte, Oct. 14, 1938, box 34; Witte to Brown, Oct. 15, 1938, box 34; "Proposed Draft, Final Report of the Advisory Council on Social Security, December 1, 1938," p. 60, box 199; Witte to Brown, Dec. 7, 1938, box 34; Witte Papers. AC *Final Report*, 25, and *passim*.

[32] AC minutes (cited note 9), April 29, 1938, afternoon, pp. 18, 30–33, 44–49. Note in Witte's handwriting attached to letter, Brown to members of the interim committee, April 7, 1938, box 199; Witte to Alanson Willcox, March 8, 1938, box 4; Witte Papers. Witte, "Thoughts Relating to the Old-Age Insurance Titles" (cited note 15), 10–14. AC *Final Report*, 6.

[33] AC minutes (cited note 9), Feb. 18, 1938, afternoon, p. 55. Linton, "Old Age Security For Everybody," *Atlantic Monthly*, 157 (April, 1936), 493. Witte, "Thoughts Relating to the Old-Age Insurance Titles" (cited note 15), 27–29. Witte to John Corson, June 4, 1938; Witte to Eveline Burns, May 20, 1938; box 4, Witte Papers.

[34] AC minutes (cited note 9), April 30, 1938, 11:30 session, p. 24. AC *Final Report*, 6.

[35] AC *Final Report*.

[36] Witte to Theresa McMahon, March 31, 1939, box 4; Witte to Geo. B. Robinson, Mar. 23, 1949, box 35; Witte to Ronald Haughton, Oct. 18, 1939, box 5; Witte Papers. "Only United Action Can End the Slump, Eccles Declares," *New York Times*, May 14, 1938.

[37] Witte to Wilbur Cohen, March 30, 1939, box 5, Witte Papers.

[38] Witte to Robert La Follette, Jr., June 15, 1939, box 34; Witte to Theresa McMahon, July 6, 1939, box 5; Witte to Thomas Norton, June 27, 1939, box 5; Witte to Wilbur Cohen, July 3, 1939, box 5; Witte Papers.

[39] Witte to Theresa McMahon, July 6, 1939, box 5; Witte to Jay Iglauer, Aug. 7, 1939, box 34; Witte to Robert La Follette, Jr., June 15, 1939, box 34; Witte Papers. For Witte's evaluation of the 1939 amendments see his article, "Social Security—1940 Model," *American Labor Legislation Review*, 29 (Sept., 1939), 101–09. For a general summary of the 1939 old age security amendments, see "Federal Old-Age and Survivors Insurance: A Summary of the 1939 Amendments," *Social Security Bulletin*, 2 (Dec., 1939), 3–16.

[40] Witte, "More Security for Old Age: The Proposals of the Committee on Old Age Security of the Twentieth Century Fund," *Social Service Review*, 12 (March, 1938), 35; Witte, "In Defense of the Federal Old Age Benefit Plan" (cited note 15), 28; Witte to C. A. Kulp, April 7, 1936, box 2, Witte Papers.

[41] Letter from Altmeyer to Arthur Vandenberg, quoted in "Senators Tackle Pension Problem," *New York Times*, Feb. 23, 1937. Witte, "The Issues Raised by the Social Security Act," synopsis of address of Oct. 1939; Witte, "Extension of Coverage—The Vitally Necessary Next Step in Old Age Insurance," address of Dec. 27, 1939; box 257, Witte Papers.

[42] Witte, "In Defense of the Federal Old Age Benefit Plan" (cited note 15), 33. Witte, "Thoughts Relating to the Old-Age Insurance Titles" (cited note 15), 25. AC minutes (cited note 9), Nov. 6, 1937, afternoon, p. 106. Linton, "Insuring the Future: The Burden of Old Age Security" (cited note 12), 547–48.

[43] AC minutes (cited note 9), April 30, 1938, 11:30 session, pp. 22–24; Cohen to Witte, Aug. 15, 1939, box 5, Witte Papers.

[44] Witte to Carl Curtis, Dec. 16, 1953, box 35, Witte Papers.

[45] Witte To Sir William Beveridge, Apr. 15, 1937, box 34; Witte to Wilbur Cohen, Nov. 6, 1943, box 8; Witte to George Bigge, Oct. 20, 1938, box 4; Witte to Harry Weiss, March 22, 1938, box 4; Witte to John A. Wolfard, March 26, 1941, box 6; Witte, "Whither Unemployment Compensation," paper dated April 10, 1940, p. 54, box 258; Witte Papers.

[46] Witte, "Economic Arguments in Support of the Constitutionality of Unemployment Compensation," paper marked "Prepared in Summer 1936 Not Published," box 257; Witte, "Factors Affecting the Economic Development of the United States," summary of address of May 3, 1956, box 259; Witte, "Experience Rating and Other Forms of Incentive Taxation," remarks of Oct. 14, 1941, box 258; Witte, "Unemployment Compensation and the General Welfare," outline of address of Aug. 16, 1941, box 258; Witte, "Experience Rating," address of May 13, 1941, box 258; Witte Papers. Witte, "Unemployment and Recovery," *Yale Review*, 26 (March, 1937), 490.

[47] Witte to John A. Wolfard, March 26, 1941, box 6, Witte Papers.

[48] Witte, "Whither Social Security," synopsis of address of July 21, 1949, box 258, Witte Papers.

[49] Witte to Wilbur Cohen, Nov. 6, 1943, box 8, Witte Papers.

[50] Witte to George B. Robinson, March 1, 1951, box 35; Witte to Altmeyer, Nov. 21, 1939, box 34; Witte Papers.

CHAPTER 9

[1] Notes in Witte's handwriting, "Government Employees and Old Age Security," for talk on Oct. 10, 1957, box 259, Witte Papers.

[2] Witte, "Public Policy on Economic Security," *Business Topics*, 5 (May, 1958), 8.

[3] Witte, "What to Expect of Social Security," *American Economic Review*, 34 (Supplement, March, 1944), 220.

[4] Witte, "The Approaching Crisis in Old Age Security," *American Labor Legislation Review*, 30 (Sept., 1940), 115–16, 120; Dickinson to Witte, Mar. 17, 22, 1941, box 6, Witte Papers.

[5] Witte to Frank Dickinson, March 19, 1941, box 6, Witte Papers. Witte, "Is the Continued Drive for Universal Pensions a Social Menace?" *American Labor Legislation Review*, 31 (March, 1941), 41–42. Witte, "What's Ahead in Social Security?" *Harvard Business Review*, 19 (Spring, 1941), 319. Notes in Witte's handwriting, "Wilbur J. Cohen on the Social Security Plank of the Democratic Platform,

1940; Information given me orally August 12, 1940," box 6; Witte, "What Should We Expect from Social Security," address of April 17, 1942, box 258, Witte Papers; Witte, "What to Expect of Social Security," 216–17.

⁶ Witte, "The Approaching Crisis in Old Age Security," 115–16. Witte to William Haber, Jan. 18, 1941, box 6, Witte Papers. Witte, "What Should We Expect from Social Security." Witte to Frederic Dewhurst, March 19, 1941, box 6; Witte, "Terms and Objectives" (Ch. 2 of his unpublished Ms. of a book on social security), 10, box 295; Witte Papers. Malcolm Scott Torgerson, "An Analysis of the Development of Old Age Assistance in the United States" (unpublished University of Nebraska Ph.D. dissertation, 1953), 157.

⁷ Witte, "Job Insurance—Its Limitations and Value," Economic Forum, 2 (Winter, 1935), 412. Witte, "The Value of Social Insurance," synopsis of address of April 19, 1935, box 257; notes in Witte's handwriting, "Maintaining Purchasing Power Through Social Security," for talk given on July 29, 1954, box 259; Witte Papers. Witte, "What Should We Expect from Social Security?" Witte to Frederic Dewhurst, March 19, 1941, box 6, Witte Papers. Witte, "Terms and Objectives," 10.

⁸ Witte, "Objectives in Social Security," synopsis of addresses of March, 1954, box 259; Witte, "Social Security in the Present Day World" (Ch. 1 of his unpublished Ms. of a book on social security), box 295; Witte, "Labor and Social Legislation," lecture of Dec., 1949, box 258; Witte, "Why Social Security—Does It Meet Our Problem?" synopsis of talk given on June 18, 1940, box 258; Witte Papers. Witte, "What to Expect of Social Security," 216. Witte to H. J. Kubiak, May 23, 1946, box 10; Witte, "Security and Economic Change," address of April 16, 1956, box 259; Witte Papers.

⁹ Witte, "Security and Economic Change." Witte, "Terms and Objectives," 7. "Problems of Aging," discussion between Witte and others in University of Chicago Round Table, no. 646 (Aug. 13, 1950), 1–10. Witte, "What is Needed for Economic Security in Old Age?" remarks of Sept. 11, 1951, box 258; notes in Witte's handwriting, "Economic Aspects of the Aged Problem," for talk on Feb. 21, 1956, box 259; Witte Papers. Witte, "Social Security Needs and Opportunities," State Government, 24, (June, 1951), 150–53. Witte, "Government's Attitude and Responsibility to an Aging Population," address of June 8, 1951, box 258, Witte Papers.

¹⁰ Arthur Altmeyer, The Formative Years of Social Security (Madison, 1966), 142–43, 148; Security, Work, and Relief Policies (Report of the Committee on Long-Range Work and Relief Policies to the National Resources Planning Board; Washington, 1942); Witte, "American Post-War Social Security Proposals," American Economic Review, 33 (Dec., 1943), 825–38; Michael Davis, "Health for the Nation," Survey Graphic, 33 (Dec., 1944), 491–93, 510–11.

¹¹ Witte, "American Post-War Social Security Proposals," 829.

¹² Security, Work, and Relief Policies, especially 545–49. Witte, "American Post-War Social Security Proposals," 825–31. Witte, "1944–1945 Programs for Postwar Social Security and Medical Care," Review of Economic Statistics, 27 (Nov., 1945), 171–88.

¹³ Witte to Mrs. C. C. Linnenberg, Jr., July 13, 1943, box 8, Witte Papers; Witte, "American Post-War Social Security Proposals," 832–38; Witte, "1944–1945 Programs," 171–88.

¹⁴ Witte to Michael Davis, Aug. 25, 1943, box 8, Witte Papers.

¹⁵ Witte to Wilbur Cohen, Apr. 6, 1942, box 7, Witte Papers.

¹⁶ Miss Brandeis to Witte, Nov. 10, 1944; Witte to Miss Brandeis, Nov. 14, 1944; box 9, Witte Papers. Witte, "American Post-War Social Security Proposals" (cited note 10), 835–37.

[17] Wilbur Cohen to Witte, Nov. 6, 1943, box 8; Witte remarks to the National Health Conference, July 20, 1938, box 257; Witte to Michael Davis, Oct. 28, 1943, box 8; Witte to Wilbur Cohen, Nov. 8, 1943, box 8; Witte Papers. Davis, "Health for the Nation" (cited note 10).

[18] Transcript of Witte's address to the Employment Service State Advisory Council, New York, Dec. 29, 1941, box 258, Witte Papers; Witte, "Labor and Social Legislation" (cited note 8); Witte to Wilbur Cohen, Feb. 15, 1941, box 6, Witte Papers; Witte, "What Should We Expect from Social Security" (cited note 5).

[19] Witte to Arthur Altmeyer, April 30, 1941, box 35; Witte to Daniel Goldy, May 23, 1946, box 10; Witte Papers. Interview with Wilbur Cohen, July 28, 1964, Washington, D. C. Cohen to Witte, Nov. 20, 1942, box 8, Witte Papers.

[20] Witte to Cohen, Nov. 9, 1942, box 8; Witte, "Social Security—1948," box 258; Witte, memo to Altmeyer, "Thoughts Regarding Amendments to the Social Security Act Which Appear Feasible in the Next Session of Congress," Aug., 1938, box 257; Witte to Ronald Haughton, Oct. 15, 1941, box 7; Witte to Wilbur Cohen, Nov. 23, 1942, box 8; Witte Papers.

[21] Witte to Wilbur Cohen, Mar. 18, 1942, box 7; Cohen to Witte, Aug. 28, 1943, box 8; Witte to Cohen, Sept. 9, 1943, box 8; Witte Papers.

[22] Witte to Cohen, Oct. 11, 1943, box 8; Witte to Miss Brandeis, May 7, 1942, box 35; Witte, "A Panoramic View of Social Security in the United States" (Ch. 5 of his unpublished Ms. of a book on social security), 1, 4, box 295; Witte Papers. Witte, "Public Policy on Economic Security" (cited note 2), 6; notes in Witte's handwriting, "Labor's Interest in Social Security," n. d., box 257, Witte Papers; Witte, "Introduction," in Dominico Gagliardo, *American Social Insurance* (New York, 1949), xvii–xx.

[23] Witte, "Public Policy on Economic Security" (cited note 2), 7.

[24] Witte, "Social Security—1948" (cited note 19); Witte, memo to Altmeyer, Aug., 1938 (cited note 20). Witte to Wilbur Cohen, March 27, 1936, box 2; Witte, "The Future of Social Security," address of Jan. 25, 1957, box 259; Witte Papers. Witte, "Objectives in Social Security" (cited note 8).

[25] Witte, "The Problem of Extending Old Age Insurance Protection to a Larger Part of the American People," confidential memo to Social Security Board, Dec., 1939, box 257; "Social Security Act Amendments," paper marked Aug. 24, 1950 (from internal and external evidence appears to be by Witte), box 258; Witte Papers. Witte, "The Future of Social Security." Witte to Altmeyer, Oct. 30, 1939, box 34; Witte, "Increase of Unemployment Insurance Benefits," address of Dec. 27, 1939, box 257; Witte, "Next Steps in Social Security," address of Sept. 28, 1940, box 258; transcrpit of Witte address, Dec. 29, 1941 (cited note 18), box 258; notes in Witte's handwriting, "The Prospects for Unemployment Insurance," for talk on June 24, 1952, box 259; Witte Papers.

[26] Witte, memo to Altmeyer, Aug., 1938 (cited note 20). Witte, "Socialized Medicine and the National Health Program," address of Sept. 22, 1939, box 257; Witte, "Health Security: Needs, Progress, and Prospects," address of April 20, 1940, box 258; Witte to Wilbur Cohen, Sept. 22, 1943, box 8; Witte to Elizabeth Brandeis, Nov. 14, 1944, box 9; Witte, "Health Security Progress," remarks of Dec. 29, 1939, box 257; Witte Papers. "Review of the Special Meeting," *Detroit Medical News,* 35 (Dec. 13, 1943), 5–7, 16–20.

[27] Altmeyer, *The Formative Years of Social Security,* 279–85; Torgerson, "Development of Old Age Assistance" (cited note 6), 157–75, 58–61. Witte, "Overall View of the Development of Social Security" (Ch. 2 of his unpublished Ms. of a book on social security), 26–28, box 295; Witte, "Old Age Security—The National Pic-

ture," paper adapted from an address of Oct. 2, 1954, box 259; Witte Papers. Witte, "Public Policy on Economic Security" (cited note 2), 5, 7.

²⁸ Outline in Witte's handwriting, "Health, Welfare, and Pension Funds," for talk on Aug. 14, 1948, box 258; Witte, "The Future of Social Security"; notes in Witte's handwriting, "Social Security," outline of address of Dec. 9, 1957, box 259; Witte Papers. Witte, "The Changing Role of Labor, Management, and Government in the Quest for Security," in *Conference on the Quest for Security—1955 Version* (Wayne University, Institute of Industrial Relations, 1955), 7–8, 13. Witte's remarks in "Collective Bargaining for Pensions," proceedings of a conference on "War Time and Long Range Issues in Collective Bargaining for Pensions," Monticello, Illinois, Feb. 16–18, 1951, pp. 24–25, box 258; Witte to Wilbur Cohen, April 6, 1948, box 35; Witte Papers. Witte, "Labor and Social Legislation" (cited note 8); Witte, "Labor's Interest in Social Security" (cited note 22); Witte, "Contributory Versus Non-Contributory Industrial Pension Plans," box 258, Witte Papers; Witte, "Social Provision for the Aged," chapter in Milton Derber, ed., *The Aged and Society* (Champaign, Ill.: Industrial Relations Research Association Publication No. 5, 1950), 115–36; Witte, "Talk at the Janesville Industrial Relations Center Institute, May 1953," box 259, Witte Papers; Witte, "Terms and Objectives" (cited note 6), 8, 13.

²⁹ Meriam, *Relief and Social Security* (Washington, 1946), 836–38, 568–70, 860; Witte, "Terms and Objectives" (cited note 6), 9; Witte, "Need for Security" (Ch. 3 of his unpublished Ms. of a book on social security), 6, box 295, Witte Papers.

³⁰ Meriam, *Relief and Social Security*, 563, 847–48. Witte, review of Meriam's *Relief and Social Security* in *American Economic Review*, 37 (Sept., 1947), 723–27.

³¹ Notes in Witte's handwriting, "The 'Baby Townsend' Plan for Old Age Security of the Chamber of Commerce of the United States," remarks of May 14, 1953, box 35, Witte Papers.

³² M. Albert Linton, "Facing Facts in Old Age Security," *American Economic Security*, 9 (Jan.–Feb., 1952), 19–27.

³³ Witte to Wilbur Cohen, Mar. 24, 1952, box 35, Witte Papers; Altmeyer, *The Formative Years of Social Security*, 202–03, 211; Witte, "The Present Danger to Social Security," outline of remarks at the National Conference on Social Security, Washington, May 14, 1953, box 259, Witte Papers; Witte, "Old Age Security—The National Picture" (cited note 27); see Ch. 8 of Altmeyer's book for more details of the history of various legislative proposals in 1953 and 1954.

³⁴ Witte, "Why Social Security—Does It Meet Our Problem?" (cited note 8); Witte, "What Should We Expect from Social Security" (cited note 5). Witte, "Whither Social Security," synopsis of address of July 11, 1949, box 258; Witte, "Old Age Security," address of March 20, 1946, box 257; Witte Papers. Witte, "Overall View of the Development of Social Security" (cited note 27), 1. Witte, "Social Security as a Major Purpose of Government," *Wisconsin State Employee* (March, 1937), 5, 19; Witte, "Social Security: A Wild Dream or a Practical Plan?" address of June 17, 1938, box 257, Witte Papers; Witte, "Labor and Social Legislation" (cited note 8), 26. Witte, "Security and Progress in the Welfare State," address of Jan. 10, 1952, box 259, Witte Papers; Witte, "The 'Bug-a-Boo' of the Welfare State," address of July 24, 1949, *Congressional Record*, 95 (81st Congress, 1st Session; Oct. 19, 1949), 15041–43.

³⁵ Witte, "Old Age Security in the Social Security Act," *Journal of Political Economy*, 45 (Feb., 1937), 39; Witte, "Government's Attitude and Responsibility to an Aging Population" (cited note 9); Witte, "What to Expect of Social Security" (cited note 3), 216. Notes in Witte's handwriting, "The Relationship of Private to Governmental Employee Security Programs," outline of address of Oct. 13,

1949, box 258; Witte, "Social Security—1951," address of Dec. 7, 1950, box 258; Witte Papers. Witte, "The Objectives of Social Security, *Review of Social Economy,* 17 (March, 1959), 25; Witte, "Need for Security" (cited note 29), 14.

[36] Calvin to Witte, Feb. 9, 24, 1938; Witte to Calvin, Feb. 15, 1934; box 34, Witte Papers.

[37] Witte to Wilbur Cohen, Nov. 6, 1943, box 8; Witte to Elizabeth Brandeis, Oct. 27, 1943, box 35; Witte to Cohen, Nov. 17, 1943, box 8; Witte Papers.

CHAPTER 10

[1] Witte, "The Present Labor Situation," address of May 18, 1937, box 255, Witte Papers.

[2] Memorandum, Witte to William Davis, Feb. 1, 1934, attached to Witte to Arthur Altmeyer, Feb. 1, 1934, box 1; Witte to Davis, Feb. 1, 1934, with attachments, box 1; Witte to Clara Beyer, Feb. 5, 11, Apr. 5, 1937, box 3; Beyer to Witte, Feb. 16, 1937, box 3; Witte Papers.

[3] Witte to Marshall Dimock, Nov. 13, 1939, box 5, Witte Papers.

[4] Witte to Clara Beyer, Apr. 5, 1937, and attached "Outline of a Suggested New Approach to State Legislation for Mediation and Arbitration in Labor Disputes," box 3, Witte Papers.

[5] Witte to T. L. Norton, Oct. 30, 1939, box 5, Witte Papers.

[6] Philip La Follette to Witte, July 14, 1937, box 3; Witte to Ronald Haughton, Feb. 27, 1939, box 5; Witte to David Saposs, Feb. 25, 1939, box 5; Witte to Martin Glaeser, Mar. 15, 1939, box 5; Witte to A. J. Glover, Aug. 2, 1939, box 63; Julius Heil to Witte, Mar. 20, 1939, box 63; Witte Papers.

[7] "Witte Resigns Labor Board," clipping marked *"Wisconsin State Journal,* 1939," in scrapbooks of Mrs. Florence Witte, Madison, Wis., Vol. II. Witte to Fred Yoder, Nov. 29, 1938, box 63; Witte, "Labor Relations as a Community Problem," address of Oct. 4, 1939, box 255; both in the Witte Papers.

[8] Witte, "Religion's Contribution to Harmonious Labor Relations," *Christianity and Crisis,* 1 (Dec. 1, 1940), 5–7; The Twentieth Century Fund, *Labor and National Defense* (New York, 1941), 121. Witte, "Labor Policies in Relation to National Defense," address of July 23, 1940, box 255; Witte to Howard Kaltenborn, July 29, 1942, box 7; Witte Papers.

[9] Salvatore J. Bella, "The National War Labor Board—A View Against the Background of Grievance Disputes," *Labor Law Journal,* 8 (June, 1957), 417–21; Witte, "Wartime Handling of Labor Disputes," *Harvard Business Review,* 25 (Winter, 1946), 171–77; Witte, "Organized Labor Confronting Wages, Prices, and Accelerated Rearmament," address of Mar. 22, 1951, box 256, Witte Papers.

[10] Bella, "The National War Labor Board," 419–20; Witte, "Wartime Handling of Labor Disputes," 171–77; Witte, memorandum to Lloyd Garrison, May 29, 1944, box 86, Witte Papers; George W. Taylor, "Voluntarism, Tripartitism and Wage Stabilization," in *The Termination Report of the War Labor Board* (Washington, 1947–1948), I, xviii; for further general description see Dexter Keezer, "Observations on the Operations of the National War Labor Board," *American Economic Review,* 36 (June, 1946), 233–57.

[11] Bella, "The National War Labor Board," 420.

[12] Witte to Orhan Yirmibesh, May 4, 1943, box 8; Witte, memorandum of conference with UAW-CIO officers, July 20, 1943, box 75; Witte to Selig Perlman, Aug. 27, 1943, box 8; Witte to John R. Commons, n. d. (from internal evidence, Aug., 1943), box 8; Witte to Herman Somers, Apr. 16, 1943, box 8; Detroit Regional War

Labor Board file, *passim,* box 84; Witte to Myron Utgard, July 19, 1943, box 8; Witte Papers.

[13] Frank Rising, "L'Envoi—or Something," document in scrapbook of Mrs. Florence Witte, Madison, Wis., Vol. III. Witte to Harry Brown, July 19, 1943; Witte to Norris Hall, Apr. 8, 1943; Witte to Orhan Yirmibesh, May 4, 1943; Witte to Sam Berger, July 13, 1943; box 8, Witte Papers.

[14] Presidential Executive Order No. 9328, Apr. 8, 1943; Witte to Theresa McMahon, Mar. 25, 1943, box 8, Witte Papers; Witte, "Wartime Handling of Labor Disputes," 182–83; Witte to Jack Todd, Nov. 4, 1943, box 8, Witte Papers.

[15] Witte to Alma Bridgman, Mar. 30, 1943, box 8, Witte Papers; Rising, "L'Envoi—or Something"; Thomas Groen, "In Labor's Hot Spot," *The Detroit News,* clipping in scrapbooks of Mrs. Florence Witte, Madison, Wis., Vol. II. marked Feb. 4, 1943.

[16] Witte to Noel Fox, Dec. 6, 1944, box 9; Witte to Charles Boyd, Feb. 14, 1944, box 8; Witte Papers.

[17] Witte to Eugene Melder, June 23, 1944; Witte to D. L. Goldy, Dec. 27, 1944; box 9, Witte Papers. National War Labor Board, *Wage Report to the President on the Wartime Relationship of Wages to the Cost of Living* (Washington, Feb. 22, 1945). Minutes of the National War Labor Board (mimeographed and unbound), June 30, 1944ff., box 77; Witte to Charles Spencer, April 9, 1945, box 9; Witte, "Observations on Present Industrial Relations Problems from the Point of View of a Public Member of the National War Labor Board," notes of Nov. 24, 1944, box 78; Witte Papers.

[18] *Passim,* box 80, Witte Papers.

[19] Documents relating to the case of the General Motors Corporation and the United Automobile, Aircraft, and Agriculture Implement Workers of America, C.I.O., No. 111-4665-D, especially two drafts of a "Summary of Issues To Be Decided by the Board, with Recommendations" and a National War Labor Board Directive Order of March 3, 1945, box 81, Witte Papers.

[20] Documents relating to Western Union Company cases, especially Witte's "Summary of the Facts Bearing on the Wage Issue" in case No. 111-17763-D and a National War Labor Board Directive Order on the same case, Dec. 29, 1945, box 86, Witte Papers.

[21] Witte to Svend Godfredsen, May 23, 1946, box 10, Witte Papers. Clark Kerr, "The Meat Packing Commission," in *The Termination Report of the National War Labor Board,* I, 1046, 1057–62. Witte, memorandum to Wm. Davis and others, Jan. 5, 1944 (but from internal evidence, *1945*), box 82; Witte to Howard Kaltenborn, Oct. 25, 1946, box 11; Witte, "Summary of the Issues To Be Decided, with Recommendations," document dealing with the cases of Swift, Armour, Wilson, and Cudahy and the United Packinghouse Workers of America, C.I.O., n.d., and a National War Labor Board Directive Order in the same cases, Feb. 20, 1945, box 83; Witte Papers.

[22] Witte to Virgle [*sic*] Wilhite, Oct. 25, 1945, box 10; Witte to Louis F. Buckley, Dec. 3, 1945, box 10; Witte to J. A. Todd, May 3, 1945, box 9; Witte to Arthur Grebler, Aug. 27, 1945, box 9; Witte Papers.

[23] Witte to Francis Haas, June 24, 1946, box 10; Witte, "Labor-Management Responsibility in a Democracy," address of June 21, 1947, box 256; Witte, "Toward Industrial Peace and Cooperation," in *3rd Annual Labor Management Round-Table Conference Program* (Kansas State College, Apr. 20–30, 1949), copy in box 256; Witte, "Trends in Collective Bargaining," address of May 9, 1946, box 255; Witte, "Industrial Labor Relations," address of Nov. 8, 1946, box 255; Witte Papers.

[24] Witte, "Some Labor Issues," address of Oct. 27, 1945; Witte, "Do We Need New Labor Relations Legislation?", address of Mar. 4, 1946; box 255, Witte Papers. For

a discussion of Congress' pre-Taft-Hartley proposals, see Harry A. Millis and Emily Clark Brown, *From the Wagner Act to Taft Hartley: A Study of National Labor Policy and Labor Relations* (Chicago, 1950), Ch. 8. Witte to Phillips Bradley, June 28, 1947, box 49; Witte, "The Current Labor Situation," address, n. d. (from internal evidence *ca.* Aug., 1947), box 256; Witte Papers. Witte, "Labor Management Relations Under the Taft-Hartley Act," *Harvard Business Review*, 25 (Autumn, 1947), 554–75; Witte, "An Appraisal of the Taft-Hartley Act," *American Economic Review*, 37 (May, 1948), 368–82.

[25] Witte, articles and addresses, boxes 255–56, *passim,* Witte Papers.

[26] Witte, "The Public Interest in Industrial Relations," address of Jan. 30, 1948, box 256; Witte, "Industrial Labor Relations," address of Nov. 8, 1946, box 255; Witte Papers.

[27] Witte, "Labor-Management Relations Under the Taft-Hartley Act," 575.

[28] Donald B. Straus, *The Development of a Policy for Industrial Peace in Atomic Energy* (Planning Pamphlet No. 71; Washington, 1950), 27–59, 63; United States Atomic Energy Commission, *Report of the President's Commission on Labor Relations in the Atomic Energy Installations* (Washington, 1949), especially p. 12; see also David B. Johnson, "Labor-Management Relations in the Atomic Energy Program" (unpublished University of Wisconsin Ph.D. dissertation, 1955).

[29] Straus, *Development of a Policy*, 64, 68–71; United States Atomic Energy Commission, *Report of the President's Commission;* Witte to Ronald Haughton, May 4, 1949, box 15, Witte Papers.

[30] Witte to George Strong, June 21, 1949, box 15, Witte Papers; "Report to the President by the Atomic Energy Labor Relations Panel, June 1 to December 1, 1952," Appendix VII in United States Atomic Energy Commission, *Thirteenth Semiannual Report* (Washington, 1953), 179; J. Keith Mann, "The Emergency is Normal—Atomic Energy," in Irving Bernstein, Harold L. Enarson, and R. W. Fleming, eds., *Emergency Disputes and National Policy* (New York, 1955), 176.

[31] Witte to Phillips Bradley, Jan. 12, 1948, box 50, Witte Papers.

[32] Ewan Clague to Witte, Oct. 30, 1947, box 50, Witte Papers.

[33] Witte, "Criteria in Wage Rate Determinations," *Washington University Law Quarterly*, 1949 (Fall, 1949), 24–43. Witte, "The Future of Labor Arbitration—A Challenge," address of Jan. 16, 1948; Witte, "Labor Arbitration from a Public Point of View," address, n. d. (marked "c. 1948"); box 256, Witte Papers.

CHAPTER 11

[1] Witte to Ronald Haughton, May 4, 1946, box 10; Witte to Maud Swett, Dec. 17, 1945, box 9; Witte Papers.

[2] Witte, *The Government in Labor Disputes* (New York, 1932); Felix Frankfurter, review in the *Columbia Law Review*, 32 (May, 1932), 920–23. For other reviews, see, for instance, Cleon Swayzee, review in *American Bar Association Journal*. 18 (Dec., 1932), 802; Edward Berman, review in *The American Economic Review*, 22 (Sept., 1932), 515–17; Nathan Greene, review in the *Harvard Law Review*, 45 (Apr., 1932), 1132–34. Christ, review in the *Journal of Political Economy*, 41 (Apr., 1933), 263–66; James Thompson to Witte, July 24, 1944, box 9, Witte Papers.

[3] Witte to James Thompson, Sept. 19, 1933, box 1; Witte to Martin Foss, Nov. 24, 1934, box 2; Witte to Thompson, Oct. 9, 1935, box 2; Witte to Alfred Fernbach, Oct. 3, 1941, box 7; Witte to Hugh Bone, May 4, 1943, box 8; Witte to Dana Ferrin, July 1, 1946, box 10; Witte to Paul Webbink, Jan. 7, 1947, box 11; Witte Papers.

[4] Witte to W. Brooke Graves, Nov. 5, 1934, box 2; Witte to Jos. Harris, May 15,

1941, box 6; Witte to Mark Ingraham, Apr. 28, 1945, box 9; Frances Q. [*sic*] to Witte, June 22, 1945, box 9; Elizabeth Brandeis to Witte, Jan. 4, 1946, box 10; Wm. Kiekhofer to Witte, June 5, 1944, box 9; Witte to Ronald Haughton, June 21, 1946, box 10; Witte Papers.

⁵ Witte, *The Development of the Social Securtiy Act: A Memorandum on the History of the Committee on Economic Security and Drafting and Legislative History of the Social Security Act* (Madison, 1963); Witte, *Five Lectures on Social Security* (Rio Piedras, P. R., 1951).

⁶ Witte, "Seven Economists Dancing on the Point of a Needle," review of Douglass V. Brown *et al., The Economics of the Recovery Program* (New York, 1934), in *New Republic*, 78 (April 11, 1934), 249.

⁷ Witte to Wilbur Cohen, Sept. 29, 1936, box 3; Witte to Verne Kaub, July 3, 1939, box 5; Witte to Emerson Schmidt, July 31, 1946, box 10; Witte to I. S. Falk, July 25, 1952, box 35; Witte to Charles Killingsworth, Nov. 12, 1941, box 7; Witte to Ronald Haughton, Nov. 24, 1941, box 7; Witte Papers.

⁸ University of Wisconsin "Instructional Reports," 1916–1954, and University of Wisconsin "Time Tables", 1953–1959; both in University of Wisconsin Archives, Madison, Wis. Witte to Grady Sloan, March 13, 1942, box 7; Witte to Jos. Harris, April 15, 1945, box 10; Witte to John Troxell, Feb. 18, 1947, box 11; Witte to Ellen Commons, Oct. 18, 1946, box 35; Witte Papers.

⁹ J. Douglas Brown to Witte, April 25, 1945, box 43; Simeon Leland to Witte, April 6, 1949, box 43; Witte, "An Economist Looks at Industrial Relations," address of April 22, 1949, box 256; Witte Papers. Witte, "Institutional Economics as Seen by an Institutional Economist," *The Southern Economic Journal,* 21 (Oct., 1954), 136, 131–33.

¹⁰ *Ibid.*, 133–35, 137–38.

¹¹ *Ibid.*, 139–40.

¹² Witte to Walter O'Donnell, Jan. 3, 1951; Witte to H. L. McCracken, Apr. 25, 1955; Witte to James Bell, Apr. 8, 1955; Witte to Geo. Stocking, July 11, 1955; Witte to Robert Barr, July 15, 1955; box 43, Witte Papers.

¹³ Witte, "Economics and Public Policy," *American Economic Review*, 47 (Mar., 1957), 1–2, 4–8, 12–13, 15, 20–21.

¹⁴ *Ibid.*, 14, 20–21.

¹⁵ John Newhouse, "Prof. Witte Knows 'Great Devotion'," *Wisconsin State Journal,* (Madison) March 24, 1957, V, p. 4.

¹⁶ *Ibid.;* Witte, "The 'Bug-a-Boo' of 'The Welfare State,' " *Congressional Record,* 95 (81st Cong., 1st Sess., Oct. 19, 1949), 15041–43.

¹⁷ Interview with Wilbur Cohen, July 28, 1964, Washington, D.C. Lloyd Ulman to Witte, March 9, 1957; Wm. Knowles to Witte, Feb. 25, 1957; both in volume of testimonial letters presented to Witte, 1957, in the possession of Mrs. Florence Witte, Madison, Wis. Ruth Schiefelbein to Witte, Sept. 10, 1937, box 3; and *passim*, Witte Papers. James S. Parker to author, June 17, 1966; Ronald Haughton to author, June 22, 1966; Merlyn S. Pitzele to author, July 7, 1966; Warren J. Baker to author, July 12, 1966; Herman Somers to author, July 14, 1966; Jos. Krislov to author, July 23, 1966. Witte to Mrs. H. V. Schwalbach, Aug. 22, 1934, box 15, Record Group 47, National Archives.

¹⁸ Stanley Williams, "Miss Perkins' Talk Makes Witte's Accomplishments Shine Brighter," *Wisconsin State Journal* (Madison), March 28, 1957; "Address of Senator Wayne L. Morse at a Luncheon Honoring Prof. Edwin E. Witte, Madison, Wisc., March, 1957," *Congressional Record*, 103 (85th Cong., 1st Sess., April 16, 1957), 5753; "Notables Praise Witte," *Daily Cardinal* (University of Wisconsin), March 28, 1957; "Social Security Held Non-Partisan," *The Capital Times* (Madison), Mar.

28, 1957; Dr. Witte Receives Friends' Plaudits," *The Capital Times* (Madison), March 28, 1957; volume of testimonial letters (cited note 17).

[19] Witte to S. L. Scheldrup, April 4, 1960, box 32, Witte Papers; interview with Mrs. Florence Witte, June 30, 1966, Madison, Wis.; medical records of Edwin E. Witte, Madison General Hospital, Madison, Wis.; medical records of Edwin E. Witte, office of Dr. A. J. Richtsmeier, Madison, Wis.; death certificate of Edwin E. Witte, Dane County Register of Deeds office, Madison, Wis.

ESSAY ON SOURCES

Introduction: the manuscript collections

The footnotes reveal the full range of sources consulted in this study, and indicate that a large proportion of them are primary documents. The most useful source has been the collection of papers that Edwin E. Witte accumulated in his lifetime, now deposited in the Manuscripts Division of the State Historical Society of Wisconsin, in Madison, Wisconsin. Witte carried on a very large volume of correspondence, collected a vast body of research materials, and consistently kept files on the numerous organizations and activities in which he was involved. Fortunately his large collection is well organized by quite specific topical categories, so that it is readily useful for investigation in specialized subjects, as well as for a general study such as the present biography.

Eighty-eight of the 296 boxes of Witte papers are taken up with correspondence, both incoming and outgoing. Since Witte habitually expressed his thoughts candidly and extensively in letters and memoranda, his "General Correspondence," occupying thirty-two boxes and including documents from 1914 to 1961, constitutes an especially valuable body of materials for a biography. Well over half of the total correspondence has been organized by subject. Especially useful have been materials grouped under the heading of social security, and selected items from categories such as labor arbitration cases, University of Wisconsin topics, and various Witte activities for the State of Wisconsin, the federal government, and numerous other organizations. Interspersed throughout both the general and the topical correspondence are many documents other than letters and memoranda, such as drafts of reports and bills. For example, most of the basic documents of the 1934–1935 Committee on Economic Security appear in the correspondence files.

A very large part of the Witte collection consists of research files. These files, which include vast numbers of clippings, government releases, and other documents, as well as Witte's own research notes, contain basic information on virtually every subject of Witte's academic and practical interests. They have been organized under detailed subject headings, under the general categories of economics, government and government's role in the economy, industrial relations, labor history and law, and social security. Completing the collection are files ranging from class lecture notes, scrapbooks, and bibliographical materials, to manuscripts of published and unpublished Witte writings. Especially useful have been nine personal diaries, and Witte's numerous articles and addresses. Many of the addresses are not available or readily accessible elsewhere. In summary, the Witte manuscript collection includes not merely personal papers, but a wide variety of basic documents in fields of his interests, organized for maximum accessibility.

273

Other collections, documents, and published items from the period under study complete the range of firsthand sources. United States Department of Labor and Social Security Administration files in the Social and Economic Branch of the National Archives, Washington, D.C., yielded extensive information, supplemented with a few items from the Franklin D. Roosevelt Library, Hyde Park, New York. Correspondence and other documents of the Wisconsin Industrial Commission and of the Wisconsin Legislative Reference Bureau, both located at Madison, Wisconsin, provided information for a period of Witte's life between 1917 and 1933 for which there are few items extant in his papers. Examination of selected items in the University of Wisconsin Archives, and in the Richard T. Ely, John R. Commons, William Leiserson, Arthur Altmeyer, and Wilbur Cohen manuscript collections at the State Historical Society of Wisconsin also helped to complement the Witte papers. Newspapers (especially the *New York Times* and Watertown and Madison, Wisconsin, newspapers) provided factual material and occasionally some interpretive comment. Most useful for contemporaries' interpretations of controversial questions and issues were records of government hearings, books written at the time of the events, and numerous articles in various scholarly journals, proceedings of organizations, and highbrow popular magazines. Numerous interviews and direct correspondence with men and women who had known and associated with Witte provided personal insights, as well as some crucial facts. Firsthand unpublished and published sources, and above all the Witte Papers, provided most of the information for the biography.

Sources revealing Witte's personal development
Numerous personal interviews, together with correspondence from Witte's surviving relatives and associates, have been invaluable for studying his personal development and habits. Eight of his nine diaries span his undergraduate and graduate years, and outline his intellectual and emotional maturation as a student at the University of Wisconsin. While his diaries offer a few comments on larger university and political matters, chiefly they record Witte's observations on his immediate experiences and problems, especially in collegiate debating and student politics. Maurice Vance's biography of the university's president, *Charles Richard Van Hise: Scientist Progressive* (Madison: State Historical Society of Wisconsin, 1960), and Merle Curti's and Vernon Carstensen's two-volume study, *The University of Wisconsin: A History, 1848–1925* (Madison: University of Wisconsin Press, 1949), provide wider perspective on the university during Witte's student years. Robert S. Maxwell's *La Follette and the Rise of the Progressives in Wisconsin* (Madison: State Historical Society of Wisconsin, 1960), describes the progressive political atmosphere of the state.

A journalistic portrait of Witte in the November 26, 1955, issue of *Business Week*, "Witte's One-Man Economics" (pp. 92–104), written anonymously by Merlyn Pitzele, reveals some of Witte's strengths, weaknesses, and style late in life. Wilbur J. Cohen's "Edwin E. Witte (1887–1960): Father of Social Security," in the *Industrial and Labor Relations Review*, 14 (Oct., 1960), 7–9, though a post-mortem eulogy, is a thoughtful sketch by a former student and close associate of Witte. Personal papers, scrapbooks, and testimonial letters in possession of Mrs. Florence Witte, Madison, Wisconsin, contained some items specific and judicious enough to be useful to the critical researcher. Interviews with Mrs. Witte were invaluable for reconstructing the personal aspects of his life and career.

Sources revealing Witte as an institutional economist
Witte seldom attempted to make explicit his basic framework of economic thought, but he said truthfully that virtually all of his ideas came from John

R. Commons. LaFayette G. Harter's *John R. Commons: His Assault on Laissez Faire* (Corvallis: Oregon State University Press, 1962) reveals the scope of Commons' interests. Commons' autobiography, *Myself* (New York: The Macmillan Company, 1934; and Madison: University of Wisconsin Press, 1963), is better for transmitting the richness of Commons' personality and thought. The four-volume *History of Labour in the United States* (New York: The Macmillan Company, 1926–1935), by Commons and his associates, provides background information and insight into Commons' contribution. Commons' and John B. Andrews' *Principles of Labor Legislation* (New York: Harper and Brothers, 1916, 1920, 1927, 1936) reveals the practical side of Commons' thought to which Witte responded most. Commons' *Industrial Goodwill* (New York: McGraw-Hill Book Company, Inc., 1919), and his *The Legal Foundations of Capitalism* (New York: The Macmillan Company, 1924), set forth principles he believed essential to a well-functioning industrial system. Two of Commons' articles, "Marx Today: Capitalism and Socialism," in *The Atlantic Monthly*, 136 (Nov., 1925), 682–93, and "Karl Marx and Samuel Gompers," 41 (June, 1926), 281–86, provide evidence of Commons' acceptance of capitalism and conservative trade unionism, as against radicalism. *Institutional Economics* (New York: The Macmillan Company, 1934) is Commons' most extensive statement of his theoretical ideas, the kernel of which appears in his "Institutional Economics," *The American Economic Review*, 21 (Dec., 1931), 647–58. A helpful interpretation of those ideas is Kenneth Parsons, "John R. Commons' Point of View," published in *The Journal of Land and Public Utility Economics*, 18 (Aug., 1942), 245–56, and in Commons' posthumous book, *The Economics of Collective Action* (New York: The Macmillan Company, 1950). Arthur J. Altmeyer's "The Wisconsin Idea and Social Security," *Wisconsin Magazine of History*, 42 (Autumn, 1958), 19–25, is also helpful, especially for setting Commons' reformism and that of the entire Wisconsin school of institutional economics in a historical perspective.

Witte's most complete and explicit statement of his own general concept of institutional economics is his "Institutional Economics as Seen by an Institutional Economist," *The Southern Economic Journal*, 21 (Oct., 1954), 131–40, in which he revealed especially the degree to which he concentrated on the practical side of Commons' thought. His 1956 presidential address to the American Economic Association, "Economics and Public Policy," in *The American Economic Review*, 47 (March, 1957), 1–21, is a further elaboration of his working assumptions and economic beliefs. Providing a broader historical and intellectual perspective on institutional economics is a 1956 paper by Kenneth Boulding, "A New Look at Institutionalism," published with critical discussion by Allan Gruchy, Forest Hill, Frank Knight, Kenneth Parsons, and Clarence Ayres in *The American Economic Review: Papers and Proceedings of the Sixty-ninth Annual Meeting of the American Economic Association*, 47 (May, 1957), 1–27.

Labor law, legislative reference, and industrial relations activities

Scholarly journals are mines of information for research on labor legislation and industrial mediation. *The American Labor Legislation Review*, organ of the American Association for Labor Legislation, spanned the most crucial period of the development of Witte's thought, and of labor legislation in the United States, with articles on virtually every substantive issue. Summarizing much of the material with which the association dealt is Lloyd Pierce's unpublished 1953 University of Wisconsin doctoral dissertation, "The Activities of the American Association for Labor Legislation in Behalf of Social Security and Protective Labor Legislation." Since the demise of the *Review* early in the 1940's the publications of the Industrial Relations Research Association, and numerous industrial relations institutes, have filled the void it left. Gertrude Schmidt's well-written but unpublished 1933 University of Wisconsin dissertation, "History of Labor Legislation in Wisconsin," sets its subject adequately in an historical and economic context, while Gordon Haferbecker's *Wisconsin Labor Laws* (Madison: University of Wisconsin Press, 1958) summarizes the development of Wisconsin labor law from its beginning to the mid-1950's.

Revealing Witte's early interest and views regarding labor disputes law are manuscripts of several orations he delivered as a university senior (Witte Papers, box 255); a report he wrote anonymously for a House Judiciary Committee minority that dissented from the proposed Clayton antitrust bill of 1914, published as Part 3 of *Antitrust Legislation*, United States House of Representatives Report No. 627 (63rd Congress, 2d Session); Witte's article, "The Clayton Bill and Organized Labor," in *The Survey*, 32 (July 4, 1914), 360; and his "The Doctrine that Labor is a Commodity," in *The Annals of the American Academy of Political and Social Science*, 69 (Jan., 1917), 133–39. Numerous unpublished reports that Witte wrote for the United States Industrial Relations Commission of 1914–1915, especially his lengthy "Injunctions in Labor Disputes," available in the National Archives, Washington, D. C. and/or in the library of the State Historical Society of Wisconsin, contain his early ideas on labor disputes law in full. In the period of the 1920's Witte set forth his substantive ideas on the labor injunction in "Results of Injunctions in Labor Disputes," in *The American Labor Legislation Review*, 12 (Dec., 1922), 197–201; "Value of Injunctions in Labor Disputes," *The Journal of Political Economy*, 32 (June, 1924), 335–56; and "Social Consequences of Injunctions in Labor Disputes," *Illinois Law Review*, 24 (March, 1930), 772–85. His " 'Yellow Dog' Contracts," *Wisconsin Law Review*, 6 (Dec., 1930), 21–32, deals with a closely related problem. He examined the history, doctrines, and practices of court interference in labor disputes more fully in his unpublished 1927 University of Wisconsin Ph.D. dissertation, "The Role of the Courts in Labor Disputes," and in his definitive 1932 book, *The Government in Labor Disputes* (New York: McGraw-Hill Book Company, Inc., 1932). In the literature paralleling Witte's labor injunction writings, Felix Frankfurter's and Nathan Greene's *The Labor Injunction* (New York: The Macmilan Company, 1930) fully supports Witte's view that court power in labor disputes cases needed to be curbed. J. Finley Christ, "The Federal Courts and Organized Labor," *The Journal of Business*, 3 (April, July, 1930), 205–49, 341–75, is a scholarly dissent from such views.

Regarding Witte's role in drafting the 1932 Norris-La Guardia Act, hearings of a 1928 Senate Judiciary subcommittee on bill S. 1482, *Limiting Scope of Injunctions in Labor Disputes* (70th Congress, 1st Session), illuminate the initial legislative problem and proposals. Documents revealing Witte's role in writing the Act are in box 1 of the Witte Papers. *The Report[s] of the Proceedings* of the annual conventions of the American Federation of Labor (1927–1931) contain the story of that organization's gradual shift to support the Norris-LaGuardia bill. Basic legislative documents in the history of the act are the 1930 Senate Report No. 1060 (71st Congress, 2nd Session), and the 1932 Senate Report No. 163 (72nd Congress, 1st Session). Witte discussed the content and history of the act after its passage in "The Federal Anti-Injunction Act," *Minnesota Law Review*, 16 (May, 1932), 638–58.

For Witte's role in administering labor law as Secretary of the Industrial Commission of Wisconsin, correspondence, minutes, and other documents in the offices of the Commission, along with its biennial published *Report[s] on Allied Functions*, provide the basic information. A pamphlet by John R. Commons, *The Industrial Commission of Wisconsin: Its Organization and Methods* (n. d.; Wisconsin Legislative Reference Library copy bears the plausible date 1913), explains the rationale of the commission. Arthur Altmeyer's *The Industrial Commission of Wisconsin: A Case Study in Labor Law Administration* (Madison: University of Wisconsin Press, 1932), is quite useful for studying the commission and early Wisconsin labor law in general.

Correspondence in the files of the Wisconsin Legislative Reference Bureau yields firsthand information on Witte's work as chief of that agency, and on many other aspects of his early career, life, and role in Wisconsin government. Of very broad value are the many indexed clippings and documents in the active collection of the Bureau's library. Writings by John H. Leek, especially his *Legislative Reference Work: A Comparative Study* (Philadelphia: University of Pennsylvania, 1925), illuminate the origins, history, and rationale of legislative reference work in general. Charles McCarthy's *The Wisconsin Idea* (New York: The Macmillan Company, 1912) contains a description of the Wisconsin agency as its architect saw it. Edward A. Fitzpatrick's laudatory biography of the architect, *McCarthy of Wisconsin* (Morningside Heights, N.Y.: Columbia University Press, 1944), and Marinus G. Toepel's more up-to-date "The Legislative Reference Library: Serving Wisconsin," in the *Wisconsin Law Review*, 1951 (Jan., 1951), 114–24, offer further historical information and some perspective on the Wisconsin bureau. Witte revealed his understanding of legislative reference work in two major addresses, "A Legislative Reference Librarian's Conception of His Job" (Oct., 1931; Witte Papers, box 259) and "The Research Work of Legislative Reference Bureaus" (Dec. 27, 1933; Witte Papers, box 257), and in several articles: "Government Agencies for the Improvement of Statute Law in Wisconsin," *Phi Beta Kappa Quarterly*, 8 (May, 1926), 47–56; "A Law Making Laboratory," *State Government*, 3 (April, 1930), 3–10; and "Technical Services for State Legislators," *The Annals of the American Academy of Political and Social Science*, 195 (Jan., 1938), 137–43. Manuscript "Report[s] of the Legislative Reference Library" for the years 1926–1933 (Witte Papers, box 108) contain factual information. A further example of Witte's contribution to orderly processes in government is his study, "The Preparation of Proposed Legislative Measures by Administrative Departments," in a publication of the 1936–1937 President's Committee on Administrative Management, *Report of the Committee with Studies of Adminisrative Management in the Federal Government* (Washington: Government Printing Office, 1937), 357–78.

A manuscript by Witte, "Outline of a Suggested New Approach to State Legislation for Mediation and Arbitration in Labor Disputes" (Apr. 5, 1937; Witte papers, box 3), reveals ideas he held in the mid-1930's for labor relations law. Offering similar information on a later period are his March, 1945, address, "Do We Need New Labor Relations Law?" (Witte Papers, box 255), and two articles, "Labor-Management Relations Under the Taft-Hartley Act," *Harvard Business Review*, 25 (Autumn, 1945), 554–75, and "An Appraisal of the Taft-Hartley Act," in *The American Economic Review*, 38 (June, 1948), 368–82. *From the Wagner Act to Taft Hartley: A Study of National Labor Policy and Labor Relations* (Chicago: University of Chicago Press, 1950), by Harry Millis and Emily Clark Brown, offers general information and perspective on labor relations law in the 1930's and 1940's. Witte's sixty-four-page booklet, *Historical Survey of Labor Arbitration* (Philadelphia: University of Pennsylvania Press, 1952), illustrates his general interest in the field of industrial mediation, while another booklet he co-authored with Robben W. Fleming, *Marathon Corporation and Seven Labor Unions* (Washington: National Planning Association, 1950), demonstrates his interest in specific industrial relations techniques.

Very ample sources of information on Witte's greatest contribution to labor relations, as a practicing mediator, are documents in his correspondence and his numerous files on separate cases. A further basic document for one of his first major industrial relations ventures is the Wisconsin Labor Relations Board's "Report Covering the Period April 28, 1937 to November 30, 1938" (mimeographed copy in the State Historical Society of Wisconsin). *The Termination Report of the National War Labor Board* (Washington: Government Printing Office, 1947–1948), I–III, summarizes the work of the agency for which he expended greatest industrial mediation efforts. In *The Terminal Report*, George W. Taylor's "Voluntarism, Tripartitism, and Wage Stabilization" (I, xv–xxi) is especially valuable for illuminating the Board's operating premises. Witte presented his ideas on wartime labor policy in "Strikes for Wartime: Experience with Controls," in *The Annals of the American Academy of Political and Social Science*, 224 (Nov., 1942), 128–34. Further interpretations and summaries of the 1942–1945 War Labor Board's work are Dexter Keezer's firsthand account, "Observations on the Operations of the National War Labor Board," in *The American Economic Review*, 36 (June, 1946), 233–47; Salvatore J. Bella's "The National War Labor Board—A View Against the Background of Grievance Disputes," *Labor Law Journal*, 8 (June, 1957), 416–35; and Witte's own "Wartime Handling of Labor Disputes," *Harvard Business Review*, 25 (Winter, 1946), 169–89. *War Labor Reports*, a periodical, is a public record of the Board's decisions. Especially useful for revealing Witte's personal role on the Board are the minutes of War Labor Board meetings and various documents Witte wrote summarizing issues and making recommendations in specific cases. Other documents, such as a mimeographed "Report and Recommendations of the Fact-Finding Board in the Meat Packing Industry Case" (Feb. 7, 1946; Witte Papers, box 83), by Witte, Clark Kerr, and Raymond J. Starr, illustrate Witte's continuing mediation efforts in the postwar period.

In *The Development of a Policy for Industrial Peace* (Washington: The National Planning Association, 1950), Donald B. Straus described the manner in which Witte and his colleagues developed a labor relations policy for the atomic energy industry in the years 1948 and 1949. An unpublished 1955 University of Wisconsin dissertation, "Labor-Management Relations in the Atomic Energy Program," by David B. Johnson, discusses the events and issues through the entire period of Witte's service on the Atomic Energy Labor Relations Panel. J. Keith Mann gave a highly interpretive account in "The Emergency is Normal— Atomic Energy," a chapter in *Emergency Disputes and National Policy* (New York: The Industrial Relations Research Association, 1955), edited by Irving Bernstein, Harold Enarson, and Robben W. Fleming. Basic primary documents relating to Witte's role in atomic energy labor relations are the 1948 "Correspondence Concerning AEC Labor Policy," the April, 1949, "Report of the President's Commission on Labor Relations at Atomic Energy Commission Installations," and subsequent "Report[s] to the President by the Atomic Energy Labor Relations Panel," published as appendices to the *Semiannual Report[s] of the Atomic Energy Commission*, 1949–1953.

Social Security

The two most important, widely accessible sources for a study of Witte's role and ideas in the field of social security are his *The Development of the Social Security Act: A Memorandum on the History of the Committee on Economic Security and Drafting and Legislative History of the Social Security Act* (Madison: University of Wisconsin Press, 1962) and Robert J. Lampman, ed., *Social Security Perspectives: Essays by Edwin E. Witte* (Madison: University of Wisconsin

Press, 1962). Though it was not published until after his death, Witte wrote *The Development of the Socal Security Act* in 1936, so that it is a primary source written near the time of the events. Although sometimes its· organization is confusing, his account offers comment on virtually ·every and ·passage of the original 1935 Social Security Act. While it gives Witte's point of view, it is objectively accurate in factual detail with only very minor exceptions. *Social Security Perspectives,* like *The Development of the Social Security Act,* is a posthumous publication. For the present biography the unabridged manuscript versions of Witte's articles and addresses have been used as sources. But Lampman has made Witte's substantive ideas and the Witte style in social security highly accessible through effectively organizing, editing, and abridging the articles and addresses on social security. A further book, giving some of Witte's most basic ideas on the subject, is Witte's *Five Lectures on Social Security* (Rio Piedras, Puerto Rico: Labor Relations Institute, University of Puerto Rico, 1951).

For general background on social security, the source materials include vast numbers of scholarly books and articles, government publications, proceedings and publications of social service agencies, and pamphlets, booklets, and releases from voluntary associations. For the pre-1935 history of the social insurance movement in America, Roy Lubove's *The Struggle for Social Security, 1900–1935* (Cambridge: Harvard University Press, 1968), is easily the best work available to date. Although Lubove has in effect joined one of the partisan camps in the pre-1935 quarrels, the camp for which Isaac Rubinow was the best spokesman, and has treated other points of view rather cavalierly, his work is a scholarly and comprehensive survey of both issues and events. *Social Security: Programs, Problems, and Policies* (Homewood, Ill.: R. D. Irwin, 1960), edited by William Haber and Wilbur Cohen, offers interpretive selections from such sources to provide various points of view. A chapter by Elizabeth Brandeis, "What Road is Forward in Social Security?" in a book edited by Thomas McCormick, *Problems of the Postwar World* (New York: McGraw-Hill Book Company, Inc., 1945), sharply contrasts two basic theories of social security. Writings of Eveline Burns provide both factual description of social security programs and interpretation: *Social Security and Public Policy* (New York: McGraw-Hill Book Company, Inc., 1956) acquaints the reader with the programs' details from the perspective of public welfare administration; "Social Insurance in Evolution," *The American Economic Review Supplement,* 34 (Mar., 1944), 199-211, provides perspicacious comment on the individualistic concept of social security that Witte held; and "Social Security in Evolution: Toward What?" in *The Social Service Review,* 39 (June, 1965), 129-40, a sequel to the earlier article, traces the development of social security ideas to the appearance of negative income tax proposals in the mid-1960s. A spate of books appearing in the 1960s and dealing with poverty offers implicit or explicit criticism of social security for failure to deal adequately with some of the most persistent problems of welfare. Of such books Michael Harrington's popular *The Other America* (New York: The Macmillan Co., 1962) set the tone; among them are such works as Richard M. Elman's *The Poorhouse State: The American Way of Life on Public Assistance* (New York: Pantheon Books, 1966), and Ben B. Seligman's *Permanent Poverty: An American Syndrome* (Chicago: Quadrangle Books, 1968).

Samuel Mencher, *Poor Law to Poverty Program: Economic Security Policy in Britain and the United States* (Pittsburgh: University of Pittsburgh Press, 1967), and Philip Klein, *From Philanthropy to Social Welfare: An American Cultural Perspective* (San Francisco: Jossey-Bass, 1968), present the development of social security in broad historical perspective, as does Arthur Altmeyer's "The Wisconsin Idea and Social Security," cited above. A very basic document is Altmeyer's *The Formative Years of Social Security* (Madison: The University of Wisconsin Press, 1966). Written by social security's leading administrator, *The Formative Years of Social Security* covers the period following the passage of the 1935 Act and emphasizes the role of administrative decisions in social security's development. Valdemar Carlson's *Economic Security in the United States* (New York: McGraw-Hill Book Company, Inc., 1962) combines historical perspective with insights from economic theory; while *Social Insurance and Allied Government Programs* (Homewood, Ill.: R. D. Irwin, 1965), by Robert J. Myers, is a more technical discussion of some of the basic concepts of insurance and social insurance financing. On the distinctions between private and social insurance, a published address of W. Rulon Williamson, *Social Insurance Legislation* (New York: The American Management Association, 1935; the association's Insurance Series Pamphlet No. 21), is instructive. More general and standard sources are the Social Security Administration's *Social Security Bulletin,* yearbooks, statistical supplements, and other publications.

An early forum for discussion of social insurance ideas was the National Conference of Charities and Corrections, later The National Conference of Social Work. Numerous papers on the subject appear in the organization's *Proceedings.* Writings of Edward T. Devine and Henry R. Seager, especially Seager's *Social Insurance, A Program of Social Reform* (New York: The Macmillan Company, 1910), represent views of early social insurance advocates with roots in the charity and social work tradition. In an unpublished 1961 Columbia University dissertation, Narayan Viswanathan has competently described "The Role of the American Public Welfare Policies in the United States, 1930–1960." For social insurance ideas of the labor legislation school of reformers, *The American Labor Legislation Review* is a basic source, supplemented by Lloyd Pierce's 1953 University of Wisconsin dissertation, "The Activities of the American Association for Labor Legislation in Behalf of Social Security and Protective Labor Legislation," which gives a summary history of early social insurance programs. Most important for studying the viewpoint of those social insurance advocates who drew their ideas chiefly from European programs are the writings of Isaac M. Rubinow and Abraham Epstein.

Rubinow's *Social Insurance, With Special Reference to American Conditions* (New York: H. Holt and Company, 1913) is an early, very full discussion of security problems and proposals. His later book, *The Quest for Security* (New York: H. Holt and Company, 1934), and Epstein's *Insecurity, A Challenge to America* (New York: H. Smith and R. Haas, 1933, 1936; Random House, 1938) are the fullest discussions to appear before passage of the Social Security Act of 1935 and contain much solid history of social insurance, despite their propagandistic tone. A publication including a wide variety of viewpoints on social insurance is the November, 1933 issue of *The Annals of the American Academy of Political and Social Science* (Vol. 170). Samuel Gompers' "Not Even Compulsory Benevolence Will Do: Infringement of Personal Liberty," in *Compulsory Health Insurance* (Annual Meeting Addresses of the National Civic Federation, Jan. 22, 1917), 5–10, is a succinct statement of organized labor's early opposition to social insurance. The writings of Frederick L. Hoffman, especially his "American Problems in Social Insurance," in the *Proceedings of the National Conference of Charities and Corrections* (1914), 346–55, and his *Facts and Fallacies of Compulsory Health Insurance* (Newark: Prudential Press, 1920) offer the views of an interested and outspoken businessman. David H. Clark's unpublished 1963 University of

Wisconsin dissertation, "An Analytical View of the History of Health Insurance, 1910-1959," is an excellent interpretive study of both public and private health insurance proposals and programs. Publications of Epstein's American Association for Old Age (later Social) Security, and Epstein's *Facing Old Age: A Study of Old Age Dependency in the United States and Old Age Pensions* (New York: A. A. Knopf, 1922) and *The Challenge of the Aged* (New York: The Vanguard Press, 1928), are documents of the crusade for old-age pensions.

For understanding the Wisconsin approach to unemployment compensation, two articles by John R. Commons, "Unemployment: Compensation and Prevention," in *The Survey*, 47 (Oct. 1, 1921), 5–9, and "Unemployment Compensation," in *The American Labor Legislation Review*, 20 (Sept., 1930), 249–53, are fundamental. Notable defenses of the 1932 Wisconsin unemployment compensation law are Paul Rauschenbush's "Wisconsin Unemployment Compensation Act," in *The American Labor Legislation Review*, 22 (March, 1932), 11–18, and an article by Harold Groves and Elizabeth Brandeis, "Economic Bases of the Wisconsin Unemployment Reserves Act," in *The American Economic Review*, 24 (March, 1934), 38–52. Isaac Rubinow's "Job Insurance—The Ohio Plan," in *The American Labor Legislation Review*, 23 (Sept., 1933), 131–136, and Abraham Epstein's "Enemies of Unemployment Insurance," in *The New Republic*, 76 (Sept. 6, 1933), 24–26, are sharp dissents from the Wisconsin approach. Further examples of the numerous discussions of unemployment insurance before the 1935 Social Security Act are Barbara Armstrong's *Insuring the Essentials: Minimum Wage Plus Social Insurance—A Living Wage Program* (New York: The Macmillan Company, 1932); *Standards of Unemployment Insurance* (Chicago: University of Chicago Press, 1932), by Paul H. Douglas; and *A Program for Unemployment Insurance and Relief in the United States* (Minneapolis: University of Minnesota Press, 1934), by Alvin Hansen, Merrill Murray, Russell Stevenson, and Bryce Stewart.

For the work of the 1934-1935 Committee on Economic Security and the legislative history of the 1935 Social Security Act, Witte's *Development of the Social Security Act* is, as noted above, easily the most important single source. The sections of the present biography dealing with the Act's origins rest very heavily also upon unpublished documents. Most of these are in the Committee on Economic Security files in Record Group 47 of the National Archives, supplemented by Department of Labor files in Record Group 174. The Franklin D. Roosevelt Library provides a few documents delineating Roosevelt's interest and role. The Witte Papers include virtually all of the most basic committee documents, including the minutes of the meetings of the committee, its technical board, and its advisory council (box 65). Interviews, especially those with Wilbur Cohen, Murray Latimer, and Arthur Altmeyer, and correspondence with Frances Perkins, supplemented these manuscripts.

Roosevelt's message of June 8, 1934, initially proposing an economic security program has been printed as *Review of Legislative Accomplishments of the Administration and Congress*, United States House of Representatives Document No. 397 (73rd Congress, 2d Session). The Committee embodied its final proposals in its *Report to the President of the Committee on Economic Security* (Washington: Government Printing Office, 1935), while further information on the Committee's work is readily available in its *Social Security in America: The Factual Background of the Social Security Act as Summarized from Staff Reports of the Committee on Economic Security* (Washington: Government Printing Office, 1937). The basic legislative documents are two volumes, each entitled *Economic Security Act*, respectively hearings before the Senate Finance Committee and the House Ways and Means Committee on bills S. 1130 and H. R. 4120 (74th Congress, 1st Session).

282   CAUTIOUS REFORMER

Retrospective accounts by the four most important participants in creating the bill appear in Frances Perkins' *The Roosevelt I Knew* (New York: The Viking Press, 1946); a 1955 address by Witte, "Twenty Years of Social Security," printed in the *Social Security Bulletin,* 18 (Oct., 1955), 15–21; Thomas H. Eliot's "The Social Security Bill 25 Years After," in *The Atlantic Monthly,* 206 (Aug., 1960), 72–75; and in Arthur Altmeyer's *The Formative Years of Social Security,* cited above.

Among other published sources, Abraham Holtzman's *The Townsend Movement: A Political Study* (New York: Bookman Associates, 1963), offers insight into the backdrop of old-age pensions agitation against which the committee worked. Of many press comments, Louis Stark's *New York Times* articles of late 1934 and early 1935 criticizing the committee's work are most notable. Outstanding dissents, particularly from the Committee's recommendations for unemployment insurance, are the "Report of the Advisory Council to the Committee on Economic Security," printed in the House Ways and Means Committee hearings, pp. 885–86, and a memorandum by twenty-four leading experts and commentators, printed in the Senate Finance Committee hearings, pp. 1138–40. Abraham Epstein sharply criticized the 1935 act in "Our Social Insecurity Act." *Harper's Monthly Magazine,* 172 (Dec., 1935), 55–66, and in the 1936 and 1938 editions of his *Insecurity, A Challenge to America,* cited above. Paul Douglas, in *Social Security in the United States* (New York: McGraw-Hill Book Company, 1936), and Eveline Burns, in *Toward Social Security: An Explanation of the Social Security Act and a Survey of the Larger Issues* (New York: McGraw-Hill Book Company, 1936), offered more temperate criticism. Examples of the extensive discussion of social security in the periodical literature of the period are the March, 1935, issue of *The Annals of the American Academy of Political and Social Science* (Vol. 178); the January and April, 1936, issues of *Law and Contemporary Problems* (Vol. 3); and the March and April, 1936 issues of the *National Municipal Review* (Vol. 25), republished as *Social Security* (New York: National Municipal League, 1936), edited by Joseph Harris. Witte meantime explained and defended the Social Security Act in numerous articles and addresses. A complete bibliography of Witte's essays on social security appears in the book of essays edited by Robert Lampman and cited above, *Social Security Perspectives,* 391–414.

For Witte's role in the discussions leading up to the social security amendments of 1939, the "Minutes of the Advisory Council of the Social Security Board," in Record Group 47 of the National Archives, are the most extensive source. Many other documents in Record Group 47, and others in the Witte Papers, provide further firsthand information. Notable public statements of Witte's views on the most troublesome issue before the advisory council are his "Financing Social Security: Reserves versus Current Taxation," in *How Shall Business Be Taxed* (New York: Tax Policy League, 1937), and his "In Defense of the Federal Old Age Benefit Plan," in *The American Labor Legislation Review,* 27 (March, 1937), 27–33. Witte's leading antagonist on the council, M. Albert Linton, expressed his views in "The Quest for Security in Old Age," *Proceedings of the Academy of Political Science,* 16 (June, 1935), 373–89; "Old-Age Security for Everybody," *The Atlantic Monthly,* 157 (April, 1936), 488–98; "The Problem of Reserves for Old Age Benefits," *The American Labor Legislation Review,* 27 (March, 1937), 23–26; and "Insuring the Future: The Burden of Old Age Security," *The Atlantic Monthly,* 162 (Oct., 1938), 544–49. The advisory council presented its final recommendations in its *Final Report,* Senate Document No. 4 (76th Congress, 1st Session). Witte's and others' testimony on the 1939 social security amendments is printed in the hearings of the Senate Finance Committee, *Social Security Act*

Amendments, and that of the House Ways and Means Committee, *Social Security* (both: 76th Congress, 1st Session). Witte presented his summary and evaluation of the changes also in his "Social Security—1940 Model," *The American Labor Legislation Review,* 29 (Sept., 1939), 101–09.

For an understanding of Witte's role as a public commentator on social security questions after 1939, the indispensable source is his articles and addresses. The complete bibliography of these public statements as it appears in Lampman's *Social Security Perspectives,* cited above, reveals the scope of the statements' content, since Witte's titles were quite accurately descriptive. Moreover, Lampman's book contains the most substantive addresses and articles. A publication setting forth some of the major social security ideas to which Witte was reacting in his last two decades was that by Sir William Beveridge, *Social Insurance and Allied Services* (American ed., New York: The Macmillan Company, 1942). A set of proposals against which Witte reacted strongly were those of the United States National Resources Planning Board Committee on Long-Range Work and Relief Policies, in its *Security, Work, and Relief Policies* (Washington: Government Printing Office, 1942). He was more favorable to wartime health insurance proposals described by Michael Davis in "Health Program for the Nation," *Survey Graphic,* 33 (Dec., 1944), 491–93, 510–11. Especially disturbing to Witte in the postwar era were proposals of Lewis Meriam in *Relief and Social Security* (Washington: The Brookings Institution, 1946); a new statement by M. Albert Linton, "Facing Facts in Old-Age Security," *American Economic Security,* 9 (Jan.–Feb., 1952), 19–27; and a United States Chamber of Commerce proposal, summarized in "Chamber Membership Approves New Social Security Policy," *American Economic Security,* 10 (Jan.–Feb., 1953), 2.

In addition to his many other articles and addresses printed or cited in Lampman's *Social Security Perspectives,* an article by Witte, "What to Expect of Social Security," in *The American Economic Review,* 34 (Supplement; March, 1944), 212–21, and his chapter, "Social Provision for the Aged," in *The Aged and Society* (Champaign, Ill.: Industrial Relations Research Association, 1950), edited by Milton Derber, are outstanding statements of his social security views as they developed in the 1940's. Witte's "The Future of Social Security," published in *U. S. Industrial Relations: The Next Twenty Years* (East Lansing: Michigan State University Press, 1958), by Clark Kerr *et al.,* and his "public policy on Economic Security," *Business Topics,* 5 (May, 1958), 1–8, are notable statements in the following decade. His final words on the subject are recorded in his manuscripts for a book (Witte Papers, box 295), unfinished at the time of his death.

INDEX

Abbott, Edith, 106
Abbott, Grace, 131
Addams, Jane, 78
Addes, George, 210
Advisory Council to 1934–1935 Committee on Economic Security: 99, 102, 130; selection of, 101; on unemployment insurance, 121, 124–125; reports of, 125
Aid to blind, 152
Aid to dependent children, 108, 129, 152, 195. *See also* Mothers' pensions, Maternity and child benefits
Altmeyer, Arthur: v, 96, 99, 101, 161, 176, 179, 193; as chairman of CES technical board, 100, 104, 111–112, 123, 124, 128, 151; on Social Security Board, 157
American Association for Labor Legislation: 17, 81–82; on old-age pensions, 85–86; "American Plan for Unemployment Reserves," 89–90, 91, 92
American Association for Old-Age Security. *See* American Association for Social Security
American Association for Social Security, 79, 85–86, 140, 154, 171
American Economic Association: 82, 224; Witte's presidency of, 225–227
American Federation of Labor: 21, 54, 65, 68, 216; on labor injunction remedy, 62–63; on social insurance, 77, 94, 160
American Liberty League, 145
American Medical Association, 82–83, 112–114, 192
American Motors Corporation, 217, 229
American Public Welfare Association, 78, 189
Amidon, Beulah, 101
Andrews, John B., 17, 28, 81, 82; on old-age pensions, 85–86; on unemployment compensation, 89–90, 92, 95, 120
Anti-trust legislation, 22–23, 28, 53. *See also* Clayton Anti-trust Act
Armstrong, Barbara, 79, 86, 108, 111, 116, 117, 119, 124, 138
Atomic energy installations: labor relations in, 215–217

Beveridge, Sir William, and Beveridge Plan, 190, 194
Bierring, Walter, 112, 113

Blaine, John J., 40–41, 45, 63, 65, 68–69
Brandeis, Elizabeth, x, 81, 88, 90, 91, 94, 122, 191, 193, 194
Brandeis, Louis, 27, 76, 92, 94, 101, 112, 115, 194, 204
British Trades Disputes Act, 28, 29, 55–56, 63
Brown, J. Douglas, 108, 111, 117, 138, 162, 173, 176
Burns, Eveline, 117, 138, 140, 141, 154, 189
Burns–Haber Report. *See* National Resources Planning Board
Business Advisory and Planning Council, Department of Commerce, 101–102, 116, 123, 140, 143, 144
Byrd, Harry F., 148–149, 162

Chamber of Commerce. *See* United States Chamber of Commerce
Child labor, 34–35
Children's Bureau. *See* United States Children's Bureau
Clayton Anti-trust Act: ix, 54–55, 62, 66, 67; Witte's dissenting report and views on, 27, 55, 62
Cohen, Wilbur J., v–viii, x, 102, 135, 180, 193–194, 229
Collective bargaining: Witte's contribution to, 212–213, 217, 219; Witte's views on, 213–214, 218. *See also* Labor relations law
Commission on Industrial Relations. *See* United States Commission on Industrial Relations
Committee on Administrative Management, 50
Committee on Economic Security: vi, 143, 144, 155, 167; appointed, 96; report of, 98, 114, 128–129; conflicts within, 99, 124–125, 130–131; organization of, 99, 101, 102, 121; staff of, 99, 100, 102, 117, 127, 130–131; editorial comment on, 100–101, 130–131; decisions on economic security program, 107, 108, 112, 114, 119–122, 125, 127, 152; rejects Lundeen Bill, 137. *See also* Advisory Council; Technical board; Economic security bill; Social Security Act (1935); *Development of the Social Security Act*
Commons, John R.: v, ix, 10, 14, 16, 17, 19, 28, 31–33, 48, 51, 58, 129, 204, 206, 220, 225, 231; biographical

284